Contents

1. In the Beginning…

"And gladly wolde he lerne, and gladly teche…"

There was a droning in the background. It was my English Literature teacher, Mr Dixon, who was excitely regaling us with Chaucer and his obvious relevance and necessity to our futures. I am in the back row on the second floor of the sixth form college building at KEVICS, in Totnes, Devon. Unfortunately for Mr Dixon his enthusiasm is being wasted on this particular scholar, as I am concentrating on events on the other side of the window behind me.

Down below, on a large green space idyllically surrounded by mature trees, a cricket match was in progress. I don't recall or never knew who the teams were, but if there ever a sight that makes you want to get up and belt out the chorus of "Jerusalem" at full whack than a cricket game in the English sunshine, then I've not yet seen it. I wanted to be out there with them, doing what they were doing. Why was I here listening to this crap?

"No empty handed man can lure a bird", Mr Dixon continued, wisely.

In a moment of enlightenment, short sightedness and immature stupidity, I packed my learning implements into my school bag, squeezing them in beside my as yet uneaten packed lunch. I got up and left, saying "I need to go" to the puzzled and annoyed looking Mr Dixon, whose passionate flow I had just rudely interrupted. I ran along the corridor and out of the building to avoid any possible confrontation and stopped on the road outside.

Having not thought past wanting to watch the cricket, I stood and pondered. My options were limited as I had no cash on me, so I decided to walk home. I had a student bus pass that was only valid on the 3.10pm, so as it was only 10.45am I started to walk. I lived in a village called South Brent, on the Southern tip of Dartmoor in Devon about eight miles from KEVICS, so I was in for a stroll.

It took me around two and a half hours. When I got home, my mother was in the kitchen preparing dinner. There was a large pile of assorted vegetables on the counter and she turned in surprise when she saw me, chopping knife still in hand.

"What are you doing home?" she said, in her wonderfully thick West Country accent.

"I've walked out on my A levels" I said. "It's not for me".

"Really?" A look of anger and disbelief descended.... "And what do you propose to do with your life now?"

Now you'd think that during the eight mile walk home, I'd have anticipated questioning along these lines and tried to come up with suitable or, at the very least, plausible responses. Not me. I remember passing the time compiling in my head as I walked first my greatest ever Arsenal XI, and then my best ever England XI... Why wasn't she asking me whether Kevin Keegan or Alan Ball should play at 7? Mum took a step towards me, one eyebrow arched and still clutching that really big knife.

"Um, I thought I'd work in restaurants" I blurted out in self preservation. I had to say something that resembled a plan. At the time, I had a part time job at The Mill at Avonwick, a local pub / restaurant just outside of South Brent. I washed dishes, did some starters and desserts, cleaned up etc. As I said it, I inwardly congratulated myself, as it sounded feasible (in my head).

"Right" Mum said. "I'll discuss it with your father when he gets home."

Next day, I had to go back to KEVICS and apologise to Mr Dixon and the Head of Year for the nature of my untimely exit. I reiterated to them both that my decision was final, and that finishing my current studies was not the path for me. They both tried to talk some sense into me, but hey, I was almost seventeen - I knew what was best...

The following day, Mother woke me up at stupid o'clock with a cup of tea.

"Come on, get up! We need to catch the 7.20 bus."

Mother and father had got me an interview with the Principle at the South Devon College of Arts and Technology in Torquay, to enrol on a course of Hotel Management and Institutional Operations. The course taught you all of the aspects involved in Hotel and Catering, both from the business side and the hands on part.

And that's how I ended up here....

2. There's Trouble at t'Mill

I always felt a bit undercooked as a kid. Slower to mature, always playing catch up. All of my peers seemed to be a bit more streetwise and cool. It didn't help that I was always the youngest (August baby) in my academic year, and usually the shortest. I don't know where the short gene came from, actually. Both brothers and my father were around the six foot mark. It has always bugged me that in my earlier years I would struggle to get girlfriends because they couldn't be seen with a short arse. Like I can help or affect my height. Imagine putting on a dating site that I refused to date any bird with a fat arse, despite the fact that she herself is responsible for all of that extra cake and sofa time. I wonder if Tinder would accept a guy stipulating "must weigh in at less than half a ton", yet they are seemingly happy for a girl to put that her prospective man "must be at least six feet, as I'm 5'9" in my heels".

It all changed at fifteen years of age (except for the height) when my best mate, Daren, helped me secure a job at The Mill at Avonwick, a lovely pub / restaurant near South Brent, my home village in Devon. All of a sudden I was in a professional, working environment. It was a loud, busy kitchen populated by people who really cared about what was being produced. There were chefs fussing over the minutest detail on a plate, waiters racing around with wine all togged out in immaculate dinner dress. Even our pot wash area, run by Daren and myself, had a source of pride about it.

When a couple of hundred covers are served on a Saturday night, with three or four courses each, plus coffee, that's a lot of crockery and cutlery. Add to that the pots, pans, trays and utensils used in the kitchen to produce this stuff, it was quite the task to keep up. One of us would be loading and unloading the commercial dishwasher, whilst the other would have his hands buried elbow deep in the giant sink, trying to keep pace with the pots and pans. Every so often, the head chef, Richard, would yell "KNIFE" and you had to jump back from the sink as a razor sharp, industrial knife would cartwheel into the water. It was a good system until it went wrong, when there would be a need for first aid and a bollocking from Richard for not being quick enough to retreat. How the new health and safety regime would review this practise today is anyone's guess.

Daren and I worked for £1 per hour. And we loved it. It was the first time either of us had ever had "serious" money, aside from the odd paper round. We worked hard, too, motivated by the noise and buzz of those around us. If we didn't mop the floor well, we were torn off a strip, so we made sure it was perfect next time. We learned from our mistakes, never making the same one twice. In time, we would move on to being allowed to help with the production of desserts, then side dishes and starters. I was immensely proud of my job there and loved every minute.

The Mill also embraced us socially. These were simpler times, the mid eighties, and along with the industry in the kitchen it was accepted that the chefs were allowed to have a beer while service was in full swing "to keep refreshed." Head chef Richard would always go through eight to ten pints of Carlsberg Export during a busy session, and end up driving home. To my eyes he was never affected by the booze, but looking back it was horrific. If Daren and I had worked our nuts off and the boss was happy, we would both be sent a pint each through the hatch towards the end of the night. Although we were fifteen or sixteen it made us feel accepted, mature and one of the team - all part of growing up.

Along with the hard work and standards came a natural education into workplace humour. Head chef Richard was always very keen to play pranks on us during the quieter sessions - usually daytimes, to both relieve his boredom and assert his superiority. I suppose I was guilty of these traits much later on in my career, so I shouldn't over criticise him at this point. He would be forever handing us hot trays across the kitchen to wash up, which would burn our fingers if we grabbed them, or try to get us to do weird, unnecessary jobs.

The best one he got me with was when he convinced me to clean the water wheel, which was a working feature situated outside the front of the restaurant. It was probably about twelve feet in diameter and used to dip into a small lake at its base as it rotated, so about ten feet of it was actually always out of the water itself. It used to turn during opening hours and be switched off at night, but on this quiet lunchtime occasion Richard switched off the rotation and asked me to try and remove the accumulated moss and lichen from the wooden struts.

Young, gullible me climbed aboard via the rocks that poked above the murky pond, armed with a bucket of hot water and scourers and proceeded to scrub the wheel with my usual enthusiastic vigour. After a couple of minutes, I looked up to see all of the kitchen staff and the owner, John, standing opposite on dry land with huge grins on their faces - and at that point, the wheel began to turn…

At that stage in my life, I was young and supremely fit, so keeping up with the speed of this wheel wasn't a problem. The issue was that it was just too quick to be able to manoeuvre off it without getting dunked, so I had to just keep going, shouting abuse and pleading for them to turn it off as I went. After a while, the bastards all filtered back inside to get on with service, so I was left doing my giant hamster impression whilst being viewed by the highly amused punters through the large front window, which was situated directly between the wheel and the restaurant dining area. After about fifteen minutes, Richard came back out with a mug of tea for me, and left it on the bank. Funny man.

Inevitably, after another ten minutes or so had passed, I gave up and took my cold bath. The experience made me a lot more wary of this type of prank, but probably in addition gave me a thirst to be able to do this stuff to others… The next time I set foot on a similar type of construction was in London about twenty years later, but on a much bigger and drier scale.

It was New Year's Eve of 1985. It had been one of the busiest services I had known and Daren and I were racing to finish before Big Ben hit midnight. Our mutual friend Joe was waiting for us in the bar and when we sat down to join him the boss, John, sent over some beers for us. As I had just finished my work and was as dry as a nun in the Sahara, I said "this won't last long". Joe responded with "I'll race you" so we chugged the lager in one. I won reasonably impressively, but John had seen us do this.

He beckoned me over, grabbed a bar cloth with "Double Diamond Works Wonders" emblazoned on it and stuffed it into the top of my shirt, so it hung down my front. He then got me to stand on a bar stool. Meanwhile, behind me as I faced the public with my back to the bar, Leonard the barman (known as Lennie the Lettuce, I never found out why…) was filling up a yard of ale vessel with Carlsberg Export.

John carefully handed the long tube to me. He showed me how to hold it, and warned me of "the bulb at the end". The crowd went "3-2-1 GO", so I went. I thought I was doing great as I drank, I was thinking how impressive I must have looked stood on that barstool, when the "bulb" hit me. You just don't expect it. You're doing fine, the beer is disappearing and then this wall of lager appears from nowhere, racing towards your eyes like a liquid amber tsunami. I swallowed as much of it as possible, but by the time I handed the vessel back to John, I was choking like an asthmatic yak, the Double Diamond was soaked through and my glasses were hanging off one ear.

I left The Mill when I started studying at a Catering College in Torquay. As part of the course, we had compulsory work assignments in various hotel establishments around the South West of England, so keeping the Mill job was impossible. I heard a couple of years after I left that Richard had died of a sudden heart attack, brought on by excessive drinking. I was terribly sad about this. He taught me much about standards and work ethic which have always stuck with me. He is by no means an unusual victim of habits and excess in this industry.

3. A College Education

Catering college was great fun. I thrived in the mature environment that we were able to learn in. It didn't feel like a school, but more of a workplace - and I was learning stuff that I was really interested in. Instead of reciting the periodic table in monotone, I learned how to produce fifty Creme Brulees for service. Instead of nailing the lid of a fly spray can to a bit of wood to make a string ball catcher, I was grilling t-bone steaks on a gueridon trolley at the table. I was taught accountancy, marketing, purchasing, staff employment law - all things relevant to the running of a catering establishment. I could even read menus in French. I was hooked, and had found my direction.

I particularly loved the practical side. There were two classes in our year, with about twenty students in each. Within the College up on the first floor we had this five star restaurant which seated about thirty five people, for which we cooked and served twice a week. For one session, my class would be the chefs. For the other class we would look after the restaurant service and wine.

Twenty chefs cooking four courses for a lunch service. We'd be in by 8am to prepare for the off at 12.30pm. The detail that went into each dish, part of a dish, a garnish, a sauce, the shape of the butter for the table... Everything was finished to a standard of incredible beauty in its intricacy and final presentation. They always used to tell us that if we are taught to produce at this level, then we will be able to cope with anything the industry has to throw at us later on. Service had to be perfect, especially when cooking the final pieces to order - the pressure when the tickets went up on the tab grabbers was both incredible and exhilarating.

As waiters, the standard of table laying, order taking and delivery of the food itself was overseen by this absolute battleaxe of a woman. You put a smudged silver knife down on that cloth and she'd smell it at forty paces. Spill a drop of wine on the table while pouring, or pick up the plate from the wrong side of the customer, and she'd tear you a new one in front of everybody. You were scared to mess up, which was probably a good thing - it certainly made me concentrate on what I was doing. You can imagine this woman's reaction one Wednesday afternoon, when I managed to cock it all up to an extraordinary level....

Back in those days, I was a cool dude. At least, that's what I thought. Doesn't every middle aged person look back on pictures of their teenage, rebellious self and cringe? My look was a kind of New Romantic. I had grown my hair to shoulder length, and had long spikes on the top of my head. As if this wasn't enough, I had done a spot of homemade bleaching with one of those kits you used to get from Boots or Superdrug, where you have this kind of Dutch cap that you pierce with holes from one end of a small brush and then coat the strands that are pulled through with a foul smelling peroxide. I used to do it in my parents bathroom looking in the cabinet mirror, whilst holding mum's make up mirror behind my head so that I could see the back of my head.

Anyway, there I was in the posh restaurant, all blonde spikes and acne and dressed like a penguin. I had my waiters cloth professionally draped over one arm and was wheeling a gueridon (a trolley used for service in five star restaurants, complete with gas burner) towards the table of four who had just all ordered crepe suzettes for their puddings. A crepe suzette is a French pancake type of dessert, with caramelised sugar, butter, orange juice and usually Grand Marnier. All of this is traditionally prepared flambe' style, in an extravagant tableside performance by your experienced silver service waiter, as you watch.

All was going swimmingly. I had caramelised the sugar with the butter and it was bubbling nicely. I slowly added the required amount of orange juice and let it simmer for a few seconds. Over my shoulder, the Battleaxe was watching intently. As there were no grunts, snorts or heavy breathing coming from that direction, I knew I was doing well. I looked up momentarily to see the four occupants of my table enraptured by my performance so far. I could almost sense their salivating...

One by one, I put the pancakes into the pan with my spoon and fork. I coated them in the sauce and neatly folded each one in quarters, as we had been trained. I now had four perfect ice cream wafer shaped crepes in my pan, all happily bubbling and just waiting to be served. I'd nailed it, I was so pleased with myself. For the final touch, you had to pour a Mississippi of Grand Marnier into the pan, slightly tilt it to encourage the flame and flambe' the dish. Unfortunately, with my new found and yet ill advised confidence in not having yet cocked up, I misjudged the amount of the liqueur that ended up with the sauce. I'd say it was more of an Amazon than a Mississippi, so consequently when I tilted the pan to catch the flame, the resulting fireball was like a bad day at Chernobyl.

Of course, with me intently looking over the dish to ensure its precision and beauty, the first thing that went up was my hair. I threw my spoon and fork up in the air and ran through the packed restaurant beating my head with my waiters cloth. I bolted through the "in" door to the kitchen and stuck my head in the giant sink used for preparing vegetables, amongst a sea of leeks. The smell of burning hair is one of the worst things you can imagine, even more so when it's yours. Moments later, the Battleaxe stormed into the kitchen and started yelling about *her* embarrassment, but even she backed off a bit when she saw the state of my new barnet. Next day, I came to college with a trendy new crew cut.

One March early morning with a biting frost on the ground, I managed to crash my mini - with my then girlfriend Ginny in the passenger seat - on the way to college. I had passed my test about two months previously, and had far more confidence in my own driving ability than any seventeen year old has the right to. I took a corner on a typical Dartmoor winding road far too fast and aqua planed over a patch of frozen mud left by an early bird tractor. I hit the roadside hedge with the passenger front side and rolled four times, spectacularly ending up on the roof in the middle of the road.

Fortunately for us, it was such a crap car that the lifting seat locks which enabled people to get into the back were broken on both sides, so that when the car went upside down the seats lifted up and jammed against the roof as we landed. This stopped the roof of the car hitting our heads and probably snapping our necks. I couldn't get out as the doors were crushed, but this guy from a South West Electricity Board van sprinted over and booted the door ajar. I unclipped Ginny, who was screaming and dangling upside down by her seatbelt, and dragged her as I was being dragged out by the nice electricity man. Seconds later, the car went up like it was Guy Fawkes night, but we were all clear of it albeit covered in glass cuts from the shattered windscreen and soaked in petrol.

We were taken to hospital in Torquay, but for both of us our injuries were superficial. Mentally, however it did plenty of damage. Poor Ginny was really freaked out - it turned her into a really nervous passenger for a long time, unsurprisingly. It was quite a few months before I was brave enough myself to get behind a wheel again, but I was forced to do so by my mother who paid for a bit of a refresher course from the village driving instructor. I am very much a better driver for having gone through this experience, but I wouldn't necessarily recommend my methods of getting to this stage.

Now without a car, in those days of my youth I was ridiculously fit. I was a cross country champion at school and always enjoyed a long run. For a bet with some of my fellow commuting student caterers, I quite regularly used to race our bus to college. I would leap off as it got into Totnes dressed in my running gear, leaving my school bag with my fellow students and run across the moors via villages such as Berry Pomeroy and Malden, arriving at the College which was located at the top end of Torquay. The aim was to beat the bus which was carrying my friends, which always took the longer and busier route via Paignton. In truth, I could only win if the bus had a bit of nasty traffic, but that occured more often than not. I look back on that now with thirty years of beer and pies having gone in and out of me and wince.

As part of the course, we were sent out to various hotels and restaurants for on the job experience. Being in Torquay, we were frequently sent out to the top hotels around the area such as The Grand or The Imperial, where we could be doing anything from silver service waiting to washing up. I think that sometimes these places used us for cheap labour rather than to further our progression, but to me it was all excellent experience as you learned to cope with a new workplace and different styles or temperament of managers.

During the Summer, again as part of the course, we had to do a long term workplace secondment for a six week period. I was sent to this incredible place called Burgh Island, which is situated off the South coast of Devon, at Bigbury on Sea. Ginny and I had somehow managed to swing it so that we were both posted together here for the Summer.

Since the second World War, the Burgh Island Hotel had fallen into disrepair - a direct hit from the Luftwaffe didn't help. In its heyday, however, it was a splendid Art Deco building, overlooking the mainland from its lofty perch high up on the island. Many dignitaries used to come here during its 1930's pomp, including Edward and Mrs Simpson, Lord Mountbatten, Winston Churchill and the aviator, Amy Johnson. Agatha Christie used to stay in the hotel for extended periods, writing two of her books here, including Evil Under the Sun.

By the mid eighties, it had been taken over by a mad couple called the Porters, who were big on dreams and ideas but rather short on knowhow. They had spent a fortune getting the hotel liveable, trying to return it to its former art deco glory. There was a small team of staff put together to do all of the running around - myself and Ginny included - and we all lived in a wooden hut with eight separate rooms situated down and to one side of the island, away from the hotel itself. There was running water in a sink in the kitchen section, cold water only from the shower room and six bedrooms. There was mice, mould, rotting walls and dirty mattresses. At 16 or 17 years of age, I guess you just accept it.

Contrast that with the hotel itself, where everything was very grand and just so. There was a beautiful Palm Court room, just off the reception, where one was to take afternoon tea. The Grand Ballroom was reserved for functions, entertainment and the service of dinner. A tuxedo and evening gown were compulsory attire. The rooms were quite boutique and beautiful, almost all with some sort of view of the sea. We, of course, would be dressed in immaculate uniforms for work, despite the fact that there was only one crappy iron to go round, and a sideboard instead of an ironing board with which to press them.

Our work would vary. We could either be in the kitchen, the restaurant or sometimes cleaning the rooms. The best job would have been serving in the Pilchard Inn, the ancient (1336AD) pub belonging to the hotel which was perched on the side of Burgh Island, but Ginny and I weren't yet eighteen, so still too young to pour alcohol. It wasn't really organised and there was a tremendous amount of firefighting with regard to the work going on, due to the inexperience of the owners. These guys were quite happy to spend £100 on the exact cushion cover that they wanted for the Lloyd Loom chair in room 3, but not the extra fiver for an ironing board. In fairness, we got by most of the time - the final product always seemed to be passable, but behind the scenes there was always chaos and arguments. Like the duck serenely gliding across the pond, but underneath, unseen, his feet are thrashing the water in order to majestically float along.

After work hours, the hut was bedlam. We had all just bust a gut to achieve the owners desired results, without thanks. Most nights, there would be a pile of cider cans to wade through, purchased from an off license on the mainland by one of us who looked over eighteen. and music would blare out from most rooms. One or two of the staff were into drugs, and one kitchen worker resorted to sniffing hair spray in a bag most nights until he passed out. Ginny and I would usually have a can or two (of cider!) before trying to retire, but sleep was limited with the noise from the rest of the place. It would bug the crap out of me today, but when you're that age you just run with it.

Burgh Island is connected to the mainland by a spit of sandy beach at low tide, but is cut off completely when the sea is at its deepest. For this reason, the hotel owned the "sea tractor", which was basically a large platform on huge tractor wheels, which would, when the tide was in, transport the pampered guest from their cars parked on the mainland to the hotel. The sea tractor was operated at all times by Jimbo, a monosyllabic local full of self importance. If there was a guest on board, Jimbo wouldn't let us mere members of staff ride. We had to wait until his next trip - it was quite pathetic. We weren't even allowed in the Pilchard on our days off, it was a real case of "seen but not heard".

One slow day, there was four of us off work for the evening. Ginny and myself, one of the waiters and the hair spray sniffer. As we weren't allowed a drink in the Pilchard, we walked across the beach to the mainland, to have a quick pint in the Smugglers Inn. One pint turned into two, two turned into....well, you know how it goes. Cut a long story short, it's one in the morning in the Smugglers, and we stagger out. Had a great time. We get back to the beach to find in the darkness that the tide is in, the lights are off in the hotel and Jimbo's gone home.

Only one thing for it. We strip to our underwear and hold the rest of our clothes and shoes above our heads. We edge into the freezing water, which has a sobering effect on certain parts of you - even at that age - almost immediately. It's about three hundred yards to the island, and the water is swirling quite strongly around our legs. We were up to our chests almost immediately, but then it stayed at that level for most of the duration. It was slow progress as walking in very cold, tidal water is, so as we were still pissed and to keep our spirits up, we started singing U2 songs at full volume.

I didn't notice it at first, but we must have been louder than we thought as one by one, a light from a hotel room on the island would come on and a silhouetted face appear at the window. I mentioned this to the others and we all agreed that they must be enjoying the show, so we sang a little louder. By the time we got to dry land on the island, the hotel was lit up like a Christmas tree and Mr Porter was there to greet us with a shotgun. When he recognised us as members of his paid employ, he went apoplectic. Not that much of it sank in at the time - we were cold and pissed and just wanted to get to our warm beds.

Next morning, with banging heads and mouths like Gandhi's flip flops, we were hauled into the office to receive the most pompous of verbal volleys, as well as the first, and only, written warning of my career.

At the end of my two year course in May of 1988, there was an option to spend another twelve months at the College upgrading my diploma from "Ordinary" to "Higher". Thinking that potential employers wouldn't really give a toss about that, I put myself out onto the job market, impatient and eager to make my way in life. I was confident in my own abilities and felt that I could make a difference somewhere. I also liked the thought of earning my own money and seeing somewhere else other than Devon. I wasn't fussy where, but I had always fancied London...

4. Skinny Face, What Happened?

I had attended one of those group assessment type days in Ashby De La Zouch, Leicestershire. My catering college had arranged it for me, as I had just finished my course and was on the lookout for gainful employment. It was for Toby Restaurants who are famous today for their help yourself Carveries, but in those days also had a Toby Grills arm - a bit like a Beefeater steak chain. Over a couple of days, there were tests on your practical skills, group bonding exercises, problem solving etc. I must have done all right, because about a week later, at home in South Brent, I got a call….

"Good morning. My name is Hunt, James Hunt."

And I'm Niki Lauda, I remember thinking.

"And I run a busy establishment in the City of London", he continued, in an Australian accent. He went on to explain that his pub / restaurant was called The Clanger and was situated on Houndsditch, a street close to Liverpool Street station in the "heart of The City".

"Apparently, you did well in the assessment day last week, and we'd like to offer you a live in position as Trainee Assistant Manager with us, at a starting salary of £5,600 per year."

I quickly did the maths. About a hundred quid a week.

"I wanted more" I responded.

There was a short silence.

"I'll have to get back to you" he said, and hung up.

Next day, he called back…

"They said no. The offer is £5,600."

Don't blame them, I thought to myself.

"I'll take it" I said. I'd have paid them to live near The Arsenal.

And so, on July 18th 1988, I moved my world to London. Bit of a culture shock, Dartmoor to the Square Mile. I was wet behind the ears, with a thick West Country accent and was largely unprepared for living in the rat race. Everybody rushed around, nobody said good morning to strangers (we do in Devon) and everyone seemed suspicious of each other. First week I was there, I got run over by a motorbike that jumped the lights outside the Phoenix cinema in East Finchley. I had just come out of a showing of Purple Rain, the movie by Prince. I was so scared I'd get in trouble, I picked up my glasses which were now nestling under the central reservation, and quickly limped into the tube station opposite. I was left with a tyre burn on the back of my calf and a bruise the size of Bournemouth on my arse. I didn't tell Mum when we spoke on our weekly phone call - she worried too much as it was. Everything seemed so fast and dangerous compared to the laissez-faire existence of rural Devon.

Being in the Square Mile, The Clanger was only open Monday to Friday. Weekends at that time was an absolute ghost town in that area, so my week was pretty similar to most people, working five days with Saturdays and Sundays off. My weekends were worked around Arsenal fixtures and being a tourist. I drank in the sights of London when my team weren't playing - there were so many famous and exciting things for a country boy to see and do. As a kid who grew up in the middle of nowhere, our capital city now became a new and special playground. Every young person from these isles should spend at least a year or two living here. It's a fabulous education, and gives one a different perspective on the world.

Samuel Johnson's famous "When a man is tired of London, he is tired of life" was, equally famously, but much later in one of my pubs, The Compton Arms, once attributed to Samuel L Jackson by a certain regular after a few pints of Camden Hells. This was the same doughnut who bet me a tenner that the sound of Bow Bells, within who's listening parameters you have to be born to be a true Cockney, was from Bow Church in London's East End. Anyone who knows their history knows that these bells belong to the church of St Mary Le Bow on Cheapside, near St Paul's cathedral. I mention this in case the doughnut buys this book, as he still owes me that tenner.

My usual working day was a 10am start, until the pub's close and subsequent clear up. Back then, I lived in Forest Gate to the east of the City, in a company staff house with about six others who were employed in various Toby Restaurant venues in London. I shared a nice ground floor bedroom that had French doors leading out to the back garden, with a massive Kiwi bodybuilder called Todd who, when he wasn't pumping iron, was pumping pints at the Tiger Tavern next to the Tower of London. Big lad, Todd, with biceps in different postcodes.

Every Wednesday, I was responsible for getting to work by 6am so that James & Patti (his wife) could have their lie in. This involved getting up at 4.45 and catching the Forest Gate to Liverpool Street train. I had bought myself an alarm clock for this purpose from Petticoat Lane the previous

Sunday - one of those old fashioned types, with the hammer that vibrates between two bells when it went off. It lived on my bedside table.

So, at 4.45am on the Wednesday my new alarm goes off. With a noise like a bear, Todd bounded out of bed and grabbed the clock. As he let forth a remarkable string of obscenities, he opened the french doors and heaved it way into the night sky, still ringing, and slammed the doors shut again. He then grabbed me by the pyjamas and said "If you ever, ever wake me up again, you'll follow it." He then went back into his bed and pulled the covers over him.

I was very much awake now, but resisted the urge to put Chris Tarrant from Capital Radio on as I got dressed. I had got that radio for my birthday previously, and still liked it. I got to work in plenty of time and regaled this tale of woe to James when he appeared later that morning. Soon after, I was transferred to other accommodation, in the George on the Strand, opposite the Law Courts. It was probably more important for James to get his lie in than save my life, but I didn't mind his motive for doing this, as I got a room of my own. I often wondered if that alarm clock has landed yet.

The Clanger was an incredibly busy venue, with three trading floors. Upstairs, there was the branded Toby Grill restaurant, which did a reasonable trade with business lunches. Had a couple of mad chefs, a Spanish waitress called Carmen and a couple of shifty Columbians also waiting tables, called Diego and Santiago. Didn't like them much, always stealing Carmen's tips.

The ground floor was a huge pub drinking area, that had a cafe' bar to one side of it. This area opened for breakfast at 8am, and was run by Gillian, a thirty something girl from Birmingham and the focus of my first older lady crush. She of course, had no time for a spotty teenager such as myself, so I didn't get too far with that one. I wasn't yet wise enough to go for someone in my league, probably because there wasn't anyone poor enough to be in my league in the City at that time. Every woman around seemed to be smoking hot in a tailor made business suit. My one suit was from Top Man, and it hung off me like I'd been ill.

The basement bar was accessed from the side of the main bar. It was like a secret club. Cool tunes from the jukebox, relaxed, private areas and a hot food counter to one side. This was run by Mo and Maggie. If ever you could imagine Eliza Doolittle as a pensioner, then Maggie was it. East End salt of the earth, said it how she saw it, and taught me a few new swear words to boot.

Mo was (is) a crazy Egyptian who managed to marry for a passport, but still struggles with English thirty years later. It was generally acknowledged that Mo was the best barman in the City, as he could serve multiple people multiple drinks, without making any mistakes. I learned a lot working beside him on busy shifts, including how not to pull women.

Despite having reputedly a pork sword the size of a baseball bat, Mo's "game" was terrible. His lack of ability in being able to string a coherent sentence together, meant that he was reduced to grunting and pointing at his cock whenever he saw female prey. I knew that this would only work a limited amount of the time for me, and then only for a select representation of the female species, so I made a mental note to ensure that my vocabulary would always give me a better crack of the whip at the fairer sex. Despite this, Mo and I got on like a house on fire, as we still do to this day. Due to the fact that he was built like a brick outhouse, I always called him "Fat Boy". In return, I was - and am - "Skinny Face".

When I first arrived, James' wife, Patti, used to be part of the management team. Working together, they got on like oil and water. I'd be sat in the office counting a till and they'd be verbally knocking lumps out of each other over my head. Soon after, Patti got employed externally doing some Human Resources stuff, which probably saved them from killing each other. Ironically, for the last quarter of a century or so, they've been exploring the world on a 40 foot yacht, and seem happy to do so together in such a confined existence.

Later on, Michael and Rachel joined the management team. Rachel started as a waitress and worked herself up to be a decent manager. She was great fun, always joined in the antics at the pub - I recall she was dating a hairy Italian bloke in those days, and had learned the language. When she left the industry, we strapped her to a barrel and covered her in squirty cream. Michael came to The Clanger from a pub hanging over the Thames called The Samuel Pepys. He was a stereotypical Irishman - big hands, luminous white skin and a great West of Ireland lilt. He knew what he was doing in a pub, too, as he ended up as Greene King royalty. Odd thing was, whenever he had a day off, there would be an IRA bomb warning somewhere on the tube network....

One late afternoon, the Clanger was packed as usual, in both the main and basement bars. We (the management) got an internal call from Mo, who wanted assistance because he was uncomfortable with a group of builders who were getting out of hand, so he had decided to stop serving them. As James was elsewhere, I went into the basement to offer my support. At the time, I was about nine stone soaking wet, and I sauntered in there swinging my keys, to give the impression that I was in charge. As I edged through the crowd at the bar, I got a tap on the shoulder. I turned 'round, and WHACK, I got nutted, and the birds started tweeting. Luckily, being still a relative shortarse, the fat thug had caught me on the forehead. Had he managed to hit my nose with that force, I would not be the handsome chap I am today. I recall being upright, but the room was spinning.... And then I could hear someone talking.

"Skinny Face, what happened?

I was unable to respond. The voice seemed to come from another room.

"Skinny Face. Hey Skinny Face..." It was Mo, shaking my shoulders. Of course it was Mo, nobody else calls me Skinny Face.

"I think I got nutted", I said, as the mists began to clear. My head hurt.

All of the builders had run out, apparently, when the brave lad had decided to lay his head on me. That was one way of getting the pub cleared, although in a straw poll taken by Trainee Assistant Managers at the time, not the most popular method. It was a cowardly act, in all reality, and exposes the harsh realism of serving alcohol for a living. Like many jobs, we are only an idiots whim away from real harm. It is a skill learned on the job to be able to diffuse a situation before it gets serious, and it was not something I had mastered at that early stage of my career.

To be honest, managing people was a skill that I lacked. Due to my training, I was already a reasonable chef, silver service waiter, barman and business person. I could do pretty much everything in the Clanger as well as any member of staff - but the real problem was, I knew it. People management skills are probably one of the most important aspects of a retail supervisors position, yet it was the last thing I was to pick up.

I suppose you can only get better through hands on experience, so jumping into a management role at eighteen years of age is not always ideal. Not many thirty or forty somethings appreciate a spotty teenager telling them to get a move on, and unfortunately I had no idea that there were different ways to impart this instruction without them wanting to punch my teeth in. People are motivated and respond to instruction in many different ways, but at eighteen, I had a one size fits all approach, which probably did my popularity ratings no favours.

I learned quickly, because I had to. I was lucky that I had excellent and experienced people around me, such as James and Mo, who both had extraordinary work ethics and broad backs, which enabled me to both progress and keep my teeth. In return, James must have seen something in myself, as I was given a lot of responsibility very quickly. This was a busy site, yet we had fun, and lots of it. The "work hard, play hard" motto was never truer than here, but whatever state we would end up in after work, no one was ever late the next day.

As an Assistant Manager, it was in James' interest to get me up to speed quickly. The sooner I was reasonably competent in all aspects of the Clangers' business, the easier his life would become. In truth, James was an authoritarian type leader, and with weekends off in the pub, he was always likely to be about, so that particular management style suited The Clanger at the time. Occasionally, although I suspect under a watchful eye, he would allow me to bloom...

We had a barman called Don, a forty something bloke from Bethnal Green in the East End, who wasn't too easy on the eye. Or nose, come to that. Firstly, he had a lazy eye, so sometimes you weren't sure if he was talking to you or looking out for the number fifteen bus down the road. I was never sure which one was the good eye, so I always felt a little uncomfortable chatting to him. Secondly, and much worse, he stank. When I say stank, I don't mean you would get the occasional waft of odour on the wind, oh no - not with Don. This bloke honked. On a bad day, it was like a rotting corpse that had been dead for six months had just been dug up and inserted into his work shirt. Other staff behind the main bar who had to work with him were retching into the glasswasher, yet Don seemed oblivious.

James didn't want to confront Don about this for two reasons. Firstly, it's a really uncomfortable and very personal subject to bring up with someone, as there is a very good chance that his feelings and pride might be damaged. Secondly, it meant getting near him. So, in James' all powerful wisdom, he decided that straws were to be drawn as to who had to have the chat with him. Of course, I lost, and so spent some time working out my strategy as to how to not hurt his feelings, yet make quite a serious point at the same time. I decided to tackle him when he went downstairs into the cellar to change a barrel, because the cellar was a really open and spacious area and had a huge fan.

"Don", I said really loudly, as it was a noisy fan.

"Yes Malcolm?" replied Don, as he climbed off the Tennent's Pilsner barrel.

"You stink", I shouted. I mean, I couldn't think of any other way to put it. Don seemed genuinely taken aback.

"Do I?" He had a shocked expression on his boat race, which I found amazing.

"Yes, you do. And we've had a load of complaints about it from other members of staff who have to work next to you. They have been begging me to force you through a car wash." I felt I was getting my point across, but was struggling with the compassion bit. Don then did something that negated the need for that. He sniffed his own armpit, as if he was trying to find out what all the fuss was about.

"Oh, fuck off Don", I said. "There's a phosphorus cloud around you right now, don't tell me no one has ever mentioned this to you". Don looked amazed, but he was bullshitting. I asked him to shower before he came to work and wear a fresh shirt every day, to which he agreed. I hoped that this would be the end of it, but within a month or two, he had another warning, a further written warning and, eventually, the sack. It wasn't as if he was a kid starting out in adulthood with a problem, this was just a long in the tooth, fully matured bloke who didn't own a bar of soap.

Unfortunately for me, Don's period of brief employment at The Clanger coincided with Arsenal's 1989 win at Anfield, when we snatched the league title from Liverpool with almost the last kick of the season. Now I had been to every game that year, home and away, but this final climax was actually played on a Friday night due to the Hillsborough disaster the previous month, so there was no way that James would let me go. Fridays were absolute bedlam here. James very kindly let me put his portable TV on the bar, facing inwards, so Don, who was also a Gooner, and myself could watch it as we poured beer.

When Mickey Thomas went through on Grobbelaar, the Liverpool 'keeper, with seconds to go, I had two pints of Tennents Extra in my hands. As he put the ball in the net, the beer went North, and I slid along the bar floor on my knees and in tears. I came to a stop under the end of the bar covered in lager and, to my horror, Don, who had jumped on me in celebration. Believe me, I was out of there and back on my feet quicker than you could say "armpit".

Usually, The Clanger would stop serving at 9.30pm. In those days, we had already taken wheelbarrows full of cash and so there was never any pressure on to meet our budgets. In addition, if you stayed open after this time, you generally got all of the dregs of the pissed up City boys, who were thrown out of the other sensible surrounding venues at 9.30 as well. Mo and I used to get everything cleaned up as smartly as we could, so that we could disappear to Collins (now called The Bull) bar on Devonshire Row, EC3 just around the corner from us.

All pubs would close by 11pm in those days in the Square Mile, so we drank as many pints as we could in the short space of time that we had, just to wind down after work. Budweiser on draught was our drink of choice back then. It was a bit of a rough pub, as it was one of the few brave enough to stay open later in the area. Mo and I saw a few punch ups in there, but never were really involved, except for this one innocuous time...

I used to do my personal laundry in the pub where there was a washing machine, and carry it to and from work and home in a plastic carrier bag. For some reason, whilst supping a Budweiser in Collins late one evening, this pissed up German bloke picked up my bag full of clean clothes and started to walk off with it. Naturally, I did a double take to check that it was my smalls he was escaping with, and yelled "Oi!". I then made a grab for the bag, but he pulled away. I dived on the bag and wouldn't let go, but the German bloke was yelling "Nichts, nichts" at me. By this time, Mo had turned around from the fruit machine and was watching this tug of war of socks between me and the pissed up German.

"Skinny Face, what are you doing?"

"This fucking Kraut's got my washing" I yelled back, and pulled even harder.

"Was?" (What?) said the German, and let go. He turned around and walked out. Mo rolled his eyes and took another gulp of his pint. Thanks for your support, pal...

To this day, I have no idea why Fritz went for my laundry. Never saw him again.

One evening, there was a very private leaving party for one of the City executives from an office around the corner. The do was to be held in the basement bar, and the arrangements were handled by James and Mo. These guys must have paid an absolute fortune for the entertainment, as there was "Foxy Boxing" and "Jelly Wrestling". We had a makeshift boxing ring to one side of the bar, where topless girls in comedy oversized gloves were knocking crap out of each other. At one point, the chap on his way out was invited into the ring, gloved and blindfolded, and the two girls proceeded to knock seven bells out of him.

Towards the other side of the bar, an arena of about twelve feet square was filled with jelly, and two more topless ladies were getting stuck into each other. My only previous live wrestling experiences were at Butlins, but I have to say this was by far the more crowd pleasing, as it seemed to get a much more positive reaction than that of the Holiday Camp variety. Mo had to stand behind the bar all evening, firstly because it was busy, and secondly because the baseball bat wouldn't subside. Had to turn the jukebox up with all of the grunting coming from behind the pumps. If you're wondering, it was raspberry jelly. Tried some.

At the end of that year, James won the Company's Manager of the Year award, which was a new Peugeot. At drinks that Friday evening, I enquired if that made me Assistant Manager of the Year.

"No." He replied.

"You're still a c*nt"."

5. Mustard and Cream

After a couple of years working at The Clanger, it was the opinion of the Area Manager that I had outgrown the pub. I had done a few reliefs (covering James & Patti's holidays) and also ran many other Toby Restaurants around London covering their managers' annual leave. I had indeed learned quickly on the job and for someone still quite young, had covered a lot of ground. I wasn't happy about the proposed move to begin with, as I loved my life at that point. I was proud of my work, enjoyed doing the odd relief and was very used to my weekends off.

Being shipped out to run other establishments for a fortnight while the managers took annual leave was a massive learning curve for me. I quickly sussed that the one size fits all approach that worked in the Clanger wasn't necessarily the way forward in other places. Every pub is different, just as every member of your employ is different, so it was a skill to quickly analyse the needs of these venues and do the best you can to meet them. Amongst others, I ran the Old Mill at Takeley, near Stansted airport, the Hayfield on the Mile End Road, the White Hart in Upminster and the Crown at Broxbourne.

All of these were different types of places with different offers and different punters, which gave a real crash course in my "pubbing" education. Realistically, my remit was just to look after the place for two weeks in the exact way that the current full time managers ran it, but naturally I found that I was able to identify flaws in their systems and would make mental notes to myself, so that I could do things better when I had the chance to be in charge somewhere full time.

It was decided in some ivory tower that I was to be transferred to The George in Enfield Town, a very busy Toby Grill that had been run by a chap called Bob and his wife for about twenty years. He was retiring, so the Company decided to put in a new team of a guy called Jonathan, a forty something who had run a Charringtons pub previously, and myself. It was a completely different type of venue to the Clanger, far more of a "locals" establishment than a City pub, so I had to learn to appreciate and look after the customers a lot more than the transient trade of the Square Mile that I was used to.

It was also obvious that Jonathan, although a really nice and well meaning chap, wasn't James. Discipline among the staff was rare, and by nature they would take advantage of this - and none more so than myself. Despite my lofty number two position, all of a sudden I was surrounded by a dozen waitresses who all wanted to mother me, and who was I to disappoint? I was like a kid in a candy store and did a lot of "growing up" in that period. Looking back, I didn't portray myself in the most moral of lights, but I was of that age where your brain is kept a long way South of your cranium, and everyone seemed very keen to be nice to me.

On a work front, The George taught me an awful lot about managing your local customers in the bar and difficult customers upstairs in the restaurant. Unfortunately for me Enfield is very much a Tottenham area, so I took an extraordinary amount of abuse over my footballing allegiance. I was in this pub when Gazza scored against us in the F.A. Cup semi final from about a mile out, and was bundled in the back bar under about twenty of them. In the main, the banter was great fun and I learned to hold my own.

The restaurant was a popular local place. It was busy almost every evening and absolutely rammed on a Sunday lunch. We were turning tables over at least twice, sometimes three times and you had to book a fair way in advance to get a table on a weekend. As well as being collectively horny, the waitresses knew what they were doing. They had their own systems, own areas and worked brilliantly as a team. My role on a busy session was generally a supervisory one - seating the guests, managing bookings etc. I would also cover for the chefs on their days off, which gave the job an enjoyable bit of variety.

It was a good team, a far better set of staff than the Clanger had (management aside). In London, especially Central London, it is so very difficult to get staff - at least those who have some sort of grasp of our language and who are prepared to turn up when they are meant to. The managers at The Clanger were always covering shifts for non shows. At The George, there was always someone willing to cover a sick person, so that side of running the show was much easier there. I suppose it's because people value their jobs more outside of big cities, or maybe there are just less jobs to go around.

It did amaze me here how rude some customers are to waiting staff. Although this was a pleasant place to have a meal, it wasn't Le Gavroche in Mayfair. Sometimes on a weekend, you'd get these people turn up in evening gowns and fur coats, and expect me to de robe them and hang it up in our non existent cloakroom. We did have a seldom used toilet upstairs, so to play along sometimes I'd chuck it in there. I once had this stuck up cow tell me that her coat was camel hair. I responded with "It's so you..." These characters would have booked a window seat, and would be clicking fingers to attract attention. Wound me right up. After being pampered all evening, this type of cretin would also be the sort to leave a 25p tip.

Kids were everywhere, too. I'd not experienced having to deal with the shorter members of our society before, as they just weren't allowed in The Clanger. It shocked me that many of them were allowed to run around the restaurant without consequence. If I had stood up in a restaurant while I was a kid - not that we went to many - I would have been whacked around the back of my head until I landed back in my chair. Not here, it was like a bloody racetrack on a Sunday afternoon.

There was this one family of Jewish people that were dining with us, all the men were wearing a kippah, including this young boy. They were just ignoring their kid as he raced about, not just around the dining room floor, but he started to run into the back areas where the kitchen was and where the waitresses prepared the desserts. Twice I went to the table and asked them really politely not to let their offspring behind the scenes, as it's quite dangerous. It wouldn't have taken much for him to collide with a waitress carrying food and cause an accident, although I quite fancied wrapping a dinner plate around his noggin, to be fair. While I was restocking the sauce carousel in the kitchen, this little shit ran into my legs. He looked at me, laughing.

"Do you like chocolate?" I said to him, sweetly. He nodded in anticipation.

"Here you go" I said, as I offered him a large spoon of brown French mustard. He snatched the spoon off me and gobbled it up. And then cried.

I led him back to his table and told his now concerned parents that he had run behind the kitchen area and stole a spoonful of mustard. "He must have thought it was chocolate" I added. I repeated that it was much safer for him to be sat down, and I left the table as he was being scolded by his parents for stealing. Little victories.

One incident that didn't go to plan was on a rammed Friday night. We were getting stuffed, it was so busy. Every table was full, and both the kitchen and waiting staff were at breaking point. I was running around, metaphorically sticking my fingers in dykes - doing a dessert here, seating people, fetching chips for the chefs, taking a payment there. At one point, Cathy asked if I could do her desserts for her - I'll always remember - it was two knickerbocker glories, a chocolate fudge cake and a banana split.

The George had this cream gun - a metallic, gas propelled canister, which made the production of desserts a lot more efficient. Basically, it turned liquid cream into whipped when you operated the gas nozzle. However, as it had been so busy, the bloody thing was empty. I delved into the fridge underneath, and took out a carton of whipping cream. I depressurised the canister, gave it a rinse and filled it up with the cream. After screwing the lid back on, I pressed the nozzle, and BOOM! The thing exploded. In my haste, I had obviously put the lid on skewed, and it wasn't having it.

I just stood there. I couldn't see, as both of the lenses on my glasses were covered in this yellowish foam. My face, hair, suit, and ears were completely caked, as well as the surrounding walls and tables. I was still holding the main body of the cream gun, but we found the head of it over by table 4 in the restaurant. There is nothing worse than a walk of shame, and the only way back to my room upstairs to shower was back through the restaurant itself. There wasn't a dry eye in the house as I squelched my way through, from either customers or staff.

After a year or more in The George, it was evident that the company weren't overjoyed with the leadership of Jonathan. Basically, he was just too nice a bloke and probably suited somewhere a little smaller and a little less hectic. A new husband and wife team were sourced for the pub which left me as a bit surplus to requirements, so I was used by the company to do some long term reliefs. This is a situation where the manager has left a business (forced or otherwise) and I was put in charge to hold it while they searched around for someone new to take over. This time frame could be a matter of weeks or months, but as I was family and commitment free at that point in my life, it wasn't really an issue. I had learned so much at the George, both personally and professionally and I felt that I was now ready to step up and be in charge by myself.

6. She Sleeps Where?

I was sent to the Thomas Kemble Toby Hotel, in Wickford, Essex, to look after it for what I thought was to be a few weeks, but ended up the best part of six months. This was a branded Toby Grill restaurant with a twenty bedroom motel type operation attached. The head receptionist here was a hottie called Lara, and it didn't take too long to make her acquaintance. In fact, I liked her so much that I ended up marrying her and we have a beautiful daughter together, Jess.

To be honest, I'm not sure how else a publican is supposed to meet anyone who doesn't work in the industry. Our hours are so skewed from the rest of the working world, that it would be very difficult to make a relationship work. She was a bubbly, fun girl, and we got on like a house on fire. She actually made my job very easy, because she knew the hotel from back to front. I was always reminded to do stuff by her that I wouldn't have thought of, as this was my first "rooms" experience.

Lara wasn't ever one for academia, but if she was shown something, it stuck. Not only that, but she'd probably find an even more efficient way of doing the task. She was like a machine, and there were very few errors ever coming from the reception side of the business. It isn't always true in this world that you must have a solid academic background to progress. In my opinion, Lara would be in my top two or three employees ever, and I've employed many hundreds over my years. At the time of writing, more than 25 years on, she is in charge of two Building Society branches in the Newcastle area. Brilliant achievement.

The hotel had a young but enthusiastic set of staff who all knew what their jobs were to a certain extent. Their main concerns were not really focussed on the work but their bizarre relationships - it was like an episode of Ex On The Beach in that workplace, as there was always someone breaking up or getting back together. I do recall having a wonderful staff Christmas Day dinner there, after all of the lunchtime punters had disappeared. We all sat around a big table in the restaurant and celebrated together, socially drinking long into the night. It was a decent bunch of people, if not totally dedicated to the industry long term.

From here, I was sent back to hold The Clanger as James & Patti had decided to take a sabbatical. As Lara and I were an established couple by then, she came with me. It was strange going back, and not really the easiest move as the staff would always view me as the eighteen year old kid, rather than the new and improved version that I had naturally become with all of the extra experience gained elsewhere. In other ways, I already knew the systems here and was confident that they worked. I ran it well for around six months or so, but it was too big and busy a site for the Company to give someone as young as I on a permanent basis, so once they had eventually found their "dream manager" for The Clanger, it was time to move on again.

I was to be given The Sutton Arms, in Carthusian Street, just off the Smithfield meat market and around the corner from Barbican tube station. I was pretty excited. It was a much smaller and quieter venue than The Clanger, although everything was, to be fair - but it was mine, permanently.

Again, due to its locality within the Square Mile, it was a Monday to Friday venue so it was back to weekends off. Just before the move from The Clanger, Lara informed me that she had fallen pregnant. By this time, the novelty of the relationship was wearing off from my side, and to say I was shocked at this news was an understatement. Lara was supposed to be on the pill, so it was really unexpected. The Area Manager at the time called it "The biggest catch since Moby Dick"...

I was quite advanced at that point in a business sense for someone of my tender years. I had come a long way in the trade very quickly, but as regards me as a human being looking back, I was still incredibly immature. I was in no way prepared or ready to have a kid and I wasn't even that happy anymore in my relationship - but what could I do? My thoughts were that my girlfriend was pregnant, so I have to make the best of it. We both moved to The Sutton Arms, with Lara choosing work at the Ear, Nose and Throat hospital near Kings Cross.

The Sutton Arms was owned by Charringtons, an historical brewery from Silvertown in the Docklands area of London which was part of Bass in those days. Soon after, Charringtons would be swallowed whole by Bass, and would cease to exist. As part of the restructure of the industry back then limiting any Company to two thousand licenses, The Sutton Arms then became one of many pubs which were purchased by Greene King, in their initial expansion outside of their East Anglian heartland.

The pub itself is a small, quirky and historical ale house, built in 1611. It gains its trade these days from the hundreds of offices and surrounding businesses, but back in older times they would have had workers from the meat market supping beer in the early hours, or the Masters from Charterhouse, which is situated just around the corner.

In the beginning, I recruited my younger brother Larry, who was at one of his loose ends. Larry always had a lot of loose ends. And screws, to be fair. He was a decent barman, and very handy with a hammer so it was a no brainer for me. He lived upstairs with Lara and I. I also advertised for new staff on an "A" board outside the pub, as all of the previous employees had disappeared with the old manager.

So this young chap, Martin walked in one morning in response to the advertisement, and explained that he was studying engineering at City University and needed to work his way part time through his academia. We had a good chat and, later that day, a good drink. He lived just around the corner, in Charterhouse Square with his psychopathic girlfriend, Clare. Martin started pulling pints for me that very week, after I got him to have a shave and we are still friends today. Indeed, he was my best man for my wedding to Wife Number Two, in 2004.

I was partly responsible for Martin's first wife, too. Caron worked on the counters at the local Barclays Bank, and Martin used to go in and flirt with her on the pretence that he had to discuss his overdraft. The problem with Martin's finances were, the more shifts he used to work for me, the more beer he used to drink. It got to the stage where his wages were used directly to cover his weekly bar tab, and then the cycle would start again on a Monday. I suppose it gave him more opportunities to go flirt. His relationship with Clare went pear shaped when she pulled out some cutlery on him, so he was best off out of that….

Now Caron was married, unhappily, to another chap. At some point, and it all happened very quickly, she ran away and hid with Martin upstairs in the pub. This went on until the shit died down, and she ended up with Martin, got married and had two kids, Will and Ellie. Years later, I would employ Will behind my bar at The Compton Arms. He's about seven foot four and built like a wardrobe these days. I always told the regulars at The Compton that I used to change Will's nappy as a baby, which always made him squirm.

On the subject of babies, my Jess arrived in April of 1993. It was the middle of the night when the waters broke, and I got a slap to wake me up for my troubles. We raced to UCH Hospital, and I managed to get a parking ticket dropping her off at 3am. Shame on you, Camden council. The labour was long, and I felt helpless. There's not a lot you can do as the father at this stage - I guess my contribution was already done and long out of the way at this point of the proceedings. Anyway, progress was slow and Lara started to fall asleep. I'd been sat there about a day, and I was starving, so I nipped out to the 24 hour KFC on Tottenham Court Road and had a Fillet Burger meal. Delicious.

Suitably energised, I raced back to Lara who probably didn't even know I'd gone. After twenty seven hours Jess decided to make her appearance, weighing in at seven pounds in weight and about twenty grand a year. For me, it was life changing. I had never felt such overwhelming responsibility as when I carried her out of the car and into our home. She was peering at me as I carried her up the stairs, and I suppose it was one of those enlightening moments in life. If I wasn't feeling mature enough to be a parent at that stage, then tough. She was there, so it had to be done. She still looks at me with that same expression today, to be fair, so I think it's all just a crafty ruse to get her way.

With Jess' arrival well before the days of extended maternity pay, Lara went back to work within weeks, which left me holding the baby and running the pub at the same time. I was lucky that she was a problem free child who loved her sleep, so I was able to keep her in a moses basket on the red wine shelf down in the cellar, while I poured pints and warmed up homemade cottage pies upstairs in the pub.

While this may sound a little bizarre (before you pick up the blower to Social Services), the logistics and layout of The Sutton Arms meant that the basket was in view at all times from behind the bar - there was just a few stairs separating us. I am unsure to this day whether being raised next to a cheeky Merlot has had any influence on her drinking habits. We generally indulge in a nice real ale when we meet up these days. If I had kept her in the fridge next to the Cumberland sausages, it would have been more of a pointer to future tastes, as she is now vegetarian.

It was very cool for me to finally have my own pub, and I strived to make sure that it was to be a success. I didn't switch off. In addition to the long opening hours, there were many tasks both before and after that required my attention which I have documented elsewhere in these pages, so it was a full on existence. Without the addition of a little humour, however, no publican could survive this unique lifestyle. Running a boozer offers plenty of opportunity for a good laugh, and as well as the comedy (intended or otherwise) which happens on the social side of the bar, I have always taken great amusement from setting my staff unlikely tasks, as I was in the beginning, in the hope that they believe that what I'm asking them to do is legitimate.

In The Sutton Arms, I had a fabulous character who had a part time bar position, who was studying at the Italia Conti school of performing arts just down Goswell Road - we'll call him Tim. Now Tim was from Northern Ireland, and if there was ever a definition of a chap "fresh off the boat", then he was it. Thick, rich Belfast accent, 18 years old and new to the lights of London.

He had a heart of gold and an unquestioning work ethic. Tim would run through a brick wall for me - not because I'd ask him to, but just because he wouldn't notice it was there in the first place. If there was a plate to be dropped, a pint to be spilled or a bag to trip over, our Tim would be first in the queue. Pull up a stool, settle down with a pint and watch the entertainment unfold. He cost me a fortune in broken crockery and stock loss, but I always maintain that Tim was one of the best value for money employees I ever had.

Now one quiet Tuesday evening, I'd had a couple and was feeling mischievous. Tim was creating havoc behind the bar, despite the relative lack of clientele and his well meaning. I beckoned him over and put on my serious face...

"We have a problem with the gas,Tim. We had a leak earlier on and we're almost out - I don't think we're going to last the night"

"Ok Boss" he replies, as this information tried to sink in to him. He had no idea gas even existed in a pub, in all probability. At that time, we used carbon dioxide in 14lb pressurised containers to assist getting the beer from the barrels in the cellar downstairs up to the pumps at the bar. In Tim's world, the beer just arrived by negative gravity, I expect. I reached over the bar and pulled out a standard cube shaped ice bucket with a lid, black in colour with Jack Daniels advertised on its side.

"I've had a chat with Bill from The Blue Posts next to Farringdon station. He says he doesn't have much but can spare us enough to last until a delivery tomorrow. Can you get him to put some in here for us?"

"No problem Boss" came the eager to please reply. "Back in a jiffy".

So off Tim goes. It's about a fifteen minute walk to the Blue Posts, but he probably did it in seven. I call up Bill to explain the situation, and he responds "Ok, leave him to me". I can sense a little eye rolling over the phone, but Bill and I were on friendly terms, as the same brewery owned both pubs and we used to socialise at area meetings.

When Tim arrived at the Blue Posts, Bill acknowledged him, took the ice bucket and lid off him and asked him to wait. He then disappeared to his cellar, filled the bucket with ice and put the lid back on. As he returned to Tim, he held the bucket from underneath with one hand and kept the lid shut with the other.

"Whatever you do, Son, don't move this lid. The slightest gap will allow the gas to escape and I don't have any more I can give you". He handed the bucket of ice back to Tim, who received it gingerly, like he was holding an unexploded doodlebug from 1942.

The fifteen minute walk back now takes half an hour. By this time, I've told both customers and staff what's going on and we are all outside peering down the road watching Tim, who, oblivious to the crowd up ahead, is gently tiptoeing towards us and holding on to that lid for dear life.

When he came back inside the pub, I took the bucket off him in a suitably over cautious fashion.

"That'll get us through, thanks a million" I said in all sincerity.

"No problem, Boss" he replied. I went downstairs and threw the ice into our ice machine. I let him go home early and never told him about the futility of his mission.

Our Tim was also victim to the occasional cellar prank. I was teaching him to spile a real ale barrel once. These were 9 gallon metal tubs that you need to put on racks on their side, with a sealed hole at the top, which needs to be pierced to allow the air in, so that the ale can start its final fermentation before tapping and serving the beer. This hole at the top would only be breached after an acceptable period of time post - racking, and was to be done with caution by releasing the pressure before finally knocking the seal completely through, so the ale would be less lively. You wouldn't open a can of coke immediately after smacking it on the concrete floor, would you? Well, you would if you wanted to get someone covered in the stuff…

So Tim is standing next to this barrel of Charrington's IPA, rubber mallet in hand. We'd just had a dray delivery about an hour previously, so this particular keg had been bounced all over the streets of London that morning, even before I had heaved it onto the rack. I hand him a wooden peg.

"Now you need to hit this firmly enough to pierce the hole - don't be shy.

I find the best method is to keep your eyes directly over the hole as you hit it, as it makes you more accurate". I took a step back.

"Ok Boss". WHACK!

In all my years of doing this job, out of all of the thousands of tubs I'd spiled, I'd not seen one go up like this. The jet of ale that came out of that barrel made the Boxing Day tsunami look like a leaky tap. Tim was thrown back backwards across the cellar on his arse as the sticky jet got him squarely on the bridge of his nose. We lost a good quarter of the barrel as it continued to spew for a good ten seconds at full pelt, drenching both the cellar ceiling and the now prostrate Tim, who was lying on his back in an ever deepening puddle of IPA. I never found the wooden peg that Tim had used, God knows where that finished up - probably in the same place as his eyeballs.

In other memorable moments, Tim has also been blown across the bar by touching a live wire protruding from a faulty glasswasher, and delivered a bacon sandwich to a fully dressed Jew by mistake, as the poor chap had only come in to let his little boy use the facilities. I even managed once to get him to look down the end of a hose in the cellar, while I stood guard at the tap, to see if he could see a blockage....!

I loved the pub lifestyle, and dived in. This was my own little corner of London, and every day lots of people came into my place wanting to spend their time and money. Trade was almost exclusively centered around office working hours here, so it was easy to predict and manage when we were going to be busy, just as it was at the Clanger, which made it relatively simpler to run than a business that attracts its customers from different strands of the community. Without realising it, however, I was diving in too deeply....

In the morning, I would carry baby Jess to the local Safeway, to pick up any ingredients I required for my food franchise. I paid Charringtons £15 per week to run the food operation myself, which consisted of a chilled food counter and a microwave under the beer pumps. I would cook trays of lasagne, or cottage pie in the domestic kitchen upstairs in the accommodation, and then heat up a portion upon request. I also sold pies and pasties from the Ginsters van that did a delivery service, plus sandwiches to order. It was only available lunchtimes, and I had a hat under the counter. It barely covered costs, but brought in a fair amount of daytime trade that we wouldn't have otherwise achieved.

At the Safeway deli counter, I used to get loads of attention carrying this cute newborn. It's the equivalent of a dog in a bag these days, I guess. The girls used to look forward to my morning visits, and come around the counter so that they could hold Jess and coo a lot. Hated every minute of it. One of these "cooers", Penny, eventually gave up her Safeway job to stay at home and become Jess' permanent baby minder, when she got too big to look after while I was working.

So I would work the lunchtimes, usually with Larry or Martin for company, and have Jess snoozing and inhaling grape fumes simultaneously in her basket downstairs. Then, in the afternoons when the lunchtime rush had dissipated, I would look after Jess upstairs with Larry or Martin looking after the pumps. When Lara came back from her work, I would go back downstairs while she had Jess.

Being still rather youthful, having like minded people around you and a cellar full of booze every day can be a lethal combination. Add this to the fact that I was now the Boss and there was no-one to pull me up, I naturally over indulged. At around four or five o'clock, the offices opened their doors and poured through mine. Regular, large groups would descend on us and started to abuse their livers. Being the "Guv'nor" of the establishment, they always insisted that I had a pint with them, so, without that maturity and foresight that comes with age and experience, I would always accept.

As there were many different groups from many different offices, I would be accepting lots of drinks - all willingly offered, and all willingly accepted. It was never "No, not for me", or "Maybe another time". I loved it, and thought it natural. I was the life and soul of the pub, and in my head I thought I was doing a great job. The punters loved my company and they came back day after day to pour money into our coffers. Isn't that what it's all about?

Looking back, I was starting to slow down. I was still doing everything required to run The Sutton Arms - the standards were still good, the figures were excellent and nobody professionally was telling me that I wasn't fantastic. I had my brother and my best friend working with me, and life was a breeze. But after drinking my bodyweight in Greene King IPA every night, the mornings were getting harder. Furthermore, I also couldn't see the damage being done to my relationship with Lara. Many a time she would bring up the state of me when I staggered upstairs, pissed out of my skull carrying the till. I used to boast about the fact that I could count the till accurate to the penny at a ridiculous speed, whilst drunk as a skunk. And I could.

I would always arrogantly shout her down, and feed her the bullshit that I was doing this for the family, and I was the one keeping a roof over our heads. In reality, I was convincing myself of this, too. The truth was, I had turned into a drunk. I drank from the afternoons until close, five nights a week, while I was "working". I would probably be knocking back upwards of fifty pints a week at that stage of my life, and the truth was it was because I was probably masking the fact that I was personally very unhappy. I was trapped in a relationship that had pretty much run its course for me even before the pregnancy, and the booze helped me to hide that unhappiness from myself.

In no way is this an excuse for what Lara had to go through. She would be upstairs with Jess every night, while I would be downstairs drinking and flirting with the office girls. I always used to deny it, and laugh it off as innocent banter, which wasn't always the case - but the truth was I was a drunk and didn't care once I was in that state. I can only imagine the pain she would have felt upstairs knowing that this went on. She is anything but stupid. I was a pig, and today I look back on those times with nothing short of horror and embarrassment.

Eventually, of course, I was caught red handed - we always are - and she rightly left me. My world fell apart as I no longer had Jess with me. I truthfully didn't really miss Lara, but they came as a package and I couldn't bear not being with my daughter. We reconciled again later on and even left the pub game for a year or two. I did a bit of lorry driving, supermarket work and even estate agency stuff, but I never really was able to find something that motivated me as much as the pub game.

Lara and I even got married, on a beach in the Caribbean a year or two later. I thought that I was doing the right thing, as Jess meant everything to me. I wanted to be with her forever so this, in my deluded and still immature mind, was the best way to go about it. Even on the sand while I was taking my vows, I was thinking to myself "What are you doing?!" I didn't love her, but here was I tying the knot. Even then, I knew it would end badly.

Just weeks later, I got caught out again, and it was over. This time, I probably wanted to get caught. While it wasn't a set up, I couldn't see any other way out of this mess that I had wholly created for myself. I was out of it, and resigned myself to weekend visits and daily phone chats with Jess. Lara was devastated and soon after moved back up North, which made visiting harder, but I still did it. I don't get absent fathers. Whatever the circumstances, it isn't the kids fault, so make the effort. The more you put in, the more you get out. Don't let them down.

Lara and I talk infrequently today. We send Christmas and birthday texts, and have met up a couple of times in recent years for Jess' graduations. Baby Jess now has a Masters in Family Law from Leeds University and later this year will become a Doctor. She lectures Law at Cardiff University. How she achieved this with her start in life next to the Merlot is anyone's guess. She always, however, had both parents solidly behind her at every step in her progression - and hopefully she could feel that. How she has turned out as such a wonderful human being, however, I'm totally attributing that to her mother.

At a random point during my tenure at The Shakespeare Tavern in Bristol, a pub business which I purchased in 2006, I began to keep a sporadic daily account of my world and its events as they happened...

Pub Diaries, Part 1.

Monday 1st October 2007.

For as long as I can remember, Monday mornings have conjured up this image of being the start of the worlds week. Any conversation you have with a normal human being will involve them saying "it's Monday, innit?"- as if it explains the way that they are feeling. It implies that the universe has, as dawn broke, released a massive handbrake and civilisation is creaking and clanking as it winds itself up for another week.

I don't have weeks. My routine does not have seven day definitions, nor set two day periods at the end of five day periods, where the rest of the world plans their social activities free from the chains of their respective labours. My week is only defined by the beginning and end of my staff rota, which is pinned behind the bar flap for my employees to plan *their* social lives around.

Mondays, to me, are days when I know that it will likely be the quietest day of my financial week. It is unlikely that the office lunchtime rush will amount to much - indeed, the word "rush" may just mean about six meals. But we always refer to that period between twelve thirty and two as the "rush". Even if we don't "rush". There will be almost no-one to serve all afternoon (although we are rarely empty) and there is another "rush" at five o'clock when the offices pour out of work, desperate to sink a pint of my fine real ale, marvelling at how they got through the prohibitive eight hour shift that loomed before them all on at dawn on a Monday.

A typical Monday morning for me is unlike any other morning, save for the stuff that happens only on a particular day of the week - for example Tuesdays is beer delivery day, which sets it apart from the other six. So, apart from the appearance of our window cleaner every Monday morning, I could be doing any other morning - Saturday and Sundays are exactly the same. Today, before the doors open at eleven, I dragged my two boys from their respective cots, changed their shitty arses, gave them both a bottle and left them in the "cage" to destroy what toys in there that they hadn't already destroyed. I then unset the alarm and went downstairs into the pub, cleaned the toilets, put the nozzles back on the pumps from their nightly soda water bath, arranged the outdoor furniture and had another forced conversation with the window cleaner.

My window cleaner annoys me. Not annoying to the degree where you want to hit him with a bar stool, but annoying like an itchy arse in a busy shopping mall. He was doing this job for a tenner a week when we bought the business. We only have three bloody windows (with twelve panes in each) so it wouldn't be a disaster if there was no window cleaner. I could get the staff to squirt the windowlene on it during the afternoons when we are virtually (but rarely completely) empty. I would save myself five hundred and twenty pounds per year, but it's got to the stage now where it would be weird to say "you're not needed anymore", because I carried on his habitual employment when I took over, which was eighteen or so months ago.

So he turns up every Monday and I hand him a tenner every Monday for about fifteen minutes work.

He always attempts weak conversation as he hands me his hand scrawled invoice: "good weekend?" or "busy?" - but he doesn't really care. I always force a standard reply like: "not bad" or "pretty quiet, really", but I don't even care for the conversation, let alone any possible meaning of the question. I just think "another tenner" and give a standard half smile of thanks as he exits my front door, two fivers richer, which will probably be used on his lunch.

Today's specials:
Coffee and a Chocolate Muffin
How Civilised
£2.50

Beef Chennai
A more up to date version of the Beef Madras.
This will make you sweat like a
cheap hooker on a treadmill.
Comes with pilau rice and naan bread.
£5.75

Grilled Salmon Salad
Well, we're trying to attract the birds. A large mixed salad, Caesar

dressing and a grilled salmon fillet. Lovely.
£5.50

**Coffees, teas or hot chocolate always available for just £1.50,
served in a mug with a kit kat for company.**

Very few people comment on my specials sheets. They are positioned one
on each bar in a Perspex stand up holder, and one on the chalkboard in the
front bar which advertises our wares in proud white paint. We do, of course
have a full menu which sits inside the wine list and goes on every table, but I
like to have a couple of specials advertised as an extra to keep things fresh.

Tuesday 2nd October

This morning, I am a tad miffed. Tonight at 7.45pm we (The Arsenal) are
playing Steaua Bucharest in the Champions League. I have no cover in the
kitchen, as it is the chef's day off and the boys bath night has fallen due today
- which means Mary (my long suffering wife, and the only other person who
"does" food) is otherwise occupied. I shall be throwing a steak pie in the
oven, dashing through to the lounge to catch a glimpse of the score on ITV4,
haring back to the kitchen to put the chips, peas and gravy on (they don't take
as long as the pie) and back to the lounge again, to see the ball go out for a
throw-in. All at once, I am likely to get three or four tickets on at once, with
three or four meals on each ticket. This is known in the industry as "being in
the shit". I then plough through the orders like a man possessed, banging the
food out with precision and care (!) only to race back in the lounge to find out
we have scored three times and their bruiser centre half has been sent off. I
arrive in time to see the ball go out for a throw-in.

It's my own fault. For some reason (and I have not, to my knowledge
ever done this) I thought Arsenal were playing on Wednesday. I got the days
wrong. Usually, the kitchen would have been thoroughly covered and the
boys would have had their bath last night. As it is, I now have a very free
Wednesday night. Bollocks.

My delivery men here all have their own footballing allegiances. This
morning, one of my draymen (who is sixty if he is a day) was chanting for
my benefit "Sven's blue army". He is an avid Manchester City fan and is
currently riding the crest of a wave as they are third in the premiership. He

has shown me three times now since he started including my pub in his rounds, that he has a Man City sticker on his windscreen. When a football fan sees something like that, he has an almost sympathetic admiration for him. Man City are a team that no-one really loves or hates (unless you are a Man Utd fan, of course) so you treat him with the irrelevant shrug that he deserves.

It must be hard for a fan to support a team that never has anything to play for past January. It says to me that he is a true fan. I have already won the price of a pint off him this season for our win over them at The Emirates and there is another pint up for grabs for the return fixture up North. This bet is probably the highlight of his season. I'll still take his money, though, with a clear conscience and a smug smile.

Tuesdays at The Shakespeare Tavern are quiz nights. This means that on a Monday or over the previous weekend I compile the questions. The format is thirty straight questions of any subject, with four or five current events thrown in. I like to try and get it so that the winner gets about twenty three or four right and everyone is capable of getting at least half. If it's too easy, there is no challenge, if it's too difficult (or perceived to be) then people don't come back the next week. It's a pound per person to enter, maximum five per team - winners get the pot. Every participant gets a plate of sandwiches and some crisps delicately emptied in the middle of the triangles. It amazes me how seriously people take this quiz. Tonight, I expect between forty or fifty people to participate, which is the pretty much the maximum you can sit inside here.

When we first arrived at The Shakespeare, they used to bring down metal containers with sausages, chips and beans. At a pre-arranged break in the questions, all participants were meant to help themselves - queue up, grab a plate etc. We just watched for the first week as about seven or eight students (who were not in the quiz) grabbed plates and "mounded" the food until it reached precarious angles before sitting on our stairs, all wild hair and chains, devouring this sorry fayre. Needless to say, only about two thirds of the contestants got fed before the grub ran out.

One particular table with an average age of well over one hundred and thirty demanded to see the manager. I was duly pointed out (thanks, Chloe) and they proceeded to demand their pounds back. I tried to point out that the food was free and the pound was for the quiz, but it cut no ice. I told him that this was our first week and promised him that it would be different next time. He said "there won't be a next time". At over one hundred and thirty, he's probably right. The following week, sandwiches were introduced. We've never looked back.

Wednesday 3rd October

Got woken up this morning by a phone call from Dad.

Dad lives the existence of someone who is determined not to miss a second of the day. He rises at around 5am, wakes up the dawn chorus and begins to squeeze out every ounce of life that there is to be squeezed. In my opinion, he squeezes too hard because he tends to nap just after lunch, again just after tea and can be in bed by eight (unless there is a whist drive on at the village hall, in which case he will have a late one - half past nine). The problem with this routine is that he is under the impression that the rest of the world should be following suit, so when you run a pub and finish around twelve thirty or one in the morning you don't always appreciate the early morning greeting. However, I must say that I look forward to my chats with Dad.

I lost my Mum just over three years ago to breast cancer. She was fifty eight, so we all felt a bit cheated at her early departure. Dad is an intensely practical man - completely emotion free - "stiff upper lip and get on with it" kind of attitude to life. Problem was he had never done anything remotely resembling housework in his whole life before - he was the breadwinner and she stayed at home and kept house - so when it came to managing on his own, it was little short of hilarious. Short of putting on his own trousers, Dad was initially pretty helpless.

It was never meant to be like that. Not to sound negative at the old man's chances, but he was about eight years older than Mum and had already suffered two strokes and a quadruple heart bypass. He was not in line to lead out our team at London 2012, if you know what I mean. It was always assumed that he would go first - whenever that may have been - and Mum would sell the family home and go and live in a flat overlooking Brixham Harbour. As it turned out, Mum was diagnosed first with diabetes, then breast cancer and was gone before we had time to synchronise our minds to the possibility that Mum leaving us was a possibility.

That was the one and only time that I have seen, or known of, Dad crying.

It was horrible - an uncontrolled wailing sound - almost inhuman, that seemed to rise from his chest and get stuck in his throat on its way out, causing a half choke to add to the confusion. It was as if he didn't know how to cry, because he probably hadn't in about fifty years or so. It was like he was unpractised at the physical process of shedding a tear. It was terrifying for me to see, but when he knew I was standing there he stopped, as if he was being ridiculous. I gave him a pat on the shoulder, like I wanted him to know that it was OK and disappeared to shed a tear myself, where no-one would discover me doing such an unmanly thing. I hope that he used his brief time alone at that moment to finish what he had started.

Since Mum's rather urgent departure, Dad has grabbed life by the udders and is furiously milking. He can use the washing machine, cook any number of meals and has added shirts and socks to his dressing repertoire. His use of the hoover, duster and mop are far too infrequent for my taste, but he is pretty happy now he has settled into his routine. Recently, he has even found himself a new "squeeze" named Vi, who is about seventy four (Dad is sixty nine). He was worried how we (his three sons) would take this news, but I am pleased that he is living his mature years how he sees fit. He has earned his retirement.

In business, Dad was a very capable, intelligent man boasting an astonishing ability with figures and numbers, probably stemming from his initial training and position in the accountancy field. He held many posts where he utilised these skills throughout his working life, with my favourite being a betting shop manager in Ivybridge, a town on the Southern edge of Dartmoor. I loved the atmosphere in the shop in the times when I was allowed to visit, hidden away in the back room. I've always loved a day at the races, too - I'm sure there's a link…

He was never a massive success in business, but always managed to do well enough to keep the family supplied, happy and in good health. The reality is, my Dad was just too nice a man - not ruthless or cut throat like maybe you need to be to make the big bucks - he would never consider stepping on someone to progress, it just wouldn't be in his moral compass. For that, I am grateful to him. I learned my ethics in business from him, never to burn bridges, never to inconvenience others, always show your best at all times and give the utmost commitment with every task you do. Without that upbringing and code of morals that my Dad possessed, I wouldn't have got anywhere in life. I can only hope that my kids are watching me as I watched him, with similar thoughts.

I speak with him on a pretty regular basis now, whereas before when I called home, it was always Mum with whom I would converse. I have more in common with my Dad than my other two brothers. The biggest connection we have is sport. Our regular chats now consist of a couple of minutes of him asking about my family and their wellbeing, a few more minutes regarding my pub business and about half an hour on the inadequacies of Paul Collingwood as the new one day cricket captain. When Mum was around, it was as if he had no time or need for these chats, but I am closer to him now than at any point in my life. This morning's conversation was standard fayre - we dissected the woeful England batting performance against Sri Lanka and waxed lyrical over The Arsenal getting an away win over the Romanians. I saw the last 15 minutes only last night, as we got completely stuffed in the kitchen - but I saw the goal, so I counted the tills a happy man.

Thursday 4th October

So this morning was my morning off. That is, I am not on any rota, my kitchen has a chef and I have two on the bar for the lunch rush. A morning off to the average publican goes something like mine did this morning...

8.05am - Baby duty. Shit, wee, bottles, cage. Nuff.

8.40 - The doorbell goes. It's the veg and salad supplier. Chef placed an order last night as she was running out of mixed lettuce. I take in the delivery, pay the man in cash (save on those bank charges) and put it all away.

9.10 - Clean toilets, set up bar etc etc. All those who have run pubs know automatically what etc etc means in this context. Your daily set up is a matter of auto pilot - it involves stuff like putting the bar towels on for a wash, hosing the cellar, removing empties, screwing on the beer nozzles, getting the papers. Most of these things are daily constants. If you ask a publican to list what he or she does every day, they would struggle - but we never seem to sit down. Coffees are taken on the run, as are half your meals during the day.

9.40 - 3663 frozen food delivery. A pain in the arse, this one. Pay the man cash, listen to his irrelevant whimpering about the state of his team (West Ham) and put the delivery away - this is always at least twenty minutes and you end up with minor frostbite at the end of it.

10.10 - Knock the wife up. I love that expression. In this context, I am merely *waking* her, but I am sure I will get round to the other half of the double entendre later.

10.30 - Breakfast with Mary (wife) and Ben & Sam (baby sons). Always a messy affair, although rather entertaining. Crumbs, juice and porridge everywhere - you would have thought being a mother of two that she would have mastered the basics of feeding herself. (Ha ha). She probably won't read this anyway.

10.40 - During breakfast, the butcher arrives. I pay her and plonk the meat in the kitchen as the chef is due in soon. She can put her own bloody delivery away.

10.55 - Phone the accountant to find out why the payroll has not yet arrived. Am informed that there is a postal strike. Lazy lefties. On yer bike, I say - and take some bloody letters with you while you're on it. So I get the accountant to email the information, so that I can put together the staff wages.

11.20 - Go to bank for change.

11.55 - Put together the staff wages.

1.10 - Chef is "in the shit". About twelve tickets have arrived in her kitchen and she's bleating like a lamb whose had a jar of mint sauce waved in its face. So I help out. I go to the fridge for baguettes to put in the oven (hot baguettes to order - this is a nice place) open the door and the tub of Beef Chennai falls out and empties itself over my one-day-old-immaculate-white-Nike's. I am noisily miffed about this, which the chef has understood. She "balanced it like that because she had to put the meat somewhere". I suggest an alternative place for the meat, which does not promote a positive vibe in the kitchen.

1.25 - Mary yells into the kitchen that she is off to her eyebrow - plucking appointment.

1.45 - Am furiously trying to wash curry out of my laces and shoes. After much scrubbing, I have stained yellow streaks down the sides of both. Chef suggests that if I buy new white laces, it would look a lot better. I enquire whether the meat has been fully put away yet, or does she need a hand? She understands again the insinuation and retreats to the relative safety of her kitchen.

2.00 - Go down to the bar to check that they have dug themselves out of the shit. Smiling barman politely enquires "how was my morning off?"

I am cooking from seven this evening, then serving the odd punter when my bar staff are looking the other way, cleaning up and counting the tills. I also intend to sink a few. Oh yes.

Homemade Bacon & Lentil Soup
Chef Pauline was influenced in her younger years by her Great Aunt Morag, who was pot wash at The Gleneagles, a back street café in the Gorbals. Anyway, that's nothing to do with this soup, which is really nice. Served with a baguette & butter.
£4.25

Beef in Beer
Chef Pauline brings you Man Food. Beer, beef, roast potatoes and seasonal vegetables. A hearty meal for real men. Bring me my slippers, woman.
£5.75

Friday 5th October

Today, I am picking up Susan, my sister-in-law, from Manchester airport. She has flown in from Vancouver to see Mary for a couple of weeks. It is a three hour journey each way from Bristol, but it was either Manchester or Gatwick - and the M25 is not the place to be on a Friday afternoon. I leave at nine, after completing my etc etc, and return at around 4.30pm. I have a quick hours kip (not as young as I used to be, you know) so that I am refreshed for whatever Friday night has in store for me.

It's nine pm and I am informed by Mary that Chef Pauline said we have sold out of specials. I whiz over to Asda (which has just gone 24 hours) and buy a load of chicken quarters and pepperoni pizzas. Our customers are in for a gastronomic feast tomorrow. It bugs the crap out of me that my chef has disappeared without ensuring that there was something to put on the specials board in the morning. I know that she has forgotten about the job the second she exits the front door, whereas I run around like a tit in a trance covering her slack. That'll teach me to have a kip - she would never have made it down the stairs if I was awake.

Pepperoni Pizza
Ever been to Rome, or Napoli? Ever tasted the homemade Italian dough,

Mamma's special tomato sauce and fresh Sicilian sausage?
You should go, really. It's great.
Until then, eat this English version, served with chunky chips.
£5.95

Chicken & Chips
Plucked, quartered and fried for your pleasure. Served with our famous chunky chips and peas (you can count the peas as one of your five, you know).
£5.50

Saturday 6th October

I love weekends, for many reasons. Firstly, and most importantly, it is when The Shakespeare Tavern takes the majority of its weekly sales. As my working week is very much seven days, I do not look upon Saturday and Sunday as times when I should be doing nothing but sightseeing or family barbeques. In this industry, we take our money when the rest of the working world take their leisure time - we are competing for everyone's leisure pound - and so I ensure that plenty of my staff are on hand to extract it from them with a cheery smile.

I work my gonads off during the week. I ensure that all of my staff get the time off that they want, so that when they are standing on my stage they give the best performance that they can give. The vast majority of their free time is inevitably taken between Monday and Thursday, because that is when I need them the least. When we are likely to take the sales that will really make a difference to my pension, I would much rather have that extra body there so that everyone gets the best possible service that they can get - and I am able to sell every pint and meal that the customers demand.

My weekends, therefore, sees me in much more of a supervisory role than a hands on one. When business dictates, I am on the floor or in the kitchen. When my highly trained (!) team can cope, I watch sport or spend time being a Dad.

Bringing up babies in a pub is not the recipe for disaster that it sounds. It is not conventional, by any stretch of the imagination. I have never, for example, seen our situation discussed in the pages of "Mother & Baby", or "Practical Parenting". My time with my children is dictated by the needs of the business - that is not to say that the business comes first - but if you are in the kitchen with a dozen meals to cook, you can't start a game of "bash the table with a plastic hammer", because the customers won't wait until you have finished.

Quality time, therefore is limited to snatches throughout the day. During quiet times, or when there are sufficient staff in, I can play for long periods - maybe go for a walk for fresh air, or even the occasional picnic when the weather allows. There are, of course, days or even weeks when it is just so busy that anything other than looking after the business is just impossible. This can put great strain on family life - Mary is left completely on her own to cope, which can be pretty tough even for the most switched on of mothers.

Ben is twenty three months and Sam eleven months, so their understanding of the stresses that their parents can be under is pretty limited at this stage. There are also instances that Mary is needed to help cook, make coffees or help clean the bar at the end of the night. She has a fantastic workload on her plate already, without the pub adding to it. Without her, the business would not be the same in standards or enjoyment - she fills in all of the gaps that need to be filled, and is very much my unsung hero. She has also bought me a brand new pair of immaculate-white-Nike's to replace the ones that Chef Pauline daubed with Beef Chennai, so today she is a sung hero.

Is a normal Dad who disappears from his young at 7.30am and reappears into their lives just before they go to bed a better example of a proper father? I am as hands on as I can be - I change nappies, dish out bottles and bounce them off the sofa at every opportunity - I imagine that my lifestyle allows me to be far less part - time than most Dads. Compared to Mary's role, however, mine is easy. My daily existence is so varied that it allows me to take the various challenges - both business and domestic - in my stride because it is made interesting by that very diversity. Mary's life, however, is predominantly one of baby talk, Playhouse Disney and the permeating whiff of Sudocrem. I couldn't do it. Big up to all you Mums out there.

Today has been the first day of the rugby World Cup quarter finals. England have shocked Australia and France have beaten New Zealand. Upset City. Tomorrow, Lewis Hamilton is racing in China trying to become World Champion in his first season (incredible), England play Sri Lanka at cricket and The Arsenal will be going back to the top of the Premier League when they whup Sunderland. I am staffed up to the hilt in anticipation of having to watch these events.

Today is also my younger brother Larry's birthday. I've sent him a card even though he never sends me one, the tight git. Mary has gone to London with her sister to increase her blood alcohol levels, and the mother in law, Theresa, has stepped in to play Mummies in her stead. I am sure to go into more detail about mother in law relationships at a later date, but it's twenty five past eleven at night and I need to start sweeping the drunks out onto the pavement.

Sunday 7th October

The Shakespeare Tavern Sunday Roast

Your choice of
Roast Turkey Breast, Lamb Shank or **Topside of Beef**
Served with roasted potatoes, cabbage, carrots, broccoli, stuffing,
Yorkshire pudding and gravy, for just
£6.95

The Dessert Trolley
Three shelves, mahogany finish and a squeaky wheel. It carries today a
sumptuous
Chocolate & Orange Profiterole Cake, a delicious **Caramel Apple
Betty** and - as it's sunny - we thought we'd try some **Xmas Pudding &
Custard.**
All desserts start from just
£3.50

Mugs of **freshly ground coffee, tea and hot chocolate**
are always available, served with a **Kit Kat,** for just
£1.50

Got out of bed at 6.30am this morning for the China Grand Prix, in great anticipation of watching Lewis Hamilton win the World Championship. Lots of coffee was the order of the morning, as I huddled on the sofa with a blanket I bought back from a Mexican holiday about ten years ago. All was going swimmingly for our Lewis, until he went straight on going into the pit lane on the way to pick up fuel instead of turning left. I don't do that getting petrol at Tescos.

Sunday evenings are always a good night for regulars. You know that the group of forty - somethings will arrive at about a quarter to nine and congregate on the table beneath the stairs. There will be three or four guys who live on their boats sitting at the back bar drinking real ale of varying description. In the front bar, on the table underneath the middle window sit Brenda and Doris, two sisters in their mid sixties who arrive at eight thirty, drink about five pints each and leave at closing time, both being picked up by their respective husbands.

These two are real characters who only come in on a Sunday night - one starts off on IPA, the other on Fosters. Both will progress to pints of Guinness as the evening wears on. When we bought the business, Mary was pregnant with Sam, which was a fascinating point of conversation for these two. When Sam was born, they gave us clothes for him and a congratulations card - it was really nice.

So last night, I am working on the bar when Doris arrives. I am serving another but greet her with my usual cheesy smile and ask "how's it going?" She replies "Could be better, love" which is most un-Doris like. The chap who I was serving - another regular - said "Don't worry, at least we won the rugby!" Doris looks down into her purse glumly and says "No, my husband died yesterday". She then looked up at me and says "IPA please, love".

Talk about a conversation stopper. These two lovely ladies come here every Sunday night, come hell or high water - nothing gets in the way of this particular routine. Later on, I went upstairs to relate the tale to Theresa who said "she would have appreciated a hug". I told her I gave her a Guinness on the house, which was probably appreciated more.

Monday 8th October

Today, the Union for the Royal Mail workers announced another forty eight hour "stoppage" from midday. I was unsure when the "startage" was from the last one to be perfectly honest, as we have had no post since last Wednesday. A Sunday night regular delivers mail in his van to Swansea and he told me that he is due holiday, which he will be taking in a couple of weeks. "Holiday from what, exactly?" was my immediate response - he hasn't delivered so much as a Visa bill to anyone in over a week. I told him that my letterbox now needs dusting and I'll be forwarding him the bill for the extra labour.

It was a rather quiet day in the pub, save for a mini rush on food at around 8pm. We have gained the trade of a load of workmen who are involved in the building of the new shopping complex in Bristol, so we tend to get busy once they have finished work and had their showers at their respective hotels. They all come in for the quiz on a Tuesday night to pool their collective brain cells in order to win the pot - but to no avail so far. Indeed, one of them came in the other night with his shirt on back to front. The jackpot on "Who Wants to be a Millionaire?" would be safe with this particular chap, no matter how much coughing went on in the background.

Mary and Susan (her sister) came back from London this afternoon armed with a box of Krispy Kreme doughnuts. This is why I married her.

Tuesday 9th October

Our food sales have gone through the roof over the past couple of months.

When we bought the business back in March of 2006, food was sold "sporadically". The pub was under tenancy to a nice guy who was also the manager of a large chain bar in the centre of Bristol. Naturally, his time was taken up with looking after that business and this was to be something on the side that would provide a second income. The problem was he couldn't find a manager reliable enough to run the pub for him and impose the standards that would make it a success.

I viewed the pub on a few occasions, before I took the plunge to plough my own cash in to buy it. On one such occasion, I was given a tour by the current tenants wife - a really pleasant lady who was also "cooking" that lunchtime. Upon visiting the kitchen, I found an industrial hotplate on one of the work surfaces which, when used, would naturally spit fat and steam upwards. The extractor hood was against the opposite wall of the kitchen (thankfully capturing the fryer oil fat) so was ineffective. The whole of the kitchen was coated in a layer of old fat and oil - all surfaces, walls, tins, windows, fridges - it was unavoidable. To compound this hygienic picture, she used to bring her dog to work - not that it contributed anything positive to the operation, you understand - but he was constantly running in and out, jumping up at her and coating himself in used fat every time he touched something. If you found a hair on your plate in those days, it probably wasn't human...

Anyway, she was pottering about, showing me where everything was, how it all worked - really quite helpful. She had done two meals that particular lunchtime (with the assistance of Fido) when she said "OK, I've got to go - we won't do any more today". So off she went, taking the canine fat brush with her. It was 12.45pm. I went downstairs to the bar staff to question the normality of this and they told me that they generally did food Monday to Thursday lunchtimes, but if there were no orders on by around 1pm, the wife would close up the kitchen.

Who in their right mind would come into the Shakespeare of a lunchtime, expecting to get a decent meal? These office people have in the main, one hour to get here, order, eat the food and get back to their desks. They need to be confident that their place of choice can deliver menu variety, value, speed and quality or they will vote with their feet and go elsewhere. Needless to say, The Shakespeare had no customers for their cuisine when we took over.

In the eighteen months or so since we have been here, we have built the food side up to around 400 meals per week - about 390 more than before, no doubt. To me, it is an integral part of my offer - when they buy a meal, they will buy a pint as well. Our menu appeals to different types of customers at different times of the day, for example our hot baguettes and jackets sell predominantly at lunchtimes Monday to Friday, when people want a typical lunch offer. In the evening, we tend to sell more main meals - traditional pub food like fish & chips, sausage & mash and that old English favourite, chicken tikka masala.

Our chilli is homemade, as are our burgers. My menu is constructed so that I have something to suit any potential customer at any time of the day or week - we do a very good tourist trade at weekends, for example, being central to Bristol's Harbourside area. Last Saturday, I convinced some American tourists that the battered fish that they had just eaten was caught fresh this morning from the docks behind the pub. They were so impressed that they went to take a photo of the water. The only thing that's been hooked out of there in the last twenty years is an Asda shopping trolley, a fluorescent pink flip flop and three suicides.

So it has got to the stage where we now need another body in the kitchen, to assist Chef Pauline, Mary and myself. I put an advertisement for a chef on a website yesterday morning, in the hope of securing someone for the weekend. By this morning, I had received just one reply from an agency offering their services. They boasted that they had James Martin, the famous TV chef on their books. I should email them back and see if I can get him for the six pounds and fifty pence per hour that I offered. If he can't operate a microwave as quickly as Chef Pauline, then I'm asking for my money back…

Wednesday 10th October

Just got back from Heathrow dropping off Theresa who is on her way home to Vancouver. Mary was very thankful that I played Mr Taxi again, but I explained that it is always a pleasure for a man to take his mother in law to the airport for the return journey.

Today was the day that had been pre-booked for about three weeks, for the change-over of Kronenbourg 1664 to Heineken. With this date set, I was able to run down my stocks of 1664 so that I wasn't stuck with it after the changeover day. Last night, during the quiz, Mary made the announcement that all 1664 was reduced to £1.45 for a pint (the price of a half) in order that we could sell it through. At close of play, we had about half of an eleven gallon barrel left. Not bad, I thought.

At 3pm today, I am on the phone to cellar services politely asking where the engineer is to implement the change. Typical response: "I'll phone the engineer and get back to you." After two further similar calls, the reply was "He can't do it today, hopefully he'll be with you tomorrow."

No apologies, no explanations. Because I am tied to this company for the purchase of my drinks portfolio, I am also tied to their cellar maintenance. Because they know this, it appears I get the lowest priority when it comes to work that needs to be done. I am not allowed to shop around or use alternatives, for that would put me in breach of contract. A tenant pays the highest prices to the brewery for their drinks, yet - certainly in this case - receives the worst service. Bottom line is, I will be running out of 1664 any minute now and not have anything to put on to replace it. The only person who looks like a tit in that situation, is me.

Talking of tits, the strip club up the road closed down recently and sold me about six boxes of their glasses for twenty quid. I asked why they were closing down and was told that they were having a complete refurbishment and re-positioning their business. "In what way?" I enquired. They were applying for a license for their strippers to go completely naked, as opposed to keeping their pants on (knickers, in America). So, if you want to watch vaguely attractive Bristol birds waving their bristols and going Full Monty in the process, you know where to go. You'll have to drink straight from the bottle, though.

Thursday 11th October

Last night, Mary and I went for an Indian meal at a new restaurant in Millennium Square, which is a white elephant area near the Harbourside. It has a statue of Cary Grant (he was from Bristol, apparently) some fountains and a lot of tumbleweed. The food was good but the service was slower than death on crutches. We eventually ended up in the casino, where we demolished a significant chunk of their vodka and gin stocks. Today is not a good day. I have a throbbing noggin and a mouth as dry as Ghandi's flip flop.

The extractor fan in the kitchen chooses today to pack up. It takes me about three quarters of an hour to get it up and running, by balancing on the hot plate and the deep fat fryer with my head inside the extraction canopy, trying to spin the fan blades with the end of a broom handle. A publican needs to be a champion multi-tasker when it comes to repairs and I know of no fan spinning, broom handle wielding man who can out spin and out wield me.

All goes well until about three o'clock, when a rainstorm hits Bristol with the force of Hurricane Nancy and knocks out the offending fan again. The biggest problem now is the fact that the hot plate and fat fryers are now red hot and there is no extraction. Muggins here puts large baking trays onto the hot plate and stands on them, with the other foot on the fryer which now has its lid on, in order to get the fan jump started. Thankfully, my spinning and wielding genius comes to the fore once again and the extraction restarts, before either foot gets fried or grilled to your liking.

Sweet Potato and Ginger Soup
Chef Pauline has been perusing the pages of Delia's Winter Recipe again.
She then ignored the lot and made this instead.
Comes with a crusty baguette and butter
£4.25

Chicken Jalfrezi
If you like your rubies rather warm, then this
is right up your alley.
It will certainly be leaving it at high speed, anyway.
Served with pilau rice and naan.
£5.95

Friday 12th October

Today is the final days filming for the cast of "Casualty", the hospital drama shown on the BBC Saturday evenings. For the duration of this week, they have been using the surrounding area as a film set, which has meant that a) we have been much busier, and b) I lost my bloody parking space.

Today at lunchtime, we got stuffed as the whole of the makeup and wardrobe department plus the extras came in all at once to eat. There were horrific injuries to be seen on table seven - apparently some kind of terrorist bomb had gone off so there were flesh wounds, broken limbs etc. The girl who had the sweet potato and ginger soup looked to be in a particularly bad way. I would not like to have been the bloke opposite who had to look at her throughout his lunch - he seemed to just pick at his fish finger baguette.

Chef Pauline is not feeling too good today. Apparently, she is going through "The Change". Us men are meant to just accept whatever behaviour comes our way from women who are going through The Change, however brutal a form this may take. Of course, being a chef, Lady Pauline has access to many knives, so I keep a discreet distance. I usually enjoy making her jump through the ceiling when she thinks there is no-one behind her. I was actually within two feet of her after lunch, armed with an industrial sized ladle and a saucepan, ready to wake the Hounds of Hell, when I remembered The Change, put down my weapons and meekly reversed from the kitchen.

This evening, I said goodbye to my daughter Jessica, who is flying to Rhodes for a fortnight's holiday with her mother, Lara (my first wife) and her maternal grandparents. Jess is a bright, switched on fourteen year old who lives in Newcastle Upon Tyne with her mum. She flies down to Bristol to stay with us during school holidays and half terms - which is never enough for me, but is all that is possible.

Being a long distance Dad is not recommended because you can never have as much influence on decisions, or be available for assistance as much as you would like. I call Jess every day if possible, but it is not the same as physically being there for her. As she has grown into young adulthood, she has matured from being my golden girl into a really pleasant, intelligent young lady. Much of this, I must emphasise, is down to genes, but the real credit must go to Lara who has done an amazing job bringing her up. Of course, we still have the teenage years to get through...

Jess now has extra reasons for wanting to visit Dad. She has two new brothers to play with and look after, which is great fun for all concerned. She is always amazed at how much each has developed in between school holidays, not realising that I feel exactly the same way when I look at her. She is no longer my baby, but a young woman. I am wondering where all the years have gone...

When Mary arrived on the scene, Jess was seven. At the time, Mary was eighteen, so there was never any conflict about being a new mum - she was more like a cool big sister. Mary had to accept the fact that I had a child from a previous marriage and did so, readily. She has never excluded Jess from any family business and always insists that our immediate family is five, not four.

Lara and I, from the time of the split, have always put the welfare of our child first. You read about bad divorces and couples using the children as weapons or pawns - but this has never been the case here. I am proud of my contribution to the upkeep of Jess, even though I am not as hands on as I feel I would like. I can't wait for my postcard...

This evening, after we closed, the staff had one or two pints to wind down. One of my staff, we'll call her Kit, who goes to West of England University, was recounting one or two memories from her past including "cow tipping", a rural teenage way of passing the time. I used to do a bit myself in the fields surrounding my village with a couple of mates. It involves waiting for the cows to fall asleep (they do so standing up) and literally tipping them over like a giant beef domino. She then came out with the line - and I quote - "cows are made of leather". Lateral thinking at its finest.

Saturday 13th October

Attention sports fans. Today at three o'clock England play Estonia at football in a European Championship qualifier at Wembley. We should wipe the floor with them, but we've been let down by an underachieving national side for so long that nothing surprises you anymore - you get numb, or immune to the disappointment. I will still be cheering them on from the comfort of my cow - covered sofa.

Eight o'clock sees England play France in Paris in the World Cup semi final of Rugby Union. We are serious underdogs here and it would be a marvellous achievement to win this one. The Sun newspaper (I don't read it, but buy it for the pub) has pictures of Jonny Wilkinson, England's Golden Boy, in typical competitive poses - "Hands off our cup" he is saying to the French, in huge red letters. Of course, half the French side probably don't speak English, so he could be saying "I must get my toes painted" for all they know. I am, amazingly, staffed up for both games...

This morning, Sam, my youngest, pushed himself upright for the first time with the help of a sofa cushion that is about the same size as him. He stood, tiny legs apart, balancing for two or three seconds like a stiff legged baby giraffe who has downed about six whiskeys. He then collapsed like a pack of cards in a heap beside the cushion. After two seconds delay, the wailing and crying started, to be comforted by willing adult hands. Sam calmed down almost immediately from his terrifying ordeal, only to crawl over to the cushion and do it all again.

10.30pm. England have just knocked out France in their own back yard to reach the Rugby World Cup Final. I am as surprised as the Queen was that time she got goosed by the Australian Prime Minister. We also won the football this afternoon, so it's been a top day if you are an English sports freak. I'm off to drink my own body weight in typical Anglo - style celebration.

Sunday 14th October

The Shakespeare Tavern Sunday Roast

Roast Leg of Pork, Lamb Shank or Roast Beef
Served with roasted potatoes, cabbage, carrots, green beans, stuffing,

Yorkshire pudding and gravy, for just
£6.95

Under Chef's Pinny
To follow your main course, we can suggest an excellent
Chocolate & Orange Profiterole Cake, or a
Sticky Toffee Pudding.
Chef Pauline has also made a splendid
Apple & Blackberry Crumble, at just **£3.50.**
You lucky customers, you.

Mugs of freshly ground coffee, tea or hot chocolate are always available,
served with a kit kat and priced at just
£1.50

Went to Bookers today, a kind of cash & carry place I use to get all of the stuff that doesn't get delivered - sauces, staff drinks, kit kats, cleaning bits etc. On the end of one aisle, piled high on a pallet, was a huge stack of "Wispa" bars. This is a re-launch of a product made by Cadburys that was a real hit in the 80's - and I loved them.

This was the smoothest, most creamy chocolate bar that one ever had the fortune to get spots with. The advert back in those days had you unwrapping the thing slowly, savouring the gentle crinkling of the purple (or is it a deep blue?) paper (I had the same trouble with the wrapper from "Banjo") and peeling the covering down the slender, dark bar like the cling wrap on a cucumber, almost drooling with anticipation at the ultimate orgasmic taste sensation to come. Gave one to Mary (who, being Canadian and far too young) had never had one. She wants a second honeymoon. Whenever we have a fight from now on, I'll just slip on my Phyllis Nelson LP at a seductively low volume, dim the lights and slide her a Wispa. Putty in my hands.

Ben has a cold, of sorts. He doesn't seem too distressed or in pain, but there are twin rivers of snot racing down his face, seemingly in an effort to beat the other to his chin. Of course, he still has bundles of pent up energy, which means that although his nose needs wiping every thirty seconds, he is never in the same place every thirty seconds. You just follow the twin trails of snot over the couch, across the dining table and up the stairs to find him so that you can attempt to stem the flow. I know how that kid who stuck his finger in the dyke felt - although I am just trying to save my lounge, as opposed to Holland.

Sunday nights we finish serving food at 6pm. By that time, we will have banged out about sixty or seventy meals - usually about forty Sunday roasts - and Chef Pauline will be on her knees. Because Sundays are my end of week financially, I need to spend a couple of hours in the office on the paperwork side, totting up sales, doing food orders, compiling the staff hours for the accountant and lots of other stuff far too tedious to be mentioning in any sort of book. So I won't.

Paperwork is, by its very nature, a very necessary evil which some find easier to cope with than others. I, for one, don't mind it. As this is my business, I have a very great interest in my own weekly "stats". When I was a manager for breweries, this would not be quite so true, unless it had some direct relation to any sort of bonus scheme which may have been up for grabs. As a manager, you are told which forms need to be filled in for the company's accountants to peruse. As a tenant, you fill them in not only for your accountant, but as an aid to your business development.

Some have a real fear of filling in forms - usually, in my experience, couriers or delivery drivers. In a previous life as a pub manager for a large chain in Brighton Marina, I was in charge of a huge site whose back delivery door was only accessible by two lifts. One day a miserable git of a delivery man was dropping off a rather large consignment of cleaning products. He had delivered there before and made it plain to me that he hated this place. I wasn't too keen on his attitude either that day, as I recall.

Into one lift from his lorry at road level he manoeuvred his pallet. It was a warmish day, and he was a porky chap at best, so the sweat was beginning to flow freely already. I pressed the "up" button on the lift (I do like to contribute) which brought the pallet load to the next level - unfortunately the lift wasn't able to take his rather generous frame at the same time, so he had to walk up the ramps.

From this platform, the load had to be transferred across a wide walkway to the next lift, so he hitched up his manual pallet truck to the stack and started to heave it from lift one to lift two. This particular hoist going up to pub level was not as big as the one coming up from the road, so he couldn't fit the actual pallet in. With much wailing, gnashing of teeth and mutterings about unions, he starts to unload the pallet and individually place the boxes into the lift. When this had been achieved, I once again swung into action and pressed the "up" button. I was being my usual cheerful self, but this chap looked like he was going to have a cardiac on the spot.

Of course, there was no room for him to get in the lift, so he had to take another long walk up a further set of ramps to get to the back door level. As the lift got to the top, my pub phone rings, so I go to answer it, leaving Mr Happy to individually unload the boxes into the pub, in "neat piles, if you could, mate, thanks". I got back to him when there were just two boxes left and a huge puddle where he was sweating like a hamster on the London Eye. "Here" I said, "let me give you a hand with that" and picked up the penultimate box to move it with the others. Wheezing, he puts down the last box with a rather too aggressive thump and stands bent over with his hands on his knees, breathing like a snotty yeti.

"Paperwork, mate?" I enquire, with genuine questioning expression.

"Didn't I give it to you already?" he breathes.

"Nope" says I. "Must still be in the lorry".

"Gracious me" he says. (Those weren't the *exact* words used, you understand, but I am sure you get the picture).

So off he drags himself, fat feet slapping on the concrete down two sets of ramps towards his lorry right down on the road. As he gets to within about six feet of his cab, I yell down to him "don't worry mate, I've found it!" I started waving the sheets in the air that I had pulled from my back pocket, which he had given to me at the start of his delivery. He turns, looks up and starts his ascent again, muttering to himself all the way up.

"Underneath this box" I say, giving one a kick as he got to the back door.

"Worst bit about this f***ing job, paperwork," he says.

Monday 15th October

Having real problems trying to get another chef. I don't actually need another *chef*, just a really switched on, organised person who can be quickly trained to get the presentation right every time, hygienically and at good speed. We are not McDonalds, but the food here is reasonably automated, in the sense that I don't want my customers to wait more than fifteen minutes for their meal from the point of ordering.

There are times, like Friday lunches, when we need to be able to dispatch around fifty meals within the lunch hour rush, so the kitchen staff need to be prepped up, organised and energetic. I don't, however, need Gordon Ramsay's youngest who could knock up pandas testicles in a champagne and bath foam sauce, delicately garnished with gnats eyeballs and a gerbil fondue.

What do you ask for in your advertisement? Whiz kid? Microwave technician? If you mention the fact that you use a microwave, most chefs seem to turn their noses away in disgust - so maybe don't ask for a chef...but I don't run a five star Michelin restaurant here - I have a proper pub, with good, honest pub food. I charge six or seven pounds for a main course, not sixty or seventy. I have gone from serving virtually no meals per week to four hundred in just eighteen months - and there has been two, yes two, complaints in that time. We are good at what we do...so why can't I find my relative Jamie Oliver to give us a hand?

One of my bar staff came to work in a Liverpool FC shirt today. He knows that I am an Arsenal supporter and that I wear the occasional branded clothing from time to time. I am not a fan of uniforms in this particular pub, as it is a relaxed City Centre local and it is essential that the character of my bar staff come to the fore in this environment. I can teach people to pour a great pint, but I can't give them a personality or the ability to naturally converse with the punters. So, my theory is: be yourself - we are not a brand.

So the guy walks in with this red scouse rag on his back and expects a little banter. I informed him that he needed to remove the offending garment, or it would be inserted into a place with limited sunlight. Why do some staff feel the need to see how far they can push the boundaries? The shirt was swapped for one advertising Abbot Ale, which was far more appropriate.

Pasta Bolognese
Homemade meaty Bolognese sauce on a bed of penne and smothered with melted cheddar. As Italian as corruption and body hair.
Served with a crusty baguette & butter
£5.75

Apple and Blackberry Crumble
There is nothing that Chef Pauline can't crumble.
Here is a fine example, served with hot, creamy custard
£3.50

Tuesday 16th October

Two aircraft had a collision at Heathrow Airport last night - on the ground whilst taxiing. Apparently, a Sri Lankan plane hit a British Airways plane "whilst manoeuvring" from behind. "It chopped off the B.A. tail fin like butter" said a Sri Lankan passenger. If he could see it, why couldn't the bloody driver have a view?

It's a bit scary when these pilots, who have absolute control over your safety, can do the equivalent of denting someone's wing in a multi-storey car park. The mother in law is an expert at such matters. Mind you, a Boeing 747 is a little easier to see than a Fiesta, plus there is a lot more room on the runway of the world's busiest airport than a parking lot and there was only one other vehicle within half a mile.

You know, I only actually dropped the mother in law at Heathrow last week, I didn't see her onto the plane itself and watch it take off...

Today, Chef Pauline and my brother, Alec (who has been here for the duration of our tenancy as an Assistant Manager) gave their notices in. They have found a live - in position in Wells, Somerset and it appears to be a good move for them. As they were living out in their jobs here, it was not particularly great financially for them, but this move is a progression on both the money front and for developing themselves - I wish them both well. Of course, that will put me deep in the fertiliser if I can't find either a chef or an Assistant Manager within the next two weeks...the advertisements are already in as I write - here's hoping for a positive response.

The quiz was too difficult tonight. The winners only got eighteen out of thirty, which is a little down on the ideal number of twenty three or four. I set the questions, which I thought were OK - that makes me damn clever or my punters damn thick. Mind you, everyone ate all of the sandwich offering - are they coming for the questions at all, or shall I stop using meat as a filling to find out?

I tend to make it down for the last hour or so on a Tuesday, after freshening up and changing from doing the kitchen. I was wearing a decent white t-shirt, virgin and crisp - that is until one of my bar staff walked into me and splashed red wine down the front. I am completely opposed to the minimum wage.

Wednesday 17th October

Day off today! Alec and Pauline generally run the shop for us on a Wednesday and then baby sit whilst Mary and I go for a meal, movie or just hang out in bus shelters.

This is certainly one aspect of them leaving that will not be good for us personally - it is difficult enough being able to get away from the business as it is. Hopefully I will be able to bed in a Duty Manager pretty quickly, to save both my sanity and marriage.

This morning I need to compile the wages, do the staff rota for next week and take in a couple of deliveries. I have already cleaned the pub (including the toilets, where I found a pair of soiled underpants in the toilet brush holder) and set up the bar ready for trading. My mindset is that I am on a day off, yet when I sit down and list my tasks for the morning it sure doesn't sound like one…is there a union I can join?

I suppose that it is the same for anyone who owns their own business - the more you put in, the more likely it is that you will reap more benefits from your endeavours. You have an extra incentive to get things right day in, day out, whereas as an employee you can virtually forget about your job when you leave at the end of your shift, until the start of your next one. Even then, for some of my previous employees, it was a job to make them think about their job whilst they were actually doing the job. That's why they are *previous* employees.

In addition, running a pub is not your average business. I am open for eighty six hours every week. I work for at least two hours before we open every day, seven days a week. I work for at least one hour after we close seven days per week (cleaning up, counting tills, balancing the safe etc). Although I would not be standing behind the bar or cooking in the kitchen for all of those hours, you still have to be there pretty much all of the time - especially without a Duty Manager.

Running a pub is your life, not just a job. You live and breathe the pub, your social life revolves around the pub, you even live above the pub so that even when you are collapsed on the sofa, you still automatically have one ear open for any unusual noises. Escaping from the day to day routine is essential - you must be able to get out of the building regularly - even a trip to Starbucks is a pleasure (especially at Christmas time when they do the gingerbread latte).

But this is all I've known. I have been doing this since I left catering college in 1988 - so that's nineteen years. If I ever get a nine to five position when I leave the industry (which I must do soon for the benefit of family life) I'll feel like a lazy part -timer.

Coffee and a Muffin
A mug of the coffee of your choice, served with a rather large muffin.
Morning glory, afternoon bliss.
£2.50

Homemade Leek and Potato Soup
Hot, wet, green and lumpy. Chef Pauline puts her very individual
slant on this most classic of soups.
Served with a crusty baguette and butter
£4.25

Thursday 18th October

Have been plagued today by a spate of cold callers, telling me that their business is essential to the well - being of my business. There should be some button installed on the mouthpiece of the telephone which, when you press it sends an electric shock through to the caller, or squirts them with cold custard.

Today, within the space of three quarters of an hour, I had three:

1/ Jenny from "The Utilities Company".

"I understand that your electricity contract is up for renewal soon".

"No, it still has six months to run".

"Yes, but if you want to change suppliers, you need to give six months notice".

"I changed suppliers six months ago and didn't give any notice."

"CLICK"

2/ Tanya from "The Till Roll Company"

"We have some really special offers on all of your till rolls and credit card rolls at the moment, and as we are your nominated supplier, we are giving you a call so you can stock up".

"You're not my supplier. I buy them from Viking on the web. They are cheaper than you and they don't cold call".

"CLICK"

When you are in the middle of doing other tasks like cleaning beer lines and taking in food deliveries, as I was this morning, these calls begin to get irritating. They are most unwelcome and time consuming. Unfortunately, the next one copped it…

3/ Emma from "Chemical Supplies".

"Can I speak to the owner of the pub, please?"

"Speaking"

"Do you have a glasswasher in the pub?"

"Yes. A midget called Phil. Been here twenty years."

"Sorry?"

"Yes, I have a glasswasher."

"Well, we have some unbelievable offers on detergent at the minute…"

"Don't believe you."

"…we have. How much do you pay for your detergents?"

"Ten bob and a pickled egg"

"Sorry?"

"Which one?"

"Glasswash detergent."

"About five or six quid from King UK. Free delivery, too - and no minimum order."

Pause…"We can do ours for about seven fifty…but it's really good…but you have to order a case of four…then there's delivery…

"CLICK"

I have no problem with people having to make a living - but there must be some other way than this…it is just annoying for small business' who are hounded daily by these script readers - and they will do anything for you to cough up.

There is a crooked company from Liverpool who constantly call us poor publicans trying to get us to spend money on advertising that does not even exist - YOU KNOW WHO YOU ARE!!!

A standard "spiel" will go something like this…

"Alright, mate" (thick Scouse accent) "can I speak to Malcolm, please?" (He knows who to ask for because the day before you get a phone call asking for the name of the business owner and then they hang up).

"Speaking"

"How's things?" (Friendly part of the script - getting you to feel comfortable chatting with them) "Business good?"

"Yes, thank you".

"That's good to hear - you must run a great pub". (Flattery…)

"Thanks…what can I do for you?"

"Well, I just phoned up to thank you, actually. You remember when I spoke to you about six months back and you agreed to take part in the advertising for the Ambulance / Police / Fire Prevention (delete as necessary - I've had all three) calendar for this year - well, they have now been produced and we just need your payment details for the space you ordered."

"Really, I ordered this - are you sure?"

"That's right, I did speak to (sound of shuffling papers in background) Malcolm and he very generously asked me to go ahead with it - so how will you be paying?"

"This was about six months ago?"

"That's right, don't you remember?"

"I've only been here three."

"CLICK"

This particular company are crooks. I fell for it the first time - you are so busy in your daily routine that you may not remember having certain conversations six months previously. You send your money, but you never get to see your advertising - they don't even produce the calendars! They have called me in every establishment I have run for the past decade - there cannot be a pub in the country who they haven't tried to fleece. Don't show any weakness, don't fall for their patter - they are reading from a script and we can see through them. Oh yes. The last call I got from them went like so…

"Alright mate" (thick Scouse accent) "can I speak to Malcolm, please?"

"Speaking"

"How's things? Business good?"

"Really good, thanks."

"That's good to hear - you must…"

"Are you Ambulance, Police or Fire Prevention?"

"Sorry?"

It's just that I've decided to plough all of my calendar advertising budget into the Page Three one this year - it may be a rip off, but at least I have something to look at."

"CLICK"

I have found these great socks from Asda. Twice the price of your normal ones, but they are ribbed around the middle part of your foot and are so supportive. Just thought I'd share that.

Friday 19th October

Took Susan (Sister-In-Law) to Manchester Airport this morning as she is going back to Vancouver after her holidays. Mary will miss her, as she has proved to be a great help with Ben and Sam and they are really close. It is quite a task for Mary to look after the Boys without any relatives close by to give her a break. Her side of the family live in Canada, which makes it a little difficult to get a babysitter from them and with my mother not with us anymore, it also rules out my side.

We are trying to find a nice day care centre in Central Bristol, but they are about as rare as bacon in a mosque. Mind you, I have plenty of maternal barmaids who would give their right ovary for a chance to look after our babies for the night - every time they are seen in the pub they are surrounded by willing hands and offers to hold them. With Alec and Pauline on their way who were our regular babysitters, we need some alternatives.

A frustrating lunch session was had in my enforced absence today. Whilst I endured the pleasures of the M5 and M6 on a Friday, my team did fifty meals in in my absence during the lunch rush - big up to them. The guy who was on the floor taking meals out, clearing tables etc suddenly announces in the middle of the bedlam that there was no cutlery left. Not "we are nearly out of cutlery" or "we will need some more cutlery in twenty minutes". This guy has been to University - why can't he think proactively, instead of standing there with a couple of Mexican burgers in his hands and expecting the customers to eat them with their feet? I repeat: I am completely opposed to the minimum wage.

There is a group of eighty eight architects staying in the Youth Hostel which is situated behind The Shakespeare. They came in last night and got absolutely plastered. They are back in tonight getting absolutely plastered. I should go and buy the manager of the Youth Hostel a beer for not having a decent bar themselves…

Saturday 20th October

It is the rugby World Cup Final today, when England take on South Africa. We are huge underdogs here, having already lost thirty six - nil to them previously in the tournament. I have a South African barman who reckons we have as much chance of winning as Britney Spears has of getting the "Hollywood Mum of the Year" award.

He even tried to book Sunday off "as he will have a massive hangover from the celebrations". Cocky tosser. I will ensure that his life will be made a misery if we win - but he's probably right, in all honesty.

One of my staff members didn't turn up at lunchtime today. She was due in at twelve midday - no phone call - just did not show. It is so frustrating that you go to the effort of integrating people into your team, treating them well and making them feel welcome, yet they have no conscience when they decide that they don't feel like turning up. Not even the courtesy of letting us know.

When someone does this, it impacts those who must fill in without notice - for example I was on my own on the bar until 1pm, which meant that Mary had to cook until then, which in turn meant that my toddlers had to be put in the cage with their toys, as there was no-one to supervise them. (I should point out that the "cage" is an eight sided playpen which we have straightened out and cornered off a section of our lounge, so you can put down the phone to social services, thank you).

So by letting us down professionally (and herself) her selfish actions have impacted my children - which is unacceptable in anyone's eyes. This is probably the fourth or fifth time she has been either late or just let us down, in the couple of months that she has been here - she has been given the benefit of the doubt and treated like an adult in all situations, but it has been made clear to her that she needs to turn up as other people depend on her doing so. She will not be working here again.

It galls me that the balance of power is heavily weighted legally in favour of the employee. I am in full support of equality in the workplace and fairness when considering possible exploitation in a job - but common sense goes out of the window when it comes to any protection the employer should have. If someone has clearly abused their employed position - as this particular woman has - then I should be perfectly within my rights to terminate her without having to tread through a minefield of employee rights. If she consistently and obviously does wrong, her rights should be forfeited.

I will illustrate this with an example from my first pub, which I joined in 1988. It was called The Clanger and was situated next to Liverpool Street Station in the financial district of London. It was about eight - fifteen in the morning and we were serving breakfasts to the early arriving commuters. One of my staff members came into my office and told me that she had just seen another employee (we'll call her Lynne) take ten pounds out of the till and put into her pocket. I counted the till in question and found it to be ten pounds down - we had only been open since eight o clock, so it looked conclusive.

I took Lynne into the office and confronted her with the evidence and the accusation and gave her the opportunity to explain. She admitted straight away that she had done it. I suspended her immediately on full pay and sent her home. I phoned my Area Manager who said that he was coming to see the pub tomorrow and would hold a disciplinary then. I phoned Lynne and arranged for her to be in attendance.

At the meeting, Lynne admitted to stealing the money and was dismissed. A couple of months later, she appealed against the decision to dismiss her. The Company settled with her one thousand pounds before it got to a tribunal, on the grounds that there was not a forty eight hour gap in between suspension and the disciplinary hearing. In summary, she admits stealing from the till, but wins an appeal against dismissal because of a technicality.

There is no common sense in this. Human resources workers will be nodding knowingly to themselves saying that it was the right decision - but there is no justice here. A thief was caught and then rewarded - nothing more or less. Although the Area Manager was at fault for not adhering to the rules by allowing a forty eight hour gap, it was not the moral outcome - common sense should be allowed to prevail in cases like this. The dodgy cow actually got away with one thousand and ten pounds in the end, as I forgot to ask for the original stolen tenner back!

My theory is that the decision to dismiss should have stood and you should - as the wronged employer - be allowed one free hit as you propel them towards the exit. Take a vote on it - you know I'm right...

Sunday 21st October

So England lost the rugby...but put up a sterling performance. I have yet to bump into my colonial friend, but I can hold my head up high. This afternoon is the Brazilian Grand Prix, where England's own Lewis Hamilton has a final chance to become World Champion in his first season. What a cracking weekend of sport this is. Unfortunately, The Shakespeare does not have any televisions in the bar, so when there are big sporting events on, we lose out, sales - wise. TV's do not fit the profile of this pub, so I make a calculated sacrifice by not having them in.

It was built in 1726 as a merchant house on the edge of Bristol's docks. Trading ships used to unload their wares into the cellars and business was conducted from the premises. The original proprietor used to provide refreshment in the form of crude alcoholic drinks to the ship workers on the side, but eventually this would form the main purpose of the building. In 1777, The Shakespeare Tavern was granted its first official license to supply alcohol to the public and has had one ever since.

Internally, the pub has changed very little from those days. The walls are internally wooden, adorned by countless pictures of Bristol from days gone by. There is a heavy maritime theme, with models of Bristolian boats and a glass case containing sailors knots in rope on the wall. The bar furniture comprises wooden tables and chairs and a few old church pews. Behind the bar, there is an old child's shoe which came from within the original front wall of the pub. It was dislodged when the Germans decided that they didn't like the look of the pub during World War 2. Apparently, a child's shoe was left in the wall cavities during construction to ward off evil spirits in years gone by - obviously bombs are not in its remit.

The longest tenancy in the pubs history is Mr and Mrs William Allen, who were in charge from 1935 to 1977 - forty two years in the same pub - quite an astonishing length of time for this industry. Of course in those days you were only allowed to sell alcohol at certain times of the day in the UK - there was no opening all afternoon or until midnight back then, so the hours would have been much easier to cope with. Rumour has it that Mrs Allen, who actually died on the premises, still walks these walls...a pub is not a proper pub without pickled eggs, pork scratchings and a ghost.

I digress...to put TV screens, any form of neon advertising, posters or space invader machines into an old fashioned public house such as this would be criminal. This is a quite stunning example of how a pub should look and feel - something that is peculiar to this corner of Northern Europe, but unfortunately a dying breed.

Last February, we decided as a nation to import bird flu from the Far East, as well as cars, toys and TV's. The Sunday Lunch menu at The Shakespeare read like so…

The Shakespeare Tavern Sunday Roast

Your choice of
Roast Turkey Breast or Roast Beef
Served with roasted potatoes, broccoli, carrots,
cauliflower, stuffing,
Yorkshire pudding and gravy for just
£6.95
Note: The turkey had a rough night with the bird flu, but we gave him a lemsip and he feels much better.

If you still have room, why not try Chef Pauline's homemade
Fruits of the Forest Crumble - £3.25
Not sure which forest, but it's been crumbled.
Served with hot custard.

There are also other desserts offered on our main menu…
Or you can ask the smiling military man behind the bar.

My elder brother Alec is the "smiling military man." He spent years in the Royal Air Force before tackling "civvy street". He is renowned for arranging all of the sauce sachets in their bowls so that they appear to stand to attention. Six ketchup, six mayonnaise and three of mustard, brown sauce and vinegar. No more, no less. Get this wrong and he will know. You will see him start to twitch before the first beads of perspiration start to appear. He doesn't even need to be on the same floor as the sachet bowls - he just senses it. The other staff just cram in the ketchups willy nilly just to see him suffer. If he was flown to Iraq when he was serving his country as cannon fodder, he would have had all of the Iraqi sauce sachets in line, let there be no doubt about that.

Monday 22nd October

Conducted a couple of interviews this morning. The first was for a part time chef position to work alongside whoever takes the full time slot. The comprehensively dreadlocked chap looked like Bob Marley's youngest (except that the guy was white). He currently works for the Bristol Ferryboat Company, who run a fleet of sightseeing boats around the harbour as well as water taxis. His hours are being cut for the Winter season, so he is looking for extra hours elsewhere to boost his reduced income. Lots of pub kitchen experience, speaks fluent English, four limbs. Sounds over qualified.

Next interviewee was for the Duty Manager slot. This is a vital one for me, as they will be my eyes and ears on the service floor, ensuring that my standards are adhered to when I am not there. This particular chap is built like a brick outhouse which automatically gives you a head start on having a presence in authority. He banged his head coming in and going out, so if he starts here I shall have to stock up on band aids or get a bigger front door. Seemed quite a switched on chap, so I offered him a position. He said he would talk it over with his fiancé, so it seems despite his size he is still in awe of the fairer sex. Being the man of the house I, of course, call the shots. But don't tell the wife.

Dinner this evening was its usual picture of family serenity. Mary and I sat down together for a meal at the dining table in the lounge at 7.30pm. This in itself may not sound too remarkable, but in this industry an undisturbed meal is a luxury. The boys had already been fed, so were milling around the lounge area in their customary leg - whirring fashion as we ate.

As I raised a fork full of delicious, buttery linguini to my mouth, a toddlers shoe from Clarks slammed down beside my left elbow, causing my pasta to slip back into the bowl. I looked around at the direction that this missile had come from to see only empty space. A tugging on my laces made me look under the table, where Sam had crawled and was now stuck in between chairs. Before I could get him out, a red and green building block appeared on the other side of my bowl as Ben had obviously decided that this was where he was going to build his new tower.

I relocated both offending offspring into the cage where they proceeded to dismantle their new environment. Despite the ruckus going on in the background, Mary and I pretended that we were having a civilised time, indulging in light, intelligent dinner conversation as best we could. After a lull in sound (always a bad sign where toddlers are concerned) the missiles started coming "over the top". First was a plastic mobile phone, followed by three rings, a brick and a stuffed Winnie the Pooh. We decided to skip dessert and coffees, for the thought of being used as target practice throughout the final course did not appeal.

My younger brother Larry paid a visit this evening for a swift half, so I got him to change the annoying light bulb in the Gents that is stuck about twelve feet up on the ceiling behind a screwed - in glass cover. We also got him to move the child's safety gate to the lounge door instead of the bottom of the stairs, as Sam has taken to crawling into the trade kitchen at every opportunity.

My DIY skills are famous around these parts for their lack of ever existing. Both brothers have this annoying ability to look at a job or repair and know exactly what needs doing and what parts you will need to achieve the desired result. I do not possess this knowledge. Furthermore, I have never had a desire to learn these things, as I am always able to read the latest copy of the Yellow Pages or, failing that, get one of my siblings to do it. If God wanted me to get oil on my hands, I would have been born with gloves on.

Tuesday 23rd October

Got an email from Olly last night accepting the position of Bar Supervisor. Olly is the rather physically imposing chap who was interviewed yesterday morning. This is a very positive move for the business as I believe he will do a good job, although he is unable to start for three weeks. I am still waiting for a reply from the albino Rasta potential part time chef...

Tonight, the Arsenal take on Slavia Prague in the Champions League. Foregone conclusion this one - which is a good thing, because I will be too busy to watch it as it is the quiz and I still have no chef for Tuesdays. I am trialling a chap who chefs for the youth hostel behind us today though, so there is a possible light at the end of a tunnel there. If this does not work, I will be forced to bow to the exorbitant prices of an employment agency. "Ouch", said the Bank Manager.

Olly came in for the quiz this evening, with friends and his fiancé. I had a look at his answers during the session and informed him that if I knew he was that thick, then I wouldn't have employed him. His woman looked pleased with this.

Fish Finger Baguette
Four fingers, no thumbs - guaranteed.
Served with chunky chips, mayonnaise,
mixed leaves and tartare sauce.
£5.25

Chicken Kiev
Straight from the streets of the Ukraine.
Chicken and garlic butter - it's like Fred and Ginger,
but without the dancing.
But with chips and peas.
£5.75

Wednesday 24th October

Arsenal won seven - nil last night. I'll repeat that - Arsenal won seven - nil last night. Oooohhh, that felt good.

Today is my day off. I have moved Alec and Pauline in for two days to run the pub before they leave on Sunday - they will answer phones, count tills, deal with problems and keep my ears free of pub business...or at least, that is the theory. This morning I cleaned the pub, including some strangely aromatic toilets, done all of the etc etc, cleaned the beer lines, placed the frozen food order and taken in two deliveries. I had also put the wages together and started to compile next weeks rota, when I was rudely interrupted by breakfast.

I am determined to be lazy for the majority of the day, although I am sure my lively offspring will see to it that the word "relaxing" isn't going to elbow its way into the schedule. Tomorrow, after Mary's dental check up (which she has to go to, as her free maternity period runs out in two weeks) we are going to my home village on Dartmoor - South Brent - to see my eighty something year old Granny Audrey. This is my Mum's mother, who moved to the village from her marital home in Plymouth when my Granddad George died, to be close to her daughter. The best laid plans...

We plan to take her out to Paignton for the afternoon as there will be places there that we can sit down for a meal, while our boys create mayhem in one of those ball ponds that you find in some eateries these days. I have always secretly fancied diving headlong into one of those things, but am always concerned that I would be ejected from the restaurant before pudding. As is the case with elderly relatives, you always become more popular when you have young children, as they want to show them off before getting worn out and handing them back.

It is also good to catch up with Audrey (I was never allowed to call her Gran / Granny / Grandma when I was a kid, as she insisted that she was too young to be a Gran - so we had to call her Audrey) as she gets little or no contact with anyone these days, save for the doctor, postman, binman and the bloke who fetches her shopping from Tesco at Lee Mill for a fiver. We call and see her as much as possible, but we run a busy pub and have two babies, so time is both precious and unobtainable for this particular family. We still feel bad when we forget to call, though.

Dad, of course, lives in the same village and probably sees her once a week to keep an eye on her, but he has his own life too, with girlfriend Vi - and Audrey is his mother in law after all...

Thursday 25th October

So last night, as part of the running the pub for two days deal, Alec and Pauline are also resident babysitters. The boys are fed, changed, into their pyjamas and plonked in front of a DVD of Baby Einstein before they are put into their respective cots. This is their normal bedtime routine and we usually feel able to depart at around 8.30pm, when they are at the Baby Einstein stage. We were determined to use up every minute of free time whilst A & P were still with us (although they have generously offered to come and babysit for us occasionally on a day off).

We went to a new lounge bar that had recently opened up on the other side of Queen Square. Nice place, plenty of potential, piano and bass player in the background - but the food was overpriced for the quality. Our chicken in chilli sauce was the sweet chilli sauce from a long glass bottle with a black lid. I know this because we buy the stuff too - but we charge six quid, not twenty, for a main course. We also use it as a dip, as it should be, as opposed to drowning an already dead chicken portion in the shallow end of the dinner plate. A side order of their new potatoes totalled four, yes four gnats testicle - sized orbs served pretentiously in what looked like an ashtray (I imagine that there are no other uses for this chinaware, now that the smoking ban has kicked in).

Anyway, disappointed. So we mosey over to the casino for a nightcap and twenty pounds worth of fifty pence chips to cover the breaks in married conversation. At about a quarter to one, I get a text from Chef Pauline, which reads - and I quote - "can you get some gravy mix, thanks". This is not a normal text which the average Joe would receive in the early hours whilst at a casino, so it threw me a tad. I asked the croupier if he had gravy mix, but, alas, he could only lay his hands on ketchup. I texted back "get it your f*!&ing self - you are supposed to be running the place". And thought no more of it.

Next morning, I learn that Chef Pauline had actually sent me that text while I was at the cash & carry the week before, but her mobile had just laid down and died, so the message did not actually leave her phone. Obviously last night Alec and Pauline were messing about with the phone in bed (their version of phone sex, I imagine - they haven't caught on yet) and the thing started to send all of the messages backed up in her outbox. There were people all over Bristol getting odd messages at one in the morning - like "I'm here - open up!" or "pick me up in five minutes!" I am sure that there is a lot more mileage in this tale if you care to think up your own lines…

Friday 26th October

Would have been Mum's birthday today, so a tad melancholic.

Got a message from the albino Rasta saying that he had changed his mind and is staying on the ferryboats full time. This puts me right up a cheffing creek without a fish slice. Next week, I have - let me count them - no chefs at all, which means that I will have to do it. I don't mind doing it, but it means that I have very little time for any other aspect of running the business - a classic fire fighting situation. The advertisements are back in the job centre and the "Bristol Gumtree", so I may get some response soon. Until then, it's head down and arse up from next week.

Last night the Spurs manager was forced to resign. For those unacquainted with footballing rivalries, Spurs are the big local rivals of Arsenal. They are in the relegation zone of the Premier League and playing like a team of one - legged schoolboys. Wonderful to watch. (That is not to offend any one - legged schoolboys that may ever read this - I'm sure you are a great player individually, it's just that a whole team of you? You would have to have right legged amputees on the left, and left legged amputees on the right, but who would play centre midfield? Of course, finding another team to play could be a task....) I digress again. My point is, Spurs have been awful this year, which is fabulous mileage for any die - hard Gooner.

Busy lunch. Food got stuffed as soon as twelve midday hit and carried on relentlessly until about a quarter to two. Friday lunchtimes are our most intense session, because it is heavily food led and everyone who comes in wants a meal. When it is just the alcohol they are after it is so much easier to cope with, but lots of food means an extra body in the kitchen and an extra pair of hands working the tables.

At the moment, we are pretty much a well oiled machine - as long as each member does his or her job while we are getting our asses kicked, then service will go smoothly and no-one waits more than fifteen minutes for their meal. If there is one weaker member working on this session, then it can all go pear - shaped pretty quickly. Today however, was a breeze. Fifty odd meals in an hour and a half or so, everyone happy, no stress. Believe me, it's not always like this in Chez Shakespeare...

Got a call from the Job Centre this afternoon regarding the advertisement for a chef, which I had placed online this morning. The chap said that the ad. was OK save for one section in which I had stated that the applicant must possess perfect written and spoken English. This is true, said I, as he or she must be able to read bar staff handwriting on the meal tickets that are sent to the kitchen, plus they also need to clearly converse with suppliers when placing food orders.

He said that the line implied that I would only employ English people. "Not true", I replied "I am happy with Welsh or Scottish, but I draw the line at a Yank". The bloke just responded with a stony silence. Absolutely no sense of humour. He insisted that the line was changed to "have the ability to communicate well in written or oral formats in English". What a tosser. Political correctness gone potty. The bloke works in an antiseptic environment, with no room for any form of individualism, humour or fun - what a bore. There is no way he could stand on his office chair and tell the joke about the nun and the aubergine in a loud voice, as he would probably get the book thrown at him for contravening the rights of aubergines.

I wouldn't employ him, for a start. Anyway, the advertisement was eventually passed, but begrudgingly, I fear.

Homemade Minced Beef Cobbler
Chef Pauline's famous concoction of minced beef, vegetables and kind of a cheesy, sconey - type crust.
Served with seasonal vegetables.
Because you're worth it.
£5.75

Homemade Salmon & Broccoli Quiche
With homemade potato salad and homemade coleslaw.
We bought the plate.
£5.25

Saturday 27th October

Interviewed a nice chap called David today for the chef's position. He grew up in a hotel on the Isle of Wight and worked in the Dover Castle pub on Harley Street, London. He will know what it feels like to be in the trade, that's for sure. Anyway, I'm going to give him a shot - he seems keen to do well and I can teach anyone who shows the minimum of ability and a good chunk of willing. Even if he turns out to be complete pants (you never really can tell until they start) it will still be a pair of hands for next week.

Jessica comes back from Rhodes today - can't wait to speak to her. We have texted a few times over the past fortnight, but it's not the same. I also received a postcard from Dad this morning - very formally written, as per usual. He appears to be having a good time with Vie, which is excellent - he should be enjoying his retirement years as much as he can. It will be good to get a call from him on Monday when he too gets back, so I can brag about the Arsenal...

On the holiday subject, we are supposed to be trying to get to Canada next year, so we need to think about booking flights now. Mary and I used to pop over to Vancouver annually, but then the boys arrived and we have not been for three years - so it is about time we did! It would be perfect if we could take Jess with us, but that usually means going in the height of Summer during the long school holidays, when they charge premium prices. Last time we went we got delayed overnight outbound - we were bussed from Gatwick to Manchester and then put up in a hotel just because something fell off the plane. Any excuse. I wrote a very civil letter of complaint and got free upgrades for our next flights, so that is something to look forward to. Who wants to fly with the working class, anyway?

Tonight, Mary and I are going downstairs to sample the magnificent old fashioned pub atmosphere that the Shakespeare Tavern offers. I am unsure whether to drink "Old Bob", a tipple from Ridley's brewery, or "Swing Low", which is a Greene King beer brewed to commemorate England's defence of the Rugby World Cup. As the tournament has finished and I still have a firkin to get through, I will probably do the dutiful business thing and sup the latter. This is Alec's last Saturday night working, so Mary and I are of a mind to get him trolleyed, but as he is also working Sunday lunch, it may not be the best idea. It doesn't take much, mind - I've seen him fall over pissed on the fumes whilst changing a barrel, the big girl.

Sunday 28th October

Yesterday morning we had three or four tourists come into the pub and enquired about our Sunday roasts. I, of course, waxed lyrical on their behalf and secured their confidence that they could bring in a party of eight today. Last night Mary got a phone call asking if the Jarvis table booked at one o'clock could be increased to eleven people. She rightly said that we do not take bookings as we are a pub as opposed to a restaurant, so it is first come, first served as regards table spaces.

There was then another call five minutes later from a Mr Jarvis which I answered. Before I had a chance to say hello, I learned that he was "very disappointed" and "quite upset" at the treatment he has got, as he had spoken to the owner this morning and confirmed a booking of eight people and it would be no problem. "Did the owner take your name" I enquired, when he was eventually forced to end his rant by breathing in.

"Yes, he did."

"And he confirmed the time?"

"That's right."

"Well, you spoke to myself - I am the owner. We discussed you coming in with eight people for Sunday lunch, but I certainly did not even know your name, nor was a time of dining discussed. As I believe my wife told your acquaintance, we are a pub that does great Sunday lunches and would be delighted if you all came in tomorrow - but if you now have eleven people, then I would recommend that you come in pretty soon after we open the doors at midday, so that you can guarantee your party a space."

"Umm, yes, good idea. It will be eleven of us tomorrow and we will have someone there early to secure a table."

"That will be wonderful, Mr Jarvis, I look forward to seeing you."

Bloody liar. Why do some people feel the need to try and impose their will on establishments when they want to eat? If they wanted a restaurant experience, then book a restaurant. This is a pub, an old fashioned English pub environment that punches above its weight when it comes to food. To start laying up tables, taking bookings etc would compromise the unique atmosphere which we proudly boast and I am not prepared to do this. Come and have a meal here and enjoy it for what it is - good, honest pub grub - big portions, honestly priced and quick service.

This morning, I got another call from "Table Jarvis":

"Hello, we are coming in for lunch today as part of a table of eleven". Here we go, thinks I...

"Hello, what can I do for you?"

"I was wondering if you allow dogs in your establishment?"

"We do indeed, but if he brings his own food, then I will have to charge corkage."

"I'm sorry?"

"Yes we do, as long as the dog stays with your party and is well behaved."

"OK, that's great, thanks. Bye!"

I like to amuse myself at customers' expense. It gives me an inner warm glow and sense of well being.

There is an Arsenal game this afternoon, away at Liverpool. Good luck to all of the fans travelling up there - hope you return with all three points and all four hubcaps.

This evening I am interviewing another chef who is moving to Bristol from London. If I manage to get two bodies in my kitchen, then this pub would be so much easier to run and I would get my life / work balance back to a more manageable level. Over the weekend, I had dotted some posters around the pub:

<u>Chef required. Today. Not tomorrow.</u>

Previous experience a must.

If you want to know what it's like here, ask the bar staff.

Food hygiene certificate essential.

**Must have good working ethic, a sense of humour,
an alarm clock and two thumbs.**

Ask for an application form from behind the bar.

The chap I am interviewing this evening got a call from his potential stepfather who lives on a narrow boat and drinks in the pub. It's amazing how some advertising works. I am pretty sure my ad. would never have passed the Job Centre political correctness criteria. I would have been chastised for not interviewing people with three thumbs.

Monday 29th October

The interviewee of yesterday evening passed with flying colours - I have high hopes that he can take my kitchen to another level. He is looking for about 45 hours a week and has all of the relevant experience. He starts on Friday so I am actually staffed up in the kitchen now, what with David climbing on board at the same time. Let's hope that neither of them turn out to be complete muppets.

Yesterday was the final day for Alec and Pauline. It was a busy Sunday lunch - we did eighty nine covers, fifty six of which were roasts - and they coped OK. Pauline even changed the oil in the fryers before she left, so they worked hard until the end. The move to Wells should suit them as a couple much better than here, because it is far more of a restaurant with a slower pace of service and more emphasis on quality of the ingredients etc. Good luck to them.

When we bought the business, I gave Alec a call to see if he was free for a month to come and decorate the accommodation, as it was an absolute disgrace. There was no way I could move my family in as it was. Alec did painting and decorating in the Royal Air Force, so he knew which end of a brush to hold - which was a step above my decorating limitations. When I took over, all but two of the staff left so I was trying to employ new people, pour the pints and cook the food at the same time. There were a few occasions that I had to yell upstairs to Alec to put his brush down and give a hand on the bar as it was a real backs to the wall effort. He at his point had never poured a pint before, but he learned quickly enough and eventually asked if himself and Pauline could both work here on a permanent basis.

Pauline has had plenty of kitchen experience in her long years, so was more than capable of operating a kitchen that had no current sales. With Alec downstairs and Pauline cooking, it freed me up to get the business off the ground. Of course, as time has progressed and trade has increased it has become necessary to shuffle the pack. I now require a number two with significant experience in the industry and my kitchen requires at least twenty more quality hours throwing at it. In turn, A & P have given eighteen months of service and gained valuable experience here, so it was a good time for them to branch out on their own and get a good live - in position for themselves, in order to put something behind them.

There are many pluses and minuses regarding the employment of family. The worst for us was the lack of privacy it gave my immediate family - A & P could walk in at any time and disturb us - not intentionally, you understand - even in our supposed time off. This was not so much a selfish act on their behalf, but the reality is that there are fewer boundaries with blood relatives than with just normal members of staff. There is no way that a kitchen porter would wander into my lounge and sit at my table when he felt like it, but that is something that is very hard to tell your brother not to do. It would also be very difficult as a relative to hear. The issue is less with them as people, but more the situation of never being able to put the job down.

On the plus side, you have a certain amount of trust and security when you know that your brother is overseeing operations instead of somebody that you don't really know. It is also very unlikely that a family member would let you down by phoning in sick. Alec had a real desire to ensure that he never cocked up in any aspect of the business, and although some tasks were sometimes carried out with a certain lack of skill or experience, his heart was in the right place. It would be good if my new Assistant had a similar drive.

Anyway, bollocks. They've gone now. Blow away the cobwebs, get out the broom - it's time for change. Let's re-ignite the business and get everyone motivated again. I'm going for coffee.

Homemade Mushroom Soup
Chef Pauline's final act as resident chef. This is made with fresh mushrooms and real tears. As she was stirring the pot, she was stroking her oven and whispering "I'll miss you…" Comes with a crusty baguette and butter.
£4.25

Homemade Cottage Pie
Made with real cottages.
Served with seasonal vegetables and gravy.
£5.95

Tuesday 30th October

On my way back up from the cellar last night, Mary told me that Alec had just called wanting to know the surname of Vi, Dad's girlfriend, as he wanted to send her a sympathy card for a family bereavement. He was to call back in a couple of minutes to speak to me, assuming that I knew. Sure enough, the phone soon rings again…

"Hi, it's only me. I want to send a card to Vi - what's her surname?"
"Oh gosh, it's an Irish name" (putting on a deep thinking tone) "I'll spell it for you…"
"Hang on, let me get a pen…OK, I'm ready"
"It's O apostrophe, L,Y,N,N,E." (Violin - see what I did there? :-))
"OK, got it, thanks"
"No problem, see you."
I returned to the bar and told Mary the conversation. I said I wondered how long that would take to sink in before he calls back. Mary couldn't believe he had swallowed it. To his credit, he phoned back within a couple of minutes, having sussed when he wrote it on the envelope. I wouldn't have let him send it, honest. She's actually called Johnstone.
It was announced today that the Government has admitted that they have

missed off three hundred thousand immigrant workers employed in the UK in their estimated figures. I can understand them being hundreds out, but three hundred thousand that they weren't aware of concerns me. Mind you, I reckon most of them applied for the part time bar person's position which I advertised last week. Out of around eighty responses online, there were five with English as their first language - and all of those were illiterate.

On the staff front, David started today. Turned up on time, seemed keen enough, worked hard and made egg mayonnaise all by himself. My favourite baguette filling of all time is crispy bacon bits, egg mayonnaise and cracked black pepper. I need to throw him a rasher and see what he can do with it. I can't stand bacon that's only half cooked - it's criminal - it just doesn't do justice to self respecting swine.

My other brother Larry is doing a few shifts for me this week behind the bar, which will neatly fill any gaps before Olly starts in a fortnight. Larry used to work for me in a pub in the early nineties in the Barbican, London called The Sutton Arms. This was a cracking little boozer next to the tube station which was only open Monday to Friday, as there was absolutely no foot traffic at weekends, being surrounded by just offices. Like Alec, Larry has a decent work ethic and is not afraid to get his hands dirty when the shit hits the fan. Actually, his first job could be cleaning the fan behind the bar, as it is full of shit.

Wednesday 31st October

So the bar was pretty steady last night, but there were four staff on plus David in the kitchen. Everyone was coping very easily, so I asked Connor if he fancied going an hour early. He was on a long shift, so he jumped at the chance. It was quiz night, so there were plenty of customers to keep everyone ticking over - we had about forty punters flexing their general knowledge muscles. At about eight - thirty, Helen goes around the bar flogging answer sheets for a pound to all and sundry, so that is her taken away from serving food and drink.

At ten to nine, this student - looking type female comes into the bar with an expression like a goldfish with its gill in a socket and asks to speak to Ginny. Our Ginny sees the dodgy look on the girl's face and goes outside to see what the matter is. I thought at the time that I now regretted sending Connor home an hour early. Ginny comes in looking a greyer shade of battleship and tells me that her mate has just been run over and is in Bristol Royal Infirmary. Of course, she wants to go and see how she is and, of course, I have to let her go knowing that I am now stuck on the bar for the rest of the evening.

It is always the way in this trade. When you are completely staffed up, it never seems busy enough yet, as soon as you are a man down, all hell breaks loose - and so it did. Some office party decided in the middle of the quiz to empty themselves into the pub. All of a sudden an extra thirty or so were at the bar demanding to be served in an already full pub - it was mayhem. It is at this point in time that you know whether you are cut out for this trade.

At seven fifteen that morning the beer delivery had arrived, followed closely by the frozen food delivery. I was then on baby duty whilst I cleaned the pub and toilets. After a snatched breakfast, I went to the bank for some change to get back in time to open up for the first hour before the staff arrived. I then went upstairs as I was the chef for lunchtime. Of course, we got stuffed (which I don't mind, as it is the reason we are here, after all) so there was lots of cleaning and prep to achieve in the kitchen post - rush. Two o'clock was the start time for David on his first shift, so there was an induction to go through and instruction for the afternoon. Customers were still ordering the occasional meal throughout the day, so I was unable to escape to my couch at this point.

Come five o'clock and the evening post work rush begins, sending a new wave of willing punters in to point frantically at my beer pumps and peruse the well - thumbed food menus. A fresh wave of custom comes in at around eight pm on Tuesdays to take part in the quiz - many have their evening meal here. At nine o'clock, the quiz begins, the kitchen closes and the sandwiches and crisps are sent downstairs to the bar. At his point, I usually have my break. The children are fast asleep in their respective cots, Mary having done a sterling job with the stun gun and chloral hydrate. I generally at this point become as one with my sofa - more liquid than solid and at peace with the world, knowing that I am at rest and my till drawers downstairs are going in and out like a cuckoo in a clock stuck on midday.

Alas, it was not to be last night. I worked my spotty arse off until close, as we went from being one too many to two too few. It was a long day, but if you can still have a smile on your face at the end of it (apart from the one you automatically get counting the tills) then this trade is probably for you.

8. Paddy was Pissing Himself

I took over an ailing Finnegan's Wake pub in Maidenhead around the turn of the millenium. An old area manager from Charrington's that we all called KC (nothing to do with the Sunshine Band) had head hunted me and thought I could do a job here. This was a smallish one bar operation, nice enough clientele but a brand that had seen its day. Finnegan's Wake was very much in the mould of the Irish O'Neill's brand, but much less well known or successful - there are still O'Neills to be found today, which probably tells you something. After a while, the brewery decided to de-brand the pub, so they took down the prints of the Irish Independent off the walls, the metallic leprechauns drinking Guinness and the hanging fiddles from the ceiling. They then painted it orange and yellow. That must have been an inebriated brainstorming meeting.

I liked the pub, personally. Had a decent set of locals in a pretty wealthy town, and they seemed to appreciate my endeavour and relative knowledge in trying to pull the pub back up by its bootstraps. The staff I inherited were pretty good, too. Usually, the characters behind the bar that are left behind after a sale, in my experience, are generally lazy, bored, thieves or institutionalised to their advantage. In this case, however, they were all ok but had probably just been mismanaged in a dying brand.

However, there was one girl who worked part time here, who took a shine to me. We'll call her Doris. This proved to be problematic for a couple of reasons, firstly because she never wanted to go home after her shift, and secondly because I wanted nothing to do with her in that way. My time as a kid with a roving eye was behind me. I had greatly matured by then, learned a few harsh lessons if you will - not to the point of being boring, but I now had an understanding of responsibility with regard to relationships and business. Furthermore, I had self imposed a "no drinking before 9.30pm" rule for myself at work, and I stuck to it.

Still with Doris, I don't think I handled her too well because as she was pretty good at her job, I didn't want to be too mean with her. So, instead of telling her to get lost at the start of all this, I would try and laugh off her advances and reject her in this way. It got to the stage where she would be ordering pizza to be delivered at closing time, when there was just the two of us left. She would then ask to share it upstairs in my flat, so I had to be brutal at this point. She then, of course, started sulking on duty and not being such a great member of staff anymore. A woman scorned....but it would get worse.

This issue was compounded when my second wife to be, Mary, applied for a position there. I was in my office upstairs when a barman came running up, saying "You've got to see the bird applying for a job downstairs. Wowzer. She's filling in an application form now." So, cool as a cucumber, I took the stairs down two at a time, before smoothly walking across the bar floor to introduce myself.

She was smokin'. Dark brown hair, dark brown eyes, body of a goddess. When she spoke I was surprised to hear a transatlantic accent, but before I called her a Yank, I found out that she was Canadian. Still smooth. Just. The interview was brief, but a formality. I asked her what went into a vodka and coke, she got it right. For just £3.60 per hour of the brewery's money, I could ogle her for as many hours as she was willing to work. She would, of course, in time prove to be far more expensive than that, but I've never begrudged a penny.

Fortunately for me, we got on like a house on fire, and she actually eventually ended up moving in with me upstairs. This was the final straw for our Doris who quit her job, but not before yelling abuse at me for not returning her love. It was unfortunate, as I went out of my way to be professional in all dealings with her, but she wouldn't accept a no. About a fortnight later, I got a package in the post. It was some intricately curled barbed wire, mounted on a wooden plinth, with an expletive laden message attached from the spurned Doris. Scary stuff.

Fast forward another week, and I got a call from the area manager of the brewery. They had received a formal complaint alleging sexual harassment against me and wanted to interview me with the HR department. Of course, I was shocked that she had taken her grudge this far as it could well have cost me my job. Fortunately for me, the other people in the pub that HR decided to interview told the same story of unreturned love, so it painted a favourable picture in my favour. Despite this, I felt I was still being treated like a criminal, but when I produced the barbed wire plinth and accompanying note it spoke volumes. She withdrew the allegation the following day.

On a lighter note, another barmaid, Kerry, used to work on a Wednesday lunch, 12-5pm shift. As with normal day shifts in the pub, we'd be busy for a couple hours for office types out for a bite and a pint, then it would die a death around two o'clock until the punters finished work and popped in for one on the way home. So, the system was that there would be a few light cleaning jobs to achieve between the hours of two and five, so that the pub stayed spick and span and the bar staff felt a) motivated, and b) awake.

However, this lazy so and so would be leaning and slouching all over the place - always in the toilet or reading a magazine when I wasn't supposed to be watching her. After one such period of non activity, I pointed to the crisp display... In Finnegan's, our crisp display stretched along the length of the back bar on a shelf perched above the optics. Six flavours of Tayto's, four facings per flavour, three deep. That's 72 packets on display.

"As it's quiet," I began, "It's a good time to Pledge the crisps."

"I'm sorry?" came the confused response.

I held up a can of Pledge. Furniture polish for wood.

"As it gets so dusty up there, we try to keep it clean and make the crisps stand out by using this stuff. Makes them shine."

I reached up and took down a packet of cheese and onion. I lifted it up so she could see and gave the bag a little squirt. With a soft yellow cloth from underneath the bar, I carefully buffed the bag.

"Make sure you get the corners" I said. "If you don't, you can really tell the difference when they're back up on the shelf with the spotlights on them." I turned the bag over, gave another careful squirt, and thoroughly buffed the second side.

Kerry looked at me as if she wasn't sure what she was seeing. I returned her look with enthusiasm.

"You won't believe what a difference this makes to the display. Take your time, but do a thorough job. I'll be back in a bit." I handed her the cloth and can of polish, and went to my office before she could see me crack up.

Twenty minutes later, I return to the scene of the crime to see Kerry stood on a chair, about halfway through the display. One of the regulars was at the end of the bar, nursing a pint of John Smiths.

"What have you got her doing?" he said to me, under his breath.

"Pledging the crisps", I replied, grinning.

"Fucking hell" he said, as he rolled his eyes and took another sip.

Unfortunately for Mary, she also fell victim to my mean streak before she got the measure and found the rhythm of English humour. Early on in our relationship in Finnegan's Wake, I was creating a special and she was peering over my shoulder. I was making a bechamel (white sauce) for a lasagne and was just finishing it up.

"Could you please just keep stirring this for me?" I asked her.

"Sure", came her eager to please response.

"It's really important that you don't leave it and keep it moving, otherwise it's going to stick like shit to a blanket."

"Ok, no problem", she said, and took the wooden spoon from me. She carried on stirring the sauce as requested, and I went downstairs to check on the pub.

Twenty minutes later, I come back upstairs to find her still dutifully moving this sauce around in the pot.

"Great job, Mary", I said. "Except I turned the heat off twenty minutes ago." She looked underneath the pan in disbelief. The ring was cold.

Another time, during a spare afternoon, we were doing a little shopping in Maidenhead town centre. She dragged me into Superdrug.

"I'm looking for some really nice bath foam", she said, enthusiastically.

"Ok then", I responded, already zoning out.

So she proceeds to go check out rows and rows of bubble bath, while I aimlessly wander the aisles of Superdrug, waiting for her to choose one. After about ten minutes, I've covered the store, so I wander back to find her unscrewing this one, sniffing it, and putting it back. Then picking up another one and repeating the procedure. For fucks sake just pick one, I'm thinking to myself... I pick up the nearest blue one, and remove the lid.

"Mmmm, how about this one?" I say, and offer her the bottle so she could drink in its floral bouquet...

As she waves her hooter over the top of the bottle, I give it a gentle squeeze. At least, I thought I did, but it must have been more urgent than I thought as this mass of blue foamy liquid shot out of the top and covered her face.

"You asshole!" she screamed, as a load of bubbles came out of her nose and mouth. I really didn't mean to get quite that much on her, but the sight of those bubbles really cracked me up. I couldn't help it.

She ran to the end of the aisle, where there was a stack of kitchen rolls beautifully displayed, and ripped open the nearest one, knocking half a dozen packs on to the floor in the process. She cleaned up her face and threw down the used stream of papers on to the floor, and stormed through the front door. On the way out, following sheepishly behind her, I complained to a checkout girl that someone had left a terrible mess on aisle 4, and it should be cleaned up before someone slips on it.

Mary's father, Steve, was a big cheese in telecommunications and had moved to Maidenhead from the family base in Canada to assist his company in the UK, which in turn had brought Mary over here too. One day, Steve asked if I'd like to accompany him on a business trip to the Monaco Grand Prix. His company were being wined and dined by a construction outfit that wanted his business and there was a spare place available - perfect for getting to know a guy who had just persuaded your daughter to move in with him.

At the time, Mary was furious that her old man had invited me and not her but KC, my Area Manager who was a huge Formula One fan, stepped in and saved the day by bribing her with a brand new DVD player to stay behind and look after the pub while I was away galavanting. Steve's motives aside, it took me all of a nano second to accept his invitation of a long weekend away watching sport in luxury, and so in May of 2001 off we went.

It was a trip full of all the bells and whistles you can imagine. Home was a luxurious 140 foot yacht for the weekend, transport was a helicopter, meals were private seven star silver service affairs. To watch the Grand Prix itself, we had moored at the point of a bend where the cars race into a tunnel, so the noise was incredible. We viewed from the top deck of the vessel, where a majestic buffet had been prepared with individually engraved, personalised binoculars for each place setting. I was terribly careful to create the right impression in this heady atmosphere, as I knew I was being assessed. If the boot was on the other foot, I would be assessing too…

The day before the Grand Prix race day, we had a free afternoon from sightseeing. On the very top of the yacht were stored some "toys". These came in the form of a motor boat, a couple of inflatables and a jet ski. Most of the business chaps chose the boat to go out onto the Mediterranean and do a spot of relaxing fishing and intelligent conversation (!) As I knew the chit chat would be centered on their shared working interests, I thought I'd branch out a bit, and have a go at the jet ski.

It was a perfect early Summer day, very little wind, nice and warm. To the distance, maybe a couple of miles away was Nice and its stunning, picturesque harbour. The yacht had dropped anchor and the fishermen were about half a mile away with a couple of rods and a few bottles of red, no doubt. A truly tranquil scene. Meanwhile, with this 70 mph top of the range machine in between my thighs, I was zipping around the Med like a wasp with his ass on fire. After a short while, a little boredom kicked in so I thought I'd give the business boys a drenching.

I opened up the throttle and hared towards them, bright yellow Arsenal away shirt billowing in the wind. My plan, loosely constructed, was to get within a few feet of them and bank it, so creating a fine spray of water as I curved majestically away from the boat. I'd seen it in a cartoon - I was sure I could do it. However, as I got towards them and leaned into the banking stage, I just carried on going sideways and plummeted towards the boat. By the time I saw six pairs of eye whites gawking at me, terrified, I knew I wasn't going to make it.

The CRUMP sound as the bottom of my jet ski crashed into the side of that fine motor boat was just awful, as middle aged men, fishing bait and chateauneuf du pape all went skywards. I was so terribly embarrassed, but they were very good about it. "Could've happened to any of us." and "Don't worry, the insurance will cover it". I've always been scared to ask Steve about his precise thoughts at that point. Some things best left unsaid, I'd wager.

That evening, dinner was served on the back of the boat in the open air. We were moored in Marseille harbour and the quayside was a hub of activity, music and dancing as the Formula One show was in town. We were tied up around this fat, flat topped cylindrical concrete bollard, just watching the entertainment around us with full stomachs and beers in hand. At one point, a rather attractive young lady wearing a very skimpy dress and clutching a hessian bag, climbed up onto our bollard and took out a ghetto blaster and two lengths of rope.

We watched her with curiosity as she set fire to the two ends of the ropes, then stood up and slipped the only item of clothing she was wearing off her shoulders and onto the floor by her feet. For the next ten minutes or so, we were treated to a quite wonderful spectacle of this naked young lady twirling and writhing these fireballs to the music playing from her system. She was given a very enthusiastic round of applause by all on board, as well as the understandably sizeable crowd that had gathered during the performance. The tip hat that she passed around was generously filled by all, which was a good thing as it was pretty obvious that she could have used a new gardener.

After a few months, trade was picking up nicely at Finnegans. Lunches were flying out, and it started to be the place to come after work, too. More local people became regulars, including a set of twins probably around sixty years of age. Word got back to me that these were a "tasty couple of blokes" in their day, and were locally feared by anyone who crossed them. To me and the rest of the staff, they were lovely men. Polite, impeccably mannered, immaculately dressed and generous in company. I and my staff were referred to by name at all times and were always offered a drink when it was their round, in addition to their own company.

One afternoon, this hairy oik came in and was drinking at the bar. Probably early forties, six feet, well built and wanted everyone to know how important he was. He had clearly consumed one or two before he got to us, and was getting louder and more aggressive the longer he stood there. After a while, one of the twins touched him lightly on the shoulder and asked him politely if he could keep the language down, as he and his brother were "in female company". The bloke told him to fuck off, and threw in one or two choice barbs to go with the advice.

The twin - we'll call him Ronnie (!) - went back to his female company and apologised to the ladies present about the language. Call it a sixth sense, but my "trouble" nose was twitching, so I hovered around the bar flap so that I could nip it in the bud if anything was to kick off. A few minutes later, the loudmouth went to the toilet. I was serving someone at the time, but out of the corner of my eye, I saw Ronnie follow him in. As I went to go through the hatch, the other twin - we'll call him Reggie (!) - stepped in front of me and said "just leave it, it'll be fine." Literally ten seconds later, Ronnie appeared wiping his hands with a handkerchief. He was unflustered, unsweating and quite nonchalant. As I went towards the toilets, he put his hand on my shoulder and said "Sorry about the mess."

I found the loudmouth spreadeagled, face down in the urinal trough. There was blood all over the wall and urinal, and broken teeth on the floor. I eventually got him and his wayward teeth up and out of the pub - to be fair, he went willingly - and got the urinal trough cleaned up. When I returned to the bar, there was a drink waiting for me and profuse apologies and handshakes from both of the twins. I still don't know what the moral of this tale is.

A far more down to earth and less scary individual was Paddy. Massive Irishman, not so much in height as girth. Lived on his own literally two hundred yards from the pub "In that house over there." Paddy would be in five or six nights a week, and drink astonishing amounts until he started singing. Maybe ten pints and half a dozen Irish whiskeys was the threshold, before "Danny Boy", or "The Irish Rover" would start to drown out the background music. Fabulous entertainment. Many a night I've had to help him home to his front door, tip him over the threshold and shut the door behind the upturned soles of his feet.

This one particular Christmas Eve night, Paddy seemed on a mission. He drank until he couldn't even sing and appeared to sag against the bar. He mumbled something about needing the toilet and began to make his way towards the Gents, inching towards them by clutching onto the bar top whilst shuffling his feet in a most unsteady fashion. Unfortunately for Paddy, he inevitably ran out of counter and with nothing to balance with but thin air he went down, straight as an arrow with the most horrific thud. This huge man lay there prone, in the middle of the floor, as if someone had pulled his plug out of its socket. Then a puddle started to form underneath him - Paddy was pissing himself.

"You get the mop, I'll call an ambulance" I said to a member of staff.

"No. You get the mop, I'll call the ambulance" came the response.

A mop and medical help were soon both acquired. They got here in less than twenty minutes (the paramedics, not the mop) in all probability, but it seemed like an age. Paddy was breathing, still, but very unconscious. As he was being monitored and prodded he suddenly sprung to life, like he had just got ammonia shoved up his nose.

"The pipes, the pipes are calling" he sat up and yelled. Everyone jumped.

"From glen to glen...."

We thought the daft bastard was dead or at the very least about to be. Scared the crap out of us. He yelled across to the bar for a Guinness from his now seated position, but he wasn't getting any more that night. The lovely paramedics ended up walking him to his door and tipping him over the threshold, just like any other night.

One Spring Saturday afternoon, we had a quite hilarious fight outside the front door. As the pub was situated on a corner of the road, there was an extended paved area out there, where there were half a dozen metallic, round tables with four folding type chairs surrounding each one. Apparently, this chap and his mate were outside with a couple of pints of Fosters, when this homeless man interrupted their schedule. He was carrying a plastic Co-op bag and a half drunk can of Tennents Super - and you could tell that it wasn't his first of the day. He looked and smelled the worse for wear and from my position inside the pub looking out, I saw that he had stopped for a chat with these two.

I imagine he was asking for a cigarette, then 50p, etc. The customer eventually got tired of the tramp and told him to fuck off. That's the first bit I heard, as I came outside doing the rounds and collecting some empties. It all escalated very quickly. In response to the guy's brutal verbal dismissing of him, the tramp kicked the chair next to where he was standing into the guys shins. The guy leapt up and took a swing at the tramp, but fell over the chair in his efforts to reach him. As he was on the floor, the tramp hit him with his carrier bag over the back of the head, which split open, and all of these apples started rolling around the floor.

Now furious, the guy leaps to his feet, grabs the offending chair and swings it at the tramps head, missing him by a mile. The tramp then shouts "Ole!" as if he was a bullfighter and puts himself into some sort of crouching, karate style pose and starts making these weird Japanese type sounds to go with it. Not wanting to make himself look like a further ass by taking a third potshot at the homeless man, the customer starts throwing the rolling apples at him. Naturally, the tramp starts chucking them back. Not wanting to see any of my windows put through by an errant Granny Smith, I decided that it was time to step in and stop the madness.

I calmed them both down, helped collect the tramps apples and also gave him three packs of smokey bacon crisps (they were out of date) and a fresh carrier bag. In those days, they didn't cost me 5p. The only real casualties from this "It's a Knockout" type skirmish was a pint of Fosters and the customers pride. I replaced one, but I bet his mate still gives him stick over the other.

After a very successful eighteen months or so at Finnegan's, the brewery decided that the pub was to be included in a package sale of disposals in a reorganisation of the company. Although I was offered a new deal to stay on by the incoming new owner, I felt that it was time to move on and try another site. Sometimes you know when you've done as much as you can somewhere, however comfortable you are at the time and it's best to get out and move on while the going is good. If only Arsene Wenger thought like that...

9. Flowers on the Underground

I was given the opportunity of a cracking site by an old area manager, Mike, from my Charrington days. I hadn't worked specifically with him, but he was a colleague of KC, who had recommended me. I cased the pub out a few times with Mary who was by now a permanent fixture and we agreed it looked idyllic.

The Flower and Firkin was not the biggest site, but it was perfectly situated within Kew Gardens tube station so it was certainly capable of taking a lot of money with a guaranteed footfall on a daily basis. Going back into London was a bonus for me and an adventure for Mary. What I didn't like was the way Mike insisted on interviewing us as a couple and making the offer of employment a joint one. I had never been put in this position before and had got to where I was in the industry as an individual.

The pub was owned by the Spirit Group, who were back in those days connected to Punch Taverns. Although I wasn't happy about the way that Spirit had organised the contract, I was initially delighted with the pub itself - perfect business setting, beautiful part of the country and promised lovely two bedroomed accommodation situated over the top of the actual railway platform, which had previously been unavailable to view. If the alarm bells weren't ringing loudly enough with the contract situation, they were blasting out like Big Ben on moving in day.

We were greeted by Peter, a sweaty chap from Middlesbrough who was already living in the accommodation, and introduced himself as the assistant manager. When questioned on this situation when Mike eventually picked up his phone, he claimed to have no idea that Peter was living in the accommodation, despite him having lived there for eighteen months previously with the last manager of the Flower. He said he'd look into it, and could we plough on until he could resolve it. I didn't believe him, and my gut feeling was that this particular job / area manager / company wasn't going to live up to expectation.

And how right I was. The culture of the Spirit Group was all about saving money, as opposed to building sales. The pub was really managed by the area managers, rather than the on-site operator such as myself. The allowance for staff wages was absolutely pitiful, which ensured that Mary,

Sweaty Peter and myself had to serve behind the bar for about fifty hours each to make ends meet. There was no room for any managerial input to improve the business from myself - I wasn't even allowed to employ anyone without the area managers say so. All the company needed at their pubs at that time were people to pull pints, cook food, clean and manage the cellar and cash.

It was now obvious why Mike had been so keen to get Mary and I onto a joint contract - because it was getting us on the cheap. By tying Mary into a salary meant that she was not getting paid even minimum wage, with the hours that she had to put in to meet our budgets due to the lack of staff costs allowed in the pub. We ran our asses off on a daily basis, free time was extremely limited, we shared a flat with a continually perspiring stranger and we were chronically underpaid. There was nothing to like.

The pub itself was typical of a venue in a wealthy London suburb such as this. While most of the layout was on the ground floor with one side of the pub a walled window bordering the train platform, the toilets were situated downstairs via a narrow staircase. Because of this isolation, it was a perfect place for the pissed up rich kids to go and snort their coke - and not the Pepsi wannabe kind. Very quickly I established that there was a real problem here, and it wasn't the odd person. Trying to stop it was almost a token gesture as it was evident that most of the evening clientele came here to secure a score. It was like going out to Starbucks with these guys for their coffee.

To add to the issues that we had walked into, Mary had a disagreement with the chef. That is, it would have been a disagreement if he had given her the time of day. His name was Khalil, and he was, I think, Algerian. Mary told me that he wasn't doing the tasks that she had set for him that day and was being rude to her face. This was odd, as every time I had dealt with this chap he had been incredibly polite, so I went to the kitchen to find out why. When I related what Mary had said to me, his response was a shrug and he said to me "Because she is a woman." I asked him to enlighten me further, and he explained that in his culture a man cannot take instruction from a woman. I told him that in this pub, Mary was a manager so he was going to have to. The chap left the next day.

We both became very unhappy at the working conditions that this Company had put us under. There was no sign of Peter being moved out of the accommodation to give us any reasonable comfort - and from his point of view, why should he? We were employed and moved in under false pretences, and nothing was going to change. The wage percent seemed to be Company wide, and all of the other managers that I met told me similar stories of woe. No investment, repairs out of petty cash, no extra staff, bonus' way out of reach. It was a shitty time. Mary confessed to me that she needed a morning vodka to go to work sometimes. I pretended to be horrified at the time, but I knew exactly where she was coming from.

Within months, I put the feelers out to people in the industry that I was looking to get out, and I got a nibble with a company called Noble House, who had a large Rat and Parrot site in trouble in Lincoln, and wanted me to go and check it out. I did that in my rare days off and liked the look of what I saw. Not a traditional type pub of my preference, but a huge City destination venue, which I thought might suit Mary better. The terms were far more generous for us both, but the position was live out, as it was a lock up operation on a retail park.

I gave Mike and Spirit two weeks notice. He was furious. Ironically, he started going on about loyalty and respecting your contract, but I didn't see him being conned into sharing his home with any sweating strangers, which, six months down the line, he had not seen important enough to address or even bring into a conversation. I pointed out to him that he didn't actually need a manager anyway, as all of the decision making for the operation was done at his level. He could just employ a couple of good barpersons on the cheap.

The Spirit group were demerged by Punch Taverns very soon after our departure. All split up into bits, and chunks of it bought by other Pub Co's. The period that we had spent running the Flower and Firkin was just the time that the Company knew that they were going to be sold and broken up, and so they were squeezing every possible penny out of their pub business'. It's unfortunate that the pub managers employed on the ground aren't privy to this kind of information, when they are asked to move their lives and homes in the hope of career progression and personal happiness.

10. What Can we Give a Vegetarian?

The journey to Lincoln was a happy one. The relief of driving away from the pressures of a no win situation at the Flower and Firkin was palpable. By now, we had sourced somewhere to live and for the time that we ran the Rat and Parrot, we resided at an older terraced house in Baggholme Road. It was great fun living off the premises, as you felt like you were putting the job down at the end of your shift. Of course, as the manager I was always on call, but to be fair I didn't get phoned much.

Our house was a couple of doors down from a great, old fashioned chip shop and a few more to a creaking local pub on the corner called the Crown. This place was like walking into a relic from the 1960's, with a bright red carpet that had seen better days, chairs and tables that had seen better days and a landlady that had....well, you know where I'm going with this. There was a small barbeque left in our back garden at the house, and sometimes after work we would cook off a load of burgers and sausages for supper. As we always would cook too much, we would have a game of "Who can hit the pub with the sausage", by trying to hurl the leftovers across the back gardens in between us and the pub.

Still, it was a new and exciting experience having our own house and our own free time after work. I found the house odd, with the bathroom to be found on the ground floor at the end of the galley type kitchen via a sliding door. I imagine that it was an extension, added later, as when the house was first built there would have been no internal plumbing.

Back at the Rat and Parrot, it was an ok business but seriously under performing. Being a flagship site on a retail park, the rent and rates on the building itself must have been huge, so as it was grossing only around eight or nine thousand at the time, it clearly needed a boost. When I take over a pub, I like to let it run the way it always did for a few days, watch and observe, and take a few notes. This gives me a chance to see what and who works, and what needs to change or be culled.

On day one, I ordered a bacon sandwich for my breakfast from the menu. The "sous chef", as he introduced himself, delivered to me a doorstep sandwich with bread not fresh, no butter, bacon only just cooked (who doesn't want it crispy?) and presented it to me just like that, no garnish, no sauce, no serviette. I asked him if he was happy with what he produced - it was about four quid to a customer - and he shrugged and said he's always done it like that. So you see my point...

I worked hard changing things - the good staff I kept, the lazy ones (including "sous") I managed out of the business. I changed the way that orders were taken, food was delivered, standards on presentation, cellar practices... in truth, there were so many quick wins, so many obvious things that could be addressed quickly, that within a month or two, sales were already building and excess expense had been trimmed. Finally, I was getting back a little of my management pride and being paid for what I was supposed to be doing. I also looked good in the eyes of the pub company, Noble House, as the figures I was giving them were already far outstripping the previous managers.

As a manager of a pub - as opposed to a tenant, or lessee - you are salaried and incentivised via a bonus situation. That is, if you hit your sales targets at the end of the financial year then you collect a bonus payment, so it was always a goal that I would keep one eye on. Key to the previously set target is the performance of the pub in the last financial year, so giving the pub company a base with which to guess future revenues. In this case at the Rat and Parrot, I was fortunate that the venue had been managed by an incompetent fuckwit, so the budget that was set was well within my grasp once I'd made the changes that were so obviously needed here. Never follow a genius. What chance did David Moyes have at Manchester United following Fergie?

On the subject of a bonus, Anheuser Busch, the European distributors for Budweiser lager at that time, held a competition while we were in Lincoln promoting their beer. The goal was to increase your percentage sales of Budweiser by the greatest amount, and tell them how it was achieved. The winners got a luxury weeks holiday to Florida with entry to Busch Gardens in Tampa, Universal Studios and Discovery Cove where you swim with dolphins. Now I'd never had any desire to bump swimming trunks with a slippery mammal, but I thought it was a pretty decent prize overall.

I was fortunate that in a storage cupboard in the pub, there was a dusty box full of old promotional Budweiser stuff from a couple of years previously. I set up a huge display of Budweiser paraphernalia in front centre of the bar. I then incentivised my own staff for a £25 weekly prize on who could sell the most Buds in the pub. I also set up a scratchcard system for the punters, so three Buds got them a Bud keychain, ten got them a Bud t-shirt. Needless to say, I managed to win the thing, so Mary and I had a lovely trip on Virgin Atlantic that Autumn.

Once the obvious quick wins to improve the pub were in place, I would hold staff meetings with my key people. Those that showed some willingness or potential when I arrived would be there, as well as any new recruits I thought could add something to the business. One chap I had misjudged by giving him a chance was the head chef, a youngish chap who we'll call Barney. Now Barney wasn't a classically trained chef, but he had clearly done enough to get to his lofty position somehow with the previous management. I noted that his work ethic was ok, and that he was just about coping with the current food offer.

What I wanted to do was to restructure the menu, to make it a bit more service friendly. Some of the items on the menu were far too laborious to be able to execute within fifteen minutes, so if a rush was on the customers could sometimes wait more than half an hour for their lunch. I sat down with Barney, Lee (who was in my eyes, way ahead of Barney, but just worked there part time during his University studies) and a couple of other key kitchen staff. I put the floor open to suggestions about what we could put on the new menu.

In truth, I had already decided on most of it, but I wanted these guys to feel involved and part of the process. A key part of motivating your team, I think, is to make them believe that their opinion matters in the direction and policy of the business and I was keen to sound out their reactions. A lot of the time this also produces a nugget or two of top ideas. As expected, Lee came up with a few logical and sensible suggestions, despite the fact that this was just a side job for him. He seemed keen and interested. In contrast, Barney sat there like a sulking lemon, as he didn't think anything needed to change. I tried to encourage him, as he was the kitchen leader - I wanted him to step up. We were bouncing ideas around at one point and I asked Barney "What can we give a vegetarian?" Barney thought for a few seconds, hand on his chin, and responded with...

"How about ham, egg and chips?"

There was a silence, and Barney looked at us looking back at him.

"What?" he said. And then, "Oh, shit, the ham!"

"Our Head Chef, Ladies and Gentlemen" I announced, with a wave in his direction.

Within a couple of months, Barney had resigned and I believe applied to be a bus driver.

Lee became full time once he graduated, and took over the running of the kitchen. There was something about the chap that I really liked. He was always so unflustered - unless Lincoln City lost on a Saturday - and was always thirsty for learning and new information. I began to give him an occasional shift elsewhere in the pub to broaden his skill base, which he lapped up.

I can't leave the Rat and Parrot story without a mention of the cleaners here. In almost every pub I've had, the cleaners have been unreliable, lazy and distant. Here, I inherited Steph and Shelley, along with their mum, Karen. They had a key to the pub and so would let themselves in at silly o'clock in the morning. By the time I got there usually around eight, most of it was already done to a great standard and they were nattering on one of the couches. It wasn't long before they knew how I took my coffee and I was invited in to their circle, which became a very welcome start to my day. Wish all cleaners were like them…

After eighteen months or so, it was job done at the Rat and Parrot, which had by now been debranded into The Glasshouse. The business was running on autopilot, the systems were in place and I was again on the lookout for a new challenge. Noble House didn't want to lose me, or so they said, and offered me an unbelievable venue that they had in Brighton Marina, which was built on pillars over the water. It had two huge trading floors and the best accommodation I've ever seen in a pub. We were off again...

11. Pub Diaries, Part 2

Thursday 1st November 2007

Ginny's friend walked across the road whilst talking on her mobile phone and got mullered by a bloke who could not stop. She has a broken collar bone, a dislocated shoulder, a fractured leg in two places plus various cuts, lumps and bumps about her person. She is off any danger list, but I doubt she'll be capable of starting the Mexican waves in ward twelve for a good while yet.

To be honest, I feel just as sorry for the driver of the car, who had this girl step right out in front of him with no warning - he had no chance. He has been inundating her with grapes since the accident, as he feels so bad about inflicting such damage on her - but at least her pain is predominantly physical. I feel that I would much rather be hit, than do the hitting.

In other news, the new chef David is doing well, for the most part. He seems to be getting a good grasp on presentation of dishes, cooking them within our time frame and working off his own steam. Last night, however, he missed off the microwaves when cleaning up, as when I opened them they seemed to be coated in a rather delicious - but rather well done - remnant of cottage pie. Not good enough, but everyone can make a mistake once…

Halloween passed without any great incident - no eggs thrown at the pub, no juvenile Bristolian in-bred trying to set fire to an outside bench or the like. Indeed, only one kid was brave enough to darken my door, so I gave him a lolly or two and shooed him on his way. Mary was saying that Halloween is so big over in Canada, but it passes here virtually whimper-free. She reckoned that she used to still be trick or treating when she was seventeen - but then she would do anything for "candy".

Apparently, one of the regulars had a bad experience a couple of years ago, when some baseball cap wearing local thug yelled "trick or treat" from a bridge, as the punter passed underneath in his boat. The said punter responded with a well aimed v-sign and was rewarded for his bravado with a couple of bags of flour all over his nice wet vessel. Apparently it took about three weeks to completely remove all of the resulting goo from the boat. He now goes under bridges on Halloween armed with candy canes and Mars

Bars, just in case…

Friday 2nd November

My other chef Nick started today - a bit of a baptism of fire being that it was a Friday lunchtime. Induction was limited to yelling stuff at him like "two sour cream dips!" and "can I get a portion of scampi in the fryer now, please?" Once the rush had died and the smoke had cleared, he was still positive and smiling - although a tad shell-shocked - and I was able to sit down with him for a more appropriate welcome. He also seemed to get on OK with David, who confided in me that "Nick was cute". Our David appears to be camper than the camp guy from "Carry on Camping". Should be fun in that kitchen…

There are four Shakespeare pubs in Bristol. Only three are in the Yellow Pages and we are the only one called The Shakespeare Tavern. There is a Ye Olde Shakespeare, a Shakespeare Inn and The Shakespeare - but we are the only Tavern. Does this stop people insisting that they have the right pub when they phone up? You would not believe how many calls we get for one of the others. The call generally goes something like this:

"Good afternoon, The Shakespeare Tavern."

"Is this the Shakespeare?"

"One of them, yes."

"Can I speak to Bob, please?"

"Do you have the right Shakespeare?"

"You know, Bob - the boss."

"You have the wrong number - there is no Bob here."

"Is that the Shakespeare in Totterdown?"

"No, Prince Street."

"Oh. What's the number for the one in Totterdown?"

"I don't know. Try Yellow Pages."

"Oh. OK"

This may seem innocuous, but this happens at least twice a week. It's bloody annoying over a period of time. Today, I had three, in the space of half an hour. The third unfortunate chap called just after my line of patience had dwindled to less than nothing…

"Good afternoon, The Shakespeare Tavern."

"Is that the Shakespeare?"

"Yes, it is."

"Is Bob there?"

"Bob who?"

"What do you mean, Bob who? The owner Bob. The landlord."

"He's not my landlord. You have the wrong Shakespeare."

"Which Shakespeare are you?"

"William. You want Bob."

CLICK.

Obviously Bob from Totterdown is too tight to splash out to put his number in the Yellow Pages. I wish he would, though, because it's getting right on my tits.

Saturday 3rd November

Today at twelve forty five, Arsenal play Manchester United at home. First place against second place, first favourite against second favourite, good against evil. This is the biggest game of the season and I am nervous - win this and I will have a hangover tomorrow. Lose this and I will have a hangover tomorrow. I am staffed up, but do not have a ticket for the game, so the sofa will have to do...

The kitchen today sees Nick learning our method of making homemade burgers and chilli con carne. He is also prepping up for tomorrow's Sunday roast, so I can get a decent look at what he can and can't do. I am hoping I will be pleasantly surprised by his capabilities and can look forward to hanging up my chef's apron.

I am noticing an increasing problem downstairs with regard to the pub's aroma. When smoking was allowed in public places in the UK up until July 1st of this year, the smell of dozens of cigarettes would mask anything else that tends to waft around an enclosed space such as ours, which would be filled with fifty or so flatulent punters. Now you have to go outside to get cancer, there is an increasing chance that the smell of furniture polish and brasso will be masked by boozed up blokes' synchronised farting and communal B.O.

It is a difficult problem to address. Our standards of cleanliness in all departments here are second to none, so I imagine it would be worse in most other establishments - but the fact is that it is not pleasant. Some sort of neutraliser that emits every twenty minutes or so could help.

We had a chap in here last week who stank. Not just a faint whiff when you are close up, but an horrific, eye-watering stench as soon as you walked into the bar. We were busy, but there was a radius of about twelve feet of empty space around this guy where no-one else could breathe. He had no idea - how, I don't know - but it was bad for business. Of course, he had been served and had ordered a meal, so we had to wait for him to finish before acting. As soon as his knife and fork hit five o'clock, I was round there holding my breath and clearing his plate at the same time, whilst spraying "Oust" all over him. When he turned around to see what I was doing, I made out I was polishing the back of his chair.

Sunday 4th November

Arsenal fought out an honourable draw yesterday with Manchester United. Excellent game, edge of the seat stuff and honours even at the end of it - sporting handshakes all round. Actually, bollocks. They were lucky, the referee was biased towards them and both of their goals were offside / fouls / fluky (delete as necessary). Roll on the next game.

My new chefs tackled Sunday lunch for the first time today, we did seventy six meals in total, forty eight of which were roast dinners (beef, lamb shank or chicken). I stayed with them in the kitchen for the first three hours to teach them our routines and then left them to it. No complaints, no wastage, no fire brigade, good clean up, prep done for tomorrow. I am not used to this efficiency. I always have had to jump in to help the kitchen out or cover shortfalls. I am going to have to learn to let go, which is not in my nature.

Had an absolutely classic drunk in the bar tonight. She has been in before, when she ran through the bar with her "clinking" carrier bag, swiping peoples drinks from their tables while they are still sat there, chugging them and then dropping the empty glass on to the floor. Tonight, James was on his own downstairs. I get a call in the office, saying can I come and help, as he was trying to throw a woman out. Interesting, thinks I, as I mosey on downstairs…

When I get there, this inebriated lady has turned a table over in the front bar, whacked a bloke sitting on a bar stool with a brass drip tray and is cowering in the corner of the seating area as James is trying to eject her. He is telling her to get out, she is responding in a crow - like voice with "Fuck off! Fuck off!" Eventually, James grabs her clinking carrier bag and walks towards the front door. Genius.

Terrified that her "clink" is no longer within her reach and disappearing outside, she leaps out of her seat and hares after him. James is now outside and she jumps at him, desperate not to lose her life blood concealed in the carrier bag, and wrestles with him to try and get it back. After thirty seconds or so, she has the bag back and is down the steps and away. James returns into the bar to catcalls such as "So was that your ex, then?" and "You can't even pull the ugly ones!"

It is incidents such as these that make this job worthwhile. I do have a pang of sympathy for someone such as this lady. She looks as if she must be in her late fifties, but I would wager money that she is no older than about forty at best. She is often seen wandering the streets of Central Bristol talking to herself or yelling at people, trying to get into pubs and immediately being ejected. She never goes without a fight, though.

It is really important that those who choose to earn a living selling alcohol take the responsibility seriously. A woman such as this would never be served anything here, but someone, somewhere is taking her money and feeding her addiction. There seems to be endless red tape and legislation heaped onto pubs with regard to the sale of alcohol, but supermarkets and off licences appear to be where people like this get their fix without any trouble. The same applies to discounted loss leading alcoholic sales to both drunks and the under age. This is where anti social behaviour problems stem from - these people are not served from pubs, I can assure you. It baffles me why off sales venues are currently exempt from censure over deep discounts, whereas it is illegal to do so in pubs. Do these legislators have blinkers on, or a hidden agenda?

Monday 5th November

Got a call from my Granny Audrey today telling me that she had had another blackout. This is a pretty common occurrence these days with her - she seems to get disorientated and fall over when she looks up suddenly, but the doctors say that there is nothing they can do about it. Apparently this time she was using the microwave, got one of her dizzy spells and ended up in between the cooker and the fridge. It is a real concern for us family members, because one day she may not be able to call for help.

She currently has one of those alarm things that is linked to a warden, or someone similar - like an old fashioned light switch on a long string from the ceiling. She has just had these new curtains installed in her front room where you pull a rope to open and shut them to avoid her looking up too suddenly. Unfortunately, it is next to one of the alarms, so she keeps pulling the wrong string: "Are you OK, Mrs Burrows?" booms the voice. "Just pulling the curtains, dear. But they haven't moved yet…"

Today, the doctor visited to check her over and sat her down for a chat. He asked her if she thought if it would be a good idea to move into a retirement home. Granny Audrey is fiercely independent, so would never entertain the idea of not being able to look after herself. "Anyway", she said to me "They play bingo in those places and I can't stand bloody bingo". Here endeth the logic.

Homemade Leek and Potato Soup
As we live so close to the Welsh border, we thought that we would boost their economy by putting on this soup. Served with a lump of coal, some close
harmony singing and a crusty baguette and butter.
£4.25

Chicken and Chips
Do you remember the good old days of pub food, where you could get chicken and chips in a basket? Well, this is it! Except for the basket. But on a plate.
£5.50

Tuesday 6th November

I must say I was disappointed with the lack of effort Bristol put on for bonfire night. Last year it was a spectacular sight from my kitchen window, which overlooks the main harbourside where there were huge displays in all directions. This year, I could only see fireworks from my lounge window, which overlooks a council car park - and the display was rubbish. Maybe I should do one from the flat roof over the gents toilet next year...

I have let one or two things slide on the preparations for Christmas. This is due to the fact that we are in the middle of re-organising our team after the departure of my chef and number two recently. It means that I have been tied to the business twenty four - seven, as I have no fully trained up key staff and it is difficult just to go out and leave them - and it would be unfair, too.

Firstly, I need to make some Christmas cakes. This is not girly. I make three or four every year, because I like them and Mary likes helping to make them. The mother in law likes them too, but I am not posting one to Canada so she is going to miss out this year. Secondly, I need to start on my Christmas shopping. Mary has almost completed hers, which smacks of serious organisation (although as the majority of her presents need to be sent to Canada well ahead of the big day, this is probably a necessity).

Before then, Ben and Sam have their birthdays. One is on the 14th and t'other 16th November, although they are a year apart. As they will only be two and one respectively, I suggested that we could ignore the fact that it will be their birthdays at all, as we will not get away with it in future years, but the suggestion was greeted with a scowl from the wife so I'd better get a cake from Costco, or somewhere similar. Won't cost much in candles, though.

Wednesday 7th November

This has been one of the quietest evenings so far during our tenure here. It is a rare sight indeed when there are just two people sat in the front bar in quiet conversation, with another outside sucking furiously on a cancer stick. There was plenty of room for the tumbleweed rolling between the bar stools...

Why do smokers put themselves through such inconvenience as to sit outside in the freezing cold or rain, in order to partake in a habit which they already know will most likely be their killer - and at fantastic financial expense to boot? I try to make it comfortable for them - seats, umbrellas etc.- but it doesn't look like much fun to me. We have a wonderful fireplace in the bar which is great to pull up a stool in front of during those chilly British Winter evenings. You can just about see it from outside the front through the windows, if you crane your neck whilst you fill your lungs with black dust.

Idiots.

It felt lethargic all evening, in truth. Even Arsenal only drew 0-0 tonight, with barely a shot on goal throughout the game. It was as if the whole world was drinking Horlicks. There was no-one in the streets, the phone did not ring, no food orders (except a ham, egg and chips at ten to nine) and my bar staff spent most of the night leaning against the pumps whilst scratching their thatching. If every night was like this, I would be in debtors prison.

Chicken Jalfrezi

Fresh chicken in a heavily spiced tomato sauce. As Indian as a bow and arrow. (Wrong Indian, Ed.) Served with basmati rice and naan bread

£5.95

Cheesy Chips

A generous helping of pure, saturated fat. Go on...

£2.75

Thursday 8th November

It is turning into Winter. Last week the clocks went back, so it gets dark at half past four now. It is also dark when I first go into the bar area in the mornings, so if some idiot member of bar staff leaves the mop bucket by the bar flap overnight, I am not going to see it and either step in it or boot it across the floor. You have to get behind the bar to reach the panel of light switches, so the initial bleary - eyed minutes of a new day are precarious indeed.

It is also colder. You really notice it when you reside in an early eighteenth century Georgian mansion - I am sure you know the feeling - as they are not exactly built with square walls or floors. You get draughts everywhere. Our particular model is flat for two - thirds of the floor space in the lounge, until it reaches a middle pillar when it slopes alarmingly downwards. Up until recently, you could roll the youngest baby from the middle of the room to the far end. You could paint a target on the wall at the point where the cage reaches the change table and see if you could hit it.

Carpeting the room was a task indeed as none of the walls or windows have true edges - they are all at varying angles. There is a chest of drawers that had to be built up by a good three inches at one end to accommodate the slope, by the carpentry expertise of Alec when we first moved in.

When it rained with any great volume, it used to start coming through our bedroom ceiling, due to the insufficient size of the guttering on the roof. The rain which falls onto the building is channelled through a gully which runs through one of the upstairs bedrooms (which is boxed off as an internal bench) so it cascades through to the rear, off the top as a mini waterfall and onto the flat roof below - which happens to be the roof of the back bar. It then, of course, seeps through to create the need for water catching buckets in three or four spots inside.

The locals take this in their stride. They have experienced this for many decades already, so to them it is just a case of moving their foaming pints of ale six inches to the left so that it doesn't get watered down any further (which is, of course the standard crack whenever it rains internally here). I don't buy the "character" theme in this case - it is not a selling point to have buckets in your back bar catching the moisture from a dripping ceiling every time it pisses down. No matter how many times the brewery come and fix it, it never seems to solve the problem. To their credit, the bedroom does not leak any more - Mary and I are always guaranteed a "dry" nights sleep these days.

However, it is time for the radiators to kick in and combat the piercing chill that Bristol has for four months of the year. The fire in the bar has already been going for a few weeks now, mainly because I think it looks great as well as warms the place. The days of wearing shorts on the job are becoming remoter, as my elegant calves won't take the icy draughts. It is also less fun for my draymen on a Tuesday morning, as they always enjoyed looking up to the pavement from my delivery hatch below, to ogle at the secretaries short skirts as they made their way to their respective offices. Now, these same ladies wrap up against the chill, with scarves, Winter coats and extra fake tan.

Friday 9th November

Booked Jessica's flights for her visit over the festive period this year. She is flying from Newcastle to Bristol on Boxing Day evening and staying until 5th January. Traditionally, she has always had Christmas with Mum and New Year with Dad - it would be fantastic to get her over Christmas Day for once, but Jess is the kind of daughter that won't want to hurt either parents' feelings by asking if they wouldn't mind Christmas without her this year. I wouldn't want to put her in that position anyway.

It is also probably true that the real excitement of Christmas has dwindled for her with age - she is not a child anymore, so the uncontrolled pandemonium that takes over young children on a Christmas morning is no longer there for my girl. It will be for Ben and Sam, of course, in a couple of years time. It is a sign of the times that Jess e-mailed me her wish list for Christmas. It was full of CD's of bands that I have never heard of, and gadgets that I could never operate.

As a child, I will always remember the gift that gave me the most unbridled joy on a Christmas morn. I would have been about eight, I suppose and it was a Kevin Keegan football. Simple, heavy duty plastic with an autograph commercially painted on. I even knew what it was before it was opened, as all of the presents for us three boys were stored under the tree (wrapped, of course) as they were purchased. This particular one was round, shaped like a football and bounced - even within its crinkly paper. Bread and butter for an eight year old super sleuth.

By Christmas Day there was a mountain of shiny parcels - all different shapes, sizes and colours with name tags stating who it was for and who it was from. My parents would be so careful to ensure that there would be an equal number of presents for each of us to avoid fights and tears. There would always be at least a dozen for the boys each, with perhaps two each for Mum and Dad. It's amazing how it never occurred to us that this may seem a tad unfair.

The vast majority would always be from Mum and Dad, with a couple from Audrey and Granddad to add to our piles. We never realised at the time how hard they all must have saved in order to do this for us - but I realise now as a parent how much pleasure you get watching your children lose themselves in the excitement of it all, during the chaos of flying paper and sellotape. It is worth every penny, believe me.

Chef Nick's first attempt at a daily special was aired today. Yesterday he was furiously perusing the pages of "Mrs Beeton's Simple Cookbook". Today, he presented to The Shakespeare regulars a rather tasty beef stew. In fairness, it was a good effort - he is really doing his best to please here - but there should have been a tad more sauce, I thought. Hey ho. It still sold out and no-one died.

Homemade Pea Soup
Chef Pauline is but a distant memory, as
Chef Nick makes his Shakespeare
culinary debut with this kind of green - coloured number.
Served with a crusty, warm baguette and butter.
£4.25

Chicken Kiev
The Ukraine's most famous export, that is except
for radioactive debris.
Served with chunky chips and salad.
£5.95

Chef Nick's Beef Stew
He worked really hard at this. So buy some. Please.
Served with roast potatoes.
£5.95

Saturday 10th November

Ordered most of Jessica's Christmas list on Amazon today. It was extremely efficient and great value for money, but I did not feel remotely festive doing it. Somehow the convenience of the internet has taken the buzz out of Christmas preparations - there is far less satisfaction in giving all of this great stuff to Jess without first having gone through the crowds and queues. What is the point of Christmas shopping for your children without having to stop at a grotto while you are doing it? I suppose soon I will be able to get "Cyber Santa Service" from online shopping sites beamed into my office via my webcam, in yet another step to further automate the festive season.

On the theme of "commercial season", I need to sort out which decorations survived last year and are willing and able to make a reappearance in the bar. There is no room for a tree downstairs, as all of the tables are pretty much full on most evenings - let alone at Christmas time - so I am unwilling to sacrifice any space for a tree which will only get systematically pulled apart anyway over the five weeks. We tend to tastefully decorate around the actual bar servery areas as opposed to the whole pub floor. We use green wreaths with stuff like pine cones attached, and plain lights. No gaudy colours, neon or inflatable reindeers. We like to keep a touch of civility and decorum in here.

There used to be a blow up Rudolph that made an annual appearance at home, when we three boys were young. It was always an integral part of the festivities for us, a sign that Christmas was imminent. There was annual consternation when the reindeer would come out of the Christmas box and not inflate - there would always be some sort of fresh puncture to repair. I'd say Rudolph would have been wise to have had shares in Elastoplast the way he looked by the time I left home.

Christmas music is always an issue with regulars and staff. You can't just not have it, because we have many offices who come in to get bladdered in celebration of the season - and they expect to hear Slade and Wizard whilst they do so. The music is always well received on December 1st and 2nd, but come later in the week both staff and locals start grinding their teeth. I tend to mix one festive CD with two or three normal ones to try and dilute the impact, but it is generally the case that the 2nd January is more than welcome here, as that is when the dust will start to gather again on the "Bing Crosby Sings Christmas" album for another eleven months.

Sunday 11th November

I always feel that it is so important to observe and respect the traditions of Remembrance Sunday. In all of the pubs I have ever been in charge of, we have always had a poppy box and collection tin behind the bar. It is a great shame that as the surviving heroes of both World Wars pass away, so the visual impact of what these people went through for us normal folk passes with them. Of course, it is not just those Wars that we are supposed to remember today, but they have always been for me the most that I feel indebted to. As the ages pass and the lessons from these conflicts are not taught as readily in the school syllabus, the true meaning of this day will inevitably mean less and less to future generations.

Today, wars are largely fought in a different way - high tech weaponry controlled from computers as opposed to hand to hand fighting. To my children's generation, it must be almost impossible to believe how things used to be done on a battlefield. To Jessica's schools credit, this past July her year was taken on a trip to France to visit the battlefields of World War I, where they were allowed to see for themselves where thousands of soldiers were sacrificed for inches of mud. Included in the visit was a trip to the war memorials and cemeteries, where Jessica said that it was an incredibly moving experience, even though she knew of no personal connection with the conflict.

I have a postcard in my possession from my Great Granddad Harry who died the year before I was born, which was written to his parents as a Christmas card in 1916. It was sent from the front line in France and was composed in the impeccable, yet quite formal English of the time - even though it was written for family. It is embroidered on the front of the card with flowers and simple lace surrounds. The thought that this brave young man braved month after month of lying in freezing mud with shells and bullets whistling inches from his helmet, just to preserve the future for his family and country sends shivers down my spine.

The majority of my generation cannot hope to appreciate fully what these men went through for our benefit, so it is a great opportunity and duty for us on this one day of the year to try and understand the magnitude of their sacrifice. It would be too much to ask for us all to learn the lessons of the past and lay down arms, of course - only beauty queens really believe that World peace is possible.

So today we got absolutely slaughtered between midday and three o'clock. We did seventy four meals in the first three hours, but only seventeen in the next three. There was a huge memorial service in the centre of Bristol, which is literally at the end of Prince Street, upon which The Shakespeare Tavern stands. At the end of the service there were hundreds of people walking past the pub on the way back to their cars, to get back home out of the drizzle. Many of these were in their uniforms, with medals proudly hanging from their chests. The majority of these veterans were quite frail, but you could somehow tell that they were once strong and still proud.

If they were just eighteen during the last year of World War II, then they would be eighty today, so it really is a dying generation. I read on The Times website that the oldest living veteran laid a wreath in Northern France today - he was one hundred and eleven - he would have been twenty two when the first World War finished. Wonder if he knew Great Granddad Harry?

Monday 12th November

The Shakespeare Tavern proudly sits on the junction of The Grove and Prince Street. The outward view from the front of the building stretches the length of The Grove, which runs alongside the dock - it's a more than pleasant view. Travelling towards the pub you can really appreciate the full majesty of the Georgian frontage - the pub itself is the middle part of a line of three original period mansions. Without the pub blackboards on the railings bordering the entrance and the branded umbrellas, we would not even look like a pub at all.

This is a Grade II listed building, which comes with heavy planning restrictions - and rightly so. You are not allowed to obscure or change any part of the front elevation, or alter the footprint of the site in any form. Practically, in this day and age, it places quite a heavy restriction on my being able to improve facilities in any way for the business. I am not allowed, for example, to put up any sort of heavy duty smoking shelter outside the front, where I have a patio area. Now the ban on indoor pollution has finally hit these shores, most other pubs have catered for the addicted at great expense with awnings, umbrellas, heaters and even plasma TV's all conveniently placed outside.

I am further not allowed to fix anything permanent to either the walls or floor. Which means that I can only have mobile umbrellas - not much use in the breeze and horizontal rain with which Bristol seems all too prone. Of course, Bristol council take their planning powers a little too seriously and have even refused hanging baskets here, at great detriment to the appearance of the pub. Since when has a well maintained floral display on a blank canvas such as ours been a negative to a pub? They do allow a tacky banner advertising beer brands to be stretched across the frontage, though. It would be nice to have a chat one day with the bureaucrats in Council Towers, but they are far too lofted to return calls to the likes of a mere publican. I wonder who goes through more gin…?

The building opposite, a beautiful old warehouse, is also a listed property. They have hanging baskets galore and have also been allowed to paint their doors a vibrant shade of red. There is no explanation for this - the warehouse has lost much of its character with the refurbishment. I would hate for something like that to happen here - but are we being penalised for actually asking for permission in the first place?

Presently, there is an application to put a smoking shelter on the flat roof at the back of the building. This would neither change the footprint nor alter or obscure the front elevation. There would be decking, heaters, fixed umbrellas and a fabulous view over the boats to boot. The probability is that there will be some technicality that will be dragged up from within their winged leather armchairs, to shoot the plans in the proverbial foot. It is a real shame because I am the last person to want to change a great pub like this, but we must all see the need for improvement and modernisation now and then. If the powers that be want to impose new laws and standards in this modern, competitive world in which we all are trying to make a living, then they must allow business' the capacity in which to interpret these changes and compete. It does not mean ruining a nugget such as ours, but just being sensible and reasonable would be a welcome start.

Tuesday 13th November

Beer delivery is late. It's never late. But it is today. I have cleaned the toilets, changed some nappies, had two large espresso's, fetched the newspapers and lost a pound or two reading a catalogue on the toilet. I usually do this stuff *after* the beer delivery. I am all out of synch - it feels like Wednesday. Think I'll have a sandwich...

As soon as my hand brushed the bread bin, all hell was let loose. Firstly, the 3663 food delivery turned up at around nine - twenty. Then both babies were emitting the smells from hell, so I was changing both bums while the food was slowly defrosting. No great panic yet, that is until the beer delivery turned up at a quarter to ten, after the second bum change, but before I could put away the food.

The beer was late apparently due to one of the draymen dropping a barrel on his foot - we won't be seeing him this side of Christmas. So after seeing in the rather sizeable stack of barrels and boxes (I am building my wet stock for Christmas) I had to finish putting away the frozen food.

It is rather typical for a publican that you haul yourself out of bed just after seven (which, you must appreciate, is quite early for someone who never finishes work before midnight) and then not get any action before twenty past nine. It is further typical that as soon as you try to relax in any way, something will happen that requires you to immediately un-relax. For example, I believe that there is a sensor on my toilet seat. Whenever I park myself there, the phone rings. Every time, I swear. Once it happened at four thirty in the morning - as if it wasn't bad enough that I had to go at that ungodly hour, some drunk called claiming that he left his phone in the bar that night. It turned out it was the wrong Shakespeare.

Chef Nick burned both his hands today, whilst trying to pick up a dish that he had taken out of the oven about ten seconds before. This sort of thing happens when there are certain levels of stress in the kitchen, with food orders piling in and dishes piling up. I tried to get the Savlon for him, but couldn't find it through the tears of laughter.

Chef David's Broccoli and Cauliflower Bake
Vegetarians rejoice. Meat is just a distant memory as we cater for all of you herbivores out there.
Served with a crusty baguette and butter.
£4.25

Pork and Guinness Casserole
What's not to like? Meat, beer, potatoes.
Food for real men. Not pretend ones.
£5.75

Wednesday 14th November

Today is Sam's first birthday. He celebrated as he always does, by guzzling a bottle of milk and filling his nappy. The young man has neither social graces nor any sense of decorum. He has received many cards and presents from various relatives, all of which he will pretty much ignore and play with the wrapping instead. Many of the gifts are joint presents, addressed to "The Mant Boys" or similar, but that is to be expected as Ben's birthday is on Friday. I have no doubt that Mummy and Daddy will be organising joint parties in the future, too.

Today we plan to escape for a touch of Christmas shopping. We have competent staff on today and Wednesday's are not the busiest of twenty four hours in our working week. It is the first time that I will have been out of the building for non work purposes in around three weeks, so I am looking forward to these precious few hours.

Heard a joke on the Chris Evans show on Radio 2 this evening, on the way back from the shopping mall: Two chickens on the pavement. One says to the other "I think I'll cross the road." The other one replies "Don't, you'll never hear the last of it."

Tickled me, anyway.

Thursday 15th November

What a crap day. You know that it is not going to go well when things do not go to plan from the off - you feel like you can't catch up and end up fire fighting for the rest of the day. Whenever you think you are straight with all that needs doing, something else happens to set you back. Eventually, you give up and go to the casino, where you drop sixty quid and come out feeling worse. Well, I did anyway.

It started off with an early morning trip to Asda. Mary usually likes to go with Ben, to give him some fresh air and give her a buggy to carry her shopping in. Unfortunately, this morning's air was completely frozen, so unless we wanted a baby ice lolly, Ben was going nowhere but the nearest radiator. So I volunteer to go in the car for her, while she takes in the two food deliveries in my stead.

This particular Asda is about the size of two football pitches. It is eight thirty in the morning and all of the shelves are packed and beautifully faced, waiting for the unemployed of Brislington to cash in their giros so that they can come in and mess it all up again. The only two gaps on the shelf in the whole store was Farleys follow - on baby formula and Weight Watchers cheese puffs - two of the absolute essentials in our household. I bought Mary the Weight Watchers cheese discs instead, but it wasn't the same, apparently. Not enough puff.

I get back to the pub as the food deliveries were being taken in - we were overcharged on our chickens, delivered way too many bananas and sent twelve bunches of chives instead of twelve chillies. Who the hell needs twelve bunches of chives? Mary suggested making chive and banana soup, but I poo-pooed that idea. We will have to make chive con carne instead and hope the punters don't notice.

I then find out that the staff wages have been sent to another pub by our accountants. To be fair, this is the first time that has happened, so I won't slaughter them in print (I find them quite indispensable, actually) but I had three or four employees coming in to get paid, to be disappointed. Although the details were e-mailed instead, it was still quite an inconvenience on the morning.

As it was the day in between my two boys birthdays, I volunteered to get a nice cake for photo purposes. We did not fancy a supermarket one, as I had had a bad experience with Jessica's first birthday all those years ago. We had bought a Thomas The Tank Engine cake - it was really good - bright blue engine, smiling face etc. Jessica duly performed for the camera by eating a couple of good slices while her parents made cooing sounds. Next morning, Jess' nappy was full of bright blue lumps in her turds, as Thomas' icing obviously did not break down too well in her juvenile system.

I drove to town, parked the car and searched for this specialist celebration cake shop on North Street, which I had found online. Unfortunately, North Street was not where I thought it would be and I ended walking about half an hour before finding it. When I got there, I was told that the next orders taken were for Wednesday pick up and there was nothing that was available to take away today. I told them that there was nothing on their website which said that I needed to pre-order, but the assistant gave me a look like I was pissing on her shoes. As she also looked like she frequently snacked on her wares and could break me in half with a single fart, I reversed meekly out of the door and back to my car half an hour away.

It was lunch time now. David was going great guns in the kitchen, so I told him to call me if he needed a hand. Unfortunately, his enthusiasm and determination to be able to cope single - handedly got the better of him and we got two complaints in one lunch time. This is very un-Shakespeare like and also completely unacceptable. Whilst I appreciate his willingness to prove himself, he does not do it at the expense of any aspect of perfect service. He served a fish and chips to a customer that only had half a fish on it - as if someone had dipped my goldfish in batter and sent it down. I was able to rectify that situation by cooking the equivalent of Jonah the whale, and presenting him with that - always exceed expectations if possible. David also managed to completely lose a ticket so two customers waited half an hour and gave up, demanding a refund. This is the first time I have not been able to turn a situation around here, which was really gutting. We lost a couple of potentially good, long term punters who will no doubt tell others.

Not good enough.

Later that afternoon, our dumb waiter (a food hoist, for the non - caterers among you, not a mute plate - runner) collapsed like a bad Yorkshire pudding when one of its cables frayed and snapped. Being Thursday after five o'clock, it meant that I could not call out an engineer until Friday morning, which meant that they wouldn't come out until Monday morning, at which point they have to order the part which takes three days, which means that it probably won't be fixed until Friday week. That is until they realise that they have been sent the wrong part, so it won't be until Tuesday week week, unless the only cable engineer who can do the job phones in sick for that week, which will make it Wednesday week week week. At best. Our lift company are crap, you may gather.

Additionally, our David has taken it upon himself to keep answering the phone. He cannot tell the difference between an outside line and an internal ring, so people are calling up to be greeted with "Yes?" or "Hello?" It is not difficult: one goes "ring, ring" like a normal phone, while the internal sound is "rriiinngg, rriiinngg." See? Even you've got it.

Mary, having bathed and put our ankle - biters to bed, kindly suggested that I get out of the building for a couple of hours to wind down - which was very considerate of her. So I did. Top wife, Mary.

Friday 16th November

Coped really well over Friday lunchtime, especially considering that we are without our dumb waiter. It was organised so that we had a couple of runners on food, up and down our original Georgian staircase, so not having a food lift costs me extra in wages - but hopefully not for too long, despite my gloomy outlook with regard to our engineers.

Ben's birthday passed without too much incident, mainly because he hasn't got a clue about it. The cake was a Marks & Spencer number, in the guise of a cuddly bear. I thought the butter icing (fur) was not as good as the marzipan (hands and feet) - but Mary thought the opposite. Ben cried when the candles were blown out and seemed rather disinterested about eating his slice. Sam, however, smeared his all over his face and hair in traditional "You've Been Framed" fashion.

Quite a busy evening, with a lull in the middle due to the England football team playing a friendly in Austria. I have never before heard of a Friday night international football match and hopefully will not again - at least as long as I run pubs. At a quarter to eight, my heaving pub became a sparsely populated one, as they all went to various boozers that show sports. Come the final whistle, everyone trooped back in to discuss our footballing mediocrity over a pint and a pork scratching. I lost two hours of peak trade, effectively, on what is generally one of my best sessions of the week. I think they should have these fixtures on Monday afternoons...

Saturday 17th November

Olly starts today. At last, I will have a replacement Assistant Manager who will (hopefully) allow myself some escape time. It gets a tad stir crazy when you are glued to the building...

Had a kitchen meeting with my two new cheffing recruits today, to iron out a few wrinkles and teething troubles - like improve the presentation, organisation of the fridges and speed of service. The thing that I like about these two guys is their enthusiasm - neither has the cooking ability of Chef Pauline, so in that aspect she is missed - but the new chaps willingness to learn and determination to be better is a real boost for my business. Invest some quality time with them and in a few weeks I will have a quality kitchen operation that will only require minimal supervision.

They both took on board the introduction of a new cleaning rota, a closing tasks list and a temperature control sheet for the fridges and freezers. They also inputted one or two ideas themselves, which was most welcome. At the end of the meeting, Nick went back to the kitchen and David to the bar, where he was doing a shift. When I enquired about the fact that he was standing behind the bar with a scarf on, he grinned at me and said "love bites". He had been on a date - his first in Bristol - and struck lucky last night. At least that is now out of his system...or in it.

The England football team were thrown a lifeline last night with some weird results in their qualifying group. All we have to do now is beat Croatia at Wembley on Wednesday and we are through to the finals. The truth is that we should already be through, but for bad results against Russia, Israel and Macedonia - hardly powerhouses of the footballing world. We have a group of massively talented individuals who are overpaid, have no team ethic and are lacking in both motivation and leadership. The fact that we will probably scrape through qualification in a poor group should not paper over the cracks. It irks me that I am not the England manager.

Coffee and a Muffin
How civilised.
£2.50

Homemade Mushroom Soup
The "champignon" of broths. Oh, stop - you're killing me.
Served with a crusty baguette and butter
£4.25

Chicken Jalfrezi
You ask any self - respecting member of the
poultry clan what they
want to be when they grow up, they'll tell you "jalfrezi".
Served with rice and naan bread
£5.95

Sunday 18th November

It is cold - very cold and wet. This will no doubt greatly affect our trade today as we rely on tourists and the elderly out for a stroll around the waterfront. Our Sunday lunches have been absolutely flying over the last six weeks or so, but no-one in their right minds is going to leave their cosy firesides on a day like this. All of the old people in Bristol will be huddled up against their electric fires with just one bar on to save electricity, with a blanket over their legs and a tin of soup ready to warm in a saucepan for their dinner.

Meanwhile, I have three bar staff and two chefs primed and ready for the onslaught that will never come, costing me about thirty quid an hour in wages. Last week, the same number struggled to cope. This week, it's all cups of tea and pocket billiards.

C'est la vie.

It is ironic that now I am finally back to being fully staffed up, with no-one on holiday and all of my vacancies filled, we have had the quietest week for a couple of months. It is amazing that when you are short of bodies in this trade, it is always the time that you tend to get your arse kicked. Staff yourself up and the customers make themselves scarce. I imagine - weather aside - that the reason for the temporary lull in trade is that people are saving for Christmas, or spending their surplus on presents instead of beer. I am sure that I will reap some rewards closer to the big day with a few office parties and the like, so I am not too distraught.

Monday 19th November

Another day full of gloom and moisture on the weather front, keeping away those "shall I shan't I" customers who, potentially may fill my lovely pub up on a night that boasts less gloom and less moisture. We had an average office lunch trade, with Chef David coping perfectly well on his own. Had this not been the case and he did not scream for my assistance, I would have stuck his head in the deep fat fryers. As it was not too busy, I made him clean them instead. In the afternoon, he used up the surplus Sunday roast veg by making a batch of very passable spicy vegetable burgers, which will be one of tomorrows specials. Big up to David.

As it was not the busiest of evenings in washed out Bristol, I allowed my South African barman, Graham, to leave at eight thirty. I still had Jo, my Polish girl behind the bar, which I figured would be more than adequate. Mary decided to take an early night while she had the chance, so it was just the two of us left to clean up. Lo and behold, at ten o'clock the World and his wife decides that The Shakespeare is the place to be on this particular Monday night and we end up running our arses off for the final hour.

All publicans know that if you let your staff go early - no matter what day it is - you will regret it. Make them stay and they will be all night twiddling their thumbs and drinking your coffee to boot. Sod's law. Whoever sod is.

The (relatively) new and unelected Prime Minister, Gordon Brown, has made his first major decision today. We have hundreds of thousands of illegal immigrants, huge areas of our major cities living below the poverty line, we are under constant threat of attack from a pissed off section of the Muslim world, large lumps of our tax money is propping up the Northern Rock bank, over two and a half million people are claiming incapacity benefit and what does our leader come up with?

He has announced (pausing for effect, clearing the throat, straightening the tie) that he wants to "put an end to one - use plastic bags".

Frankly, I was hoping for more. This is a fabulously intelligent and very educated citizen, who has risen like a shit rich in fibre to the top of the political toilet bowl. With a nation's problems resting on his shoulders, I feel that maybe announcements such as these could be delegated - is there not a Minister for Carrier Bags? If not, why not? To save taxpayers money, maybe there should be a Minister for All Bags - why narrow the field of responsibility? Organise yourself, Gordon.

Tuesday 20th November

Chef Nick seems to be a very determined young man. He appears to be absolutely desperate to get everything 100% in his workplace, so when something occurs that is not according to plan, you can hear a short, sharp aggressive cursing from our lounge, which is situated on the other side of the wall to the commercial kitchen. Mary and I have taken to betting each other a pound on what may have just happened to provoke one of these outbursts. The most popular guesses so far are (in no particular order) cutting himself, dropping food, a burn or scald, or the lift tripping out.

At the time of writing, Mary is one pound up, due to me giving her "a cut" when Chef Nigel actually grated his thumb whilst crumbling a wedge of stilton. I could have stuck to my guns and claimed a no result, as technically he did not cut himself, but as there was blood drawn, I magnanimously conceded. It is a long road, however and I fully expect to draw level during Chef Nick's next shift.

Our lift has yet to be fixed. I reported a snapped cable first thing Friday morning, when the "emergency hotline" that the brewery runs opened up for the day. It was deemed an urgent call out because of the precarious nature of running hot food down a Georgian staircase. So Friday afternoon, an engineer (who is a dead ringer for Captain Mainwaring from Dad's Army) came out and pronounced "Can't do anything here - I've got no cable on the van." I enquired as to why a call out for a snapped lift cable could possibly be fixed without a new cable. He shrugged and said "I'll be back on Monday".

Monday comes, but Captain M doesn't. After three calls to the "emergency hotline" at regular intervals during the day, I finally get a return call from the lift company themselves, promising me that their man was on another job but would definitely be with me today. I locked the doors and alarmed the building at around midnight, still peering into deserted streets waiting for him.

Tuesday morning sees him here by ten in the morning, armed with two small bags containing lengths of cable - each long enough to tie a pretty bow around a single gnats testicle. I pointed out that there was at least fifteen feet between the bar floor and the kitchen floor, with the cable looping up and down the other side - which would require at least two lengths of thirty feet. He shot me a filthy look and proceeded to climb into the lift shaft itself and start to rummage around inside with a torch and a spanner. After much grunting and cursing (which gave a curious echo from within the void) he reappeared after about ten minutes. "They've sent me the wrong f***ing cable". He promised to return later that day with a mate, so that they could cock it up in tandem.

Amazingly, Captain M and pal both came back at eight thirty in the evening, just as the quiz night was about to start. The place was packed and the lift is situated behind the bar, with barely enough room for all of the staff, let alone two engineers. Luckily, it was only my skinny staff working, so it was manageable. Come closing time, they had managed to replace one of the cables and promised to be back tomorrow morning.

Wednesday 21st November

It's eleven thirty in the morning and still no sign of "Team Captain M."

Tonight, England take on Croatia in the final match of the European Football Championship. Win or draw and England qualify. Lose and the rest of Europe will collectively belly laugh. Why are we hated so?

Also tonight is The Shakespeare Tavern staff piss up, where all of our staff go on a crawl of the worst pubs, bars and clubs that Bristol has to offer, ending up at three in the morning lying face down in a gutter puking their eyeballs out whilst waiting for a cab. Mary has organised the "beano", which means that I have to stay behind to babysit. All who are on the rota for working tomorrow have been reminded of their responsibilities…

At precisely seven thirty this evening (those who were present will remember the moment for the rest of their days) our lift was finally declared fixed. Banners were erected, car horns were blaring, youngsters climbed the nearby lamp posts - there were young women kissing complete strangers and children were dancing up and down the steps at the front of the pub. Even old Mrs Mack, the deaf lady next door who owns the green recycling bin with the squeaky wheel, was to be seen hastily baking shortbread and fairy cakes in her kitchen to hand out to all and sundry.

Actually, none of this happened. Captain Mainwaring turned up, gave the cables a tweak and a fiddle, sprayed them with WD40 and f***ed off. Miserable git. It amazes me that people choose to do jobs that they most obviously dislike. I know I whinge a bit at the many downsides of my chosen career - but I cannot imagine doing anything else. This job suits me - it suits my personality and I have adapted the way I run this business to suit bringing up a family. If I did not enjoy this world that I choose to live in, then I would do something else. Captain M must dread going to work every day of his life. What a sucker.

Thursday 21st November

The entire English nation was awoken this morning to the sound of raucous belly laughing drifting across the Channel. We were embarrassed last night by a Croatian side that, quite frankly, were better than us. Despite us having far superior, better paid and more famous "stars" in our side, we once again proved that we are to teamwork what Stephen Hawking is to Irish dancing. Bad management, bad attitude, bad team. On the plus side, it also means that my pub won't be empty every time there is a big game at the European Championships in the Summer, because we won't even be there.

The aftermath of the staff night out was more than annoying. Firstly, Mary came home looking like she had consumed the entire contents of the Smirnoff distillery. She couldn't remember coming in, setting the alarm or getting undressed. I wouldn't let her touch any light switches for fear of her breath igniting. She fell over three times taking off her boots and couldn't find her mouth with her birth control pill.

Between two and two thirty a.m., I got four separate phone calls from David and Jo, asking for telephone numbers for other members of staff. I eventually had to tell them to stop calling, as both babies were being disturbed. This morning, both D and J were absolutely mortified that they had done this - neither can remember anything. I recall when I was that age getting plastered and losing touch with reality, but I don't think I would ever have been quite so trolleyed as to call up my boss in the early hours of the morning, asking for random phone numbers.

However, no-one got injured or died and much was achieved in a team bonding sense, so the plusses of the exercise probably outweighed the irritations. I believe in a strong team ethic for this business - we all are in the frame of mind to help each other and not let anyone down, so nights like this help to reinforce that kind of spirit in

our camp.

Talking of camp, Daniel managed to gain another number from a like-minded chap during the evening's frivolities. I believe he is beginning to enjoy living in Bristol. He should try Brighton, mind.

Just after lunch, a pinging sound was to be heard in the vicinity of the bar area. Upon further investigation, the end of a cable was found to be poking out of the lift shaft. Captain Mainwaring, where are you? British workmanship at its renowned best.

Lamb Korma

Korma facts: 1/ It originates from the 16th century.
2/ It has roots in the Mogulese cuisine of Northern India.
3/ Tescos sell it. 4/ It rhymes with Norma.
5/ It comes with pilau rice and naan bread.
£5.75

Chicken & Mash

Half a roasted chicken, mash, gravy and peas.
It's like being at your Mum's table.
But with beer, too.
£5.95

Friday 23rd November

Wow. This was one of the busiest days since we took over here. From the time we opened our doors, it was constant - a terrific food rush over lunch, an Irish stag party walked in at five o'clock and a really busy Friday night session to top it off. This is the reason that the staff have been re-organised recently - it all went swimmingly with no complaints and no panics. For the first time ever in this pub, we did one hundred meals - a fabulous achievement. The only sour point was the Irishmen, who were found to be smoking something other than Benson and Hedges on the front terrace so they were immediately ejected. Other than that, a splendid day.

On the sporting front, the England football manager was sacked today, along with his assistant. His has been the shortest reign of any previous boss, ending in abject failure from not qualifying for the European Championships in 2008. Apparently, he is getting a two and a half million pound payoff from the Football Association for being dismissed. I remember the old days when if you were crap at what you did for a living, you got sacked and booted out the door with a kick up the pants on the way out.

Getting a seven figure bonus for being really bad is obscene, immoral and unjust - but highly symptomatic of the game today. To be fair to the ex-manager, the players that were at his disposal were also victims of the same malaise - far too wealthy far too early in life and much too high an opinion of their own worth, which inevitably leads to a lack of real motivation and desire when it comes to the crunch of top competition. The evening that England were ejected from the competition, every single member of the squad - millionaires every one - would have gone home to their six bedroom detached houses in one of their fleet of top of the range cars, to be greeted by a trophy wife or girlfriend, nanny, cleaner, agent etc. Some of these are still kids of twenty one - they know no different. They have not had to scrap for a living like your average Joe - or any of the Croatian team that humbled them on Wednesday. The fire in your belly that comes from survival in the gutter, does not even remotely smoulder in today's top English footballers.

Homemade Broccoli and Stilton Soup
Moist, warm and lumpy. Not Chef David, but his soup.
Served with a crusty baguette and butter.
£4.25

Homemade Vegetarian Burgers
It has always irked me that vegetarians have products such as pretend bacon. Well, these only contain real vegetables
- you can just pretend it's beef.
Served in a floured bap with mayo, salad and chunky chips.
Bacon's an extra 50p.
£5.50

Saturday 24th November

Due to the hammering we took on the food front yesterday, I needed to take a trip to the cash & carry to top up on supplies. So, after my morning tasks were completed and I had consumed a quite wonderful bacon and egg roll provided by Mary, I set off to Bookers in Avonmouth. The route I have to take to get there - along the A4 West out of Bristol, is the one where I have been caught twice for speeding since I have lived here. The particular stretch of road in question goes from a forty miles per hour limit to thirty at a certain point, goes for two hundred yards and then back up to forty.

Quite frequently, the police have a mobile camera set up at the point where the limit reduces, for those who do not drop quickly enough. Like a lamb to the slaughter, I have been caught twice. I now have six points on my license for forty two and forty three miles an hour respectively. Although the mobile unit is within the thirty zone, the photos that it takes are of vehicles before they get to that point - very sly.

What really annoys me about all of this is the blatant money making objective. I cannot argue as I was above the permitted speed - I knew the road limit, but was marginally over. I was driving perfectly safely for the road and its conditions, but the restrictions are set by others and have to be abided by - rightly or wrongly. However, the morality of setting up a police van at that point is highly questionable - it is purely for financial gain, not road safety.

Furthermore. there are officers of the law tied up with this when they could be far more productive doing other things. My car has been vandalised four times since I have lived here, by youngsters coming out of the club across the road - not once has an officer deemed it important enough to investigate, or even check CCTV cameras which point in that direction. I have had people steal from the staff locker room during opening hours three times - but the police are always too busy to try to catch these people - even with descriptions. It just does not register with them as a valid use of their time - maybe it doesn't affect the right set of statistics. Catching someone two or three miles over the speed limit is far more important than dealing with burglaries, vandalism or anti-social behaviour, as we all agree. How would the council pay for their caviar and merlot without consistent sixty pound donations from your average motorist? It's a worthy cause....

Sunday 25th November

There has been a touch of fallout from the staff party this week. Apparently, Graham the South African barman has had designs on Ginny the Irish barmaid for quite some time. After much groundwork over the previous few weeks, he had decided that the staff party was to be the time when he would try to have more than just designs with her. All was going to plan during the evening, as Ginny was getting gradually numb from the flavoured vodka shots in the "Eighties" bar that they all ended up in - Graham was gambling on the fact that she would be losing a little more than her inhibitions...

After much juvenile touching and light petting on a couch by the corner of the dance floor, Ginny goes outside with the others for a cigarette while Graham discusses his next move with another male member of staff. To his horror, when he finds her again, she is playing tonsil tennis with our loyal chef Nick, who has somewhat stolen poor Grahams thunder. The evening ends up with Ginny disappearing with Nick to go back to the boat where he was currently staying with his mother's boyfriend (who was elsewhere at the time).

According to legend, Nick was too pissed at this point to do a lot of things. Firstly, he could not open the locked door of the aforementioned boat. Out of sheer frustration, Ginny takes the key off him and snaps it in the lock. As you do in these situations, they make their way back to her flat instead, in an effort to resume the drunken frolicking. When they get inside the door, Nick treads on her laptop and breaks it (of course it was on the floor - she's a bloody student) which kind of pissed Ginny off.

With all of the shenanigans in actually trying to get to the point where they can get "down to business", Nick has sobered up enough to have a conscience about doing the dirty on Graham. He breaks off from whatever form of entanglement that they were practising at the time, to explain that he does not want to lose a friend over getting involved, by using the term "Mates Before Muff". As you can imagine this went down like a drunken Santa in Saudi Arabia with our Ginny, who boots him out into the night.

Since then, Graham hasn't spoken to Nick, who hasn't been spoken to by Ginny, who isn't being spoken to by Graham. It is actually quite hilarious, until it (as it will) starts to affect my business. I will be restoring a touch of maturity to the proceedings tomorrow, but it was fun while it lasted and will provide plenty of ammunition for me in future liaisons with all three.

Monday 26th November

Lots of pub records broken yesterday. Most meals in a day (122), biggest food sales in a week, biggest overall revenue in a week... and biggest wage bill in a week. I guess they all go hand in hand.

It is very pleasing to see that we are still growing as a business despite the significant setbacks of mid 2007, when the smoking ban was introduced and at the same time we lost a huge office next door, which held about two hundred alcoholics. They moved to a bigger office the other side of Bristol town centre, although we still get occasional evenings or Friday lunchtimes when their hardcore reappear for old times sake. I would love to run a pub next door to somewhere where they held Alcoholics Anonymous meetings. I am pretty sure that I could market my business successfully to suit my immediate potential custom.

I have booked a nice little trip for myself next week. The Arsenal have a midweek game in Newcastle, so I have got a ticket for that and will also take the opportunity to see Jessica at the same time. It is amazing how a quick one night trip can escalate in cost, when you add up all of the incidentals involved. Plane ticket, airport parking, car hire at the other end, hotel for a night and match ticket. I am sure that my parents would have paid a lot less than that when I was a kid when we had a fortnight's holiday in Cornwall for our family of five.

Really quiet night. It is sometimes good to have a non stressful day like this, after the week that has just gone. If you do not have the occasional session where you can take your foot off the gas, then it can get quite overwhelming as a lifestyle. Ended up watching Dragons Den and Have I Got News For You on TV, in the company of my wife and a quite excellent Indian takeaway. Perfect.

Tuesday 27th November

The damn dray turned up at ten past eleven today. The usual time is generally around the seven thirty mark, which means that you do not really want to start anything in case it turns up - so a bit of a wasted morning really. Of course, the brewery did not have the courtesy to call me in advance and let me know of the delay - that would indicate both good service and that it actually mattered to them. Because of the beer tie, I am obliged to spend around five thousand pounds every week with them on their products, as I cannot buy anywhere else. You would think that with that sort of spending commitment, they would go out of their way to ensure that I felt valued as a very good customer - but it is really the opposite.

As a tenant - and I am sure that this is the case for all breweries - you are there (from their point of view) to make the company money. All of the risk is heaped on the individual - rather than shared - and a percentage of those accepting the challenge will end up bankrupt. You can be sure that the big boys do not lose in the same devastating manner when a business fails. An ex Area Manager of mine from about ten years ago, now works as a Regional Manager for one of the big tenancy and leasehold companies. He told me that they actually build into their business model a certain percentage for those who will be made bankrupt.

It is similar to banks having a bad debt allowance in the world of finance. The difference here is that the Regional Managers are encouraged to fill a vacant site with the first person who has the finance - but not necessarily the best candidate for that particular pub. A vacant business is just money down the drain for the brewery, so the objective is always to fill the site as quickly as possible, irrelevant of the fact whether that candidate is deemed capable of actually making a go of it.

In the old days, you used to hear of footballers who used to retire in their early thirties without the immense earnings behind them of today's spoilt lot. They would have a few quid from their testimonial with which they would buy a pub. The theory is that they would then spend their retirement years sat at the end of the bar with half a lager permanently stapled to their palms, to while away their ever expanding middle years. You would read about them in the inside back pages of the News of the World one day, passed away at fifty five of a heart attack brought on by staple poisoning.

Today, pubs are serious businesses. It would be ridiculous for me to see anyone who has a few quid behind them, just buy a pub and expect it to be successful without the necessary training or experience. I was a Manager for seventeen years before I ploughed my savings into my own business - I knew the trade inside and out - the hours, the pitfalls and the benefits. Always make your mistakes with other people's money. To all of my previous employers - I apologise. Really. No, honest.

Wednesday 28th November

It has been one of those days...

Firstly, we had a leak on one of our superb guest ales - Batemans XXXB. Wonderful character, nutty aftertaste, deep rust colour - all pissing out over my cellar floor. Olly my assistant is built like a fridge and when he tightens a real ale tap, it stays tightened. I think that he has twisted this one a tad too far and, to put it technically, buggered it up.

Next, the thermostat on one side of the kitchen griddle refused to turn off, so it ended up glowing like a smacked arse. We had to unplug that particular area and work with half the space for the rest of the session. Simultaneously, there was a small pop and one of the microwaves (the best one, of course) gave up the ghost. James the barman is, however, an electronics wizard and quickly diagnosed an internal fuse while its innards were spread all over the salad chopping board.

Finally - and most disgustingly - the gents toilet began to shed water. Upon further investigation, the pan itself was found to be rocking from too many drunken bums sitting and swaying at the same time. The screws had come loose that were bolting it to the floor, which had worked the external pipe out of its casing and also started a crack which ran from the floor to calf level (when seated).

To summarise, today I have I lost about £100 of beer, spent £300 on a griddle, £273 on a new toilet (mostly exorbitant emergency plumber hourly rates, of course) and 30p on a new 1.25 amp fuse. Only one of these do I consider value for money.

On the plus side, I convinced our camp cook David that I had just been called up on the phone by the Government Gay Quota people. I informed him that we were being checked on for how many people were homosexual in our workplace. As we had twelve employees, our quota for lesbians and gays was two. His eyes widened in horror at the injustice of this and he started to cry sexual discrimination. I tried to pacify him by saying that if we could employ another six staff, then we would have room for another one, but this did not appear to cut any ice with him.

He said that it should not matter about anyone's sexual orientation as long as they can do the job, but I told him that there must be Government guidelines, or they wouldn't be calling me in the first place. He was furious about this, so I let him rant for five or ten minutes while he took it out on a cucumber. Apparently, according to Nick, who was with him in the kitchen for the duration of the rant, he will be writing to his MP and calling up the local papers in the next day or so. Mary thinks that I should tell him the truth about the call, but Olly and Nick don't. I think that I should let my conscience decide, but no doubt Mary is bound to tell him first.

Shakespeare Fried Chicken
Secret recipe, protected over the years and handed
down through the generations.
Father to son, son to embryo.
We serve it with chips and peas too.
£5.50

Beef Madras
If you aren't keen on the roof of your mouth,
then this is the dish for you.
Strips paint, this one - you'll love it.
You will also love the pilau rice and naan bread, no doubt.
£5.75

Chef Luigi's Homemade Lasagne
Layers of Bolognese sauce, sheets of pasta, a creamy béchamel and
cheese.
Served with a mixed salad and coleslaw.
(FYI Chef David didn't sound right).
£5.95

Thursday 29th November

The World is a funny place. Today in the Sudan, a middle aged English woman has been sentenced to fifteen days in prison, for allowing her class of five year olds to vote on a name for the class teddy bear. They decided on the name Muhammad, which evidently pissed off a certain section of the Islamic world in the country. She was accused in a Sudanese court today of "insulting religion", "inciting hatred" and "showing contempt for religious beliefs".

According to the BBC, Sudan's top clerics called for the full weight of the law to be used against her and have labelled her actions as part of a Western plot against Islam.

If it was, I would be disappointed if this would be the best plot that we could come up with. It perturbs me greatly that those in Muslim communities who stand for moderation, logic and tolerance don't stand up and be counted, as opposed to letting the extremists always have their voice. It is obvious that it was a completely innocent act of the naming of a teddy - the poor woman didn't even choose the name herself. If it was a class pig, however...

I had a letter from a group of workmen who have been fixing pipes in the road outside yesterday, stating that my water supply, along with the rest of the road, will be switched off between eleven in the morning until eight pm today. Obviously, nine hours without water would have meant the closure of the pub. This morning I make all of the workmen mugs of coffee with kit kats. My supply was back on by midday. British morality at its finest.

We also had a walk in visit from Trading Standards this morning. They bought two double shots of Bells whisky and proceeded to take them as random samples. The shots were divided into three specimen bottles, then wrapped, sealed and signed for. I enquired what exactly they were looking for and was told that they were checking that it is actually Bells in the bottle, in addition to seeing if the spirit was watered down. I told him that it would have been, but they have just turned off my water supply. The bloke just looked at me deadpan - not a flicker of humour. At least I amuse myself, I suppose.

Friday 30th November

Another busy Friday, especially on the drinking side. Food was steady enough, but nothing that caused mass panic in the kitchen. We were never going to run out of cutlery, or have one of the chefs jump out of the window during a stress induced hysterical fit. I must buy more cutlery...

No, it was the drinkers of Bristol who most generously contributed to the pension fund today. We sold a quite astonishing amount of Abbot Ale, which is our most potent hand pull on offer. You always can gauge how busy you are (without counting the till, of course) by how often you find yourself running up and down the cellar steps during the course of a day. With ten different draught products on sale here, the chances are that at least a couple of barrels will need a change even on the quietest of days, but when you change the same product three times (in this pub) then you know you have got hammered.

It did not help that Polish Jo started her shift at five o'clock and then declared herself too sick to work at a quarter to six. When someone does that, you have absolutely no chance of covering as everyone else has made their plans for the night. Had she phoned me at three in the afternoon and said that she was not well, then I would have a fighting chance of finding someone - but I suppose most staff don't think of the consequences of their actions on the business when they are unwell. They are paid to do a certain job - which Jo does very well - and anything else outside of that bubble is irrelevant.

On a lighter note, Olly the assistant manager who I entrust my business to when I am off, was reading the specials sheet and said "So does Chicken Kiev come from Kiev, then?"

"No", I replied, "Munich."

I am trying to encourage Olly not to think out loud.

12. Sticky Fingers

At the time of me selling up my last public house venture, in May of 2018, the percentage for my sales settled by credit or debit cards had nudged 60%. Which also meant that the other portion of the take was in cold, hard cash. Over the preceding three or four years the acceleration of card payments has been astonishing, as when I bought into The Compton in 2011, it was probably only around 15% of my revenue. No doubt this figure would be much higher if my business was more food and restaurant based, as most table service type experiences are settled with a card these days.

Over the thirty years of doing the trade though, it is certainly one of the biggest changes. At this rate (is it something to do with a Moore's Law type acceleration?) cash will be obsolete in pubs with a few years. I even read only last week that a brave landlord near Ipswich has taken the step to become the first traditional pub in Britain to stop money as a source of payment. His rationale for doing this was quite sound - a huge reduction in bank charges (banks charge you to pay in cash into your own account as a small business, and also charge when you buy change in coins), a reduction in insurance premiums as cash is no longer kept on the premises, and a massive reduction in "leakage" as it's known in the trade - stock loss, or stealing.

Despite the fact that our groundbreaking landlord in Ipswich pays up to 1.5% in credit card fees for every transaction, what this chap is saving on other fees and thievery far outweighs this cost. The temptation to skim off the top when standing behind the pumps in this traditionally cash rich environment, proves too much for many workers in pubs. In the course of my career, I have dismissed dozens for stealing. I have probably missed catching hundreds.

When I first started back in 1988 in The Clanger, the tills were the latest in technology. All singing, all dancing for the time - which meant that it wasn't much better than ringing in the amount for a pint - indeed, it still had that facility. For example, a pint of Carling back then was £1.32. As a dishonest bar person, you could ring in 0.32 and slip a pound into your sky rocket. Basic example, but that's the gist. With the advent of products being put onto buttons, it gets a little trickier, but by not ringing in every fifth pint, for example, the sticky fingered bartender could make some extra in this way.

In the back office, all of the accounts were done in the traditional manner by hand in 1988, just as they would have been by Scrooge and Marley during Dickensian times - there had been little evolution or progress since then in basic accounting. With the acceleration of computing soon after, the tills and back office systems became commonplace, and the thievery moved with the times. In reality, as long as there is loose cash flying around the workplace, the temptation to rob the employer will always be present - and it's up to the systems put in place by the business owner and the diligence of the on site manager to try and stem the flow of leakage. You won't be able to completely stop it, but you can make it very difficult - prevention is always better than cure.

In my pub in Lincoln, The Rat and Parrot, I suspected this chap - we'll call him Mark - of not being a straight shooter. I had been having some real problems on stocks, showing unreasonably large deficits, and was trying to get to the bottom of it. My instincts told me that he was stealing. When he was on shift, his tills never took as much as the others, but he didn't appear to be any lazier or slower - I guess you always work harder for yourself. Upon investigation, I found that on one session the previous evening, there were 53 "no sales" on his till. I had deliberately separated him from the others, giving him his own till, justifying it by telling him that he was the fastest, so I didn't want anyone in his way.

A "no sale" is generally only done by a manager. It can be for a couple of reasons, maybe if a customer has asked for change for the cigarette machine, or the manager is checking for coins or doing a till drop. In reality, you wouldn't expect to see more that four or five no sales in a session. So this chap Mark is basically not ringing his drinks in, and just pocketing the money.

Next session, I got a friend to sit at the bar, order a pint and watch him no sale it. When confronted with the evidence, this Mark chap was never seen again. They never are. The mentality is in their own heads is that they aren't really doing anything wrong, until judgement day falls and the threat of prosecution looms, at which point the reality of their actions hits.

A similar situation happened in The Shakespeare, with a South African called Graham. Behind the bar, we used to sell electric cards costing a tenner, for the people who lived on boats in the harbour. Graham would be operating a similar scheme to Mark, by under ringing his drinks this time, as opposed to using the no sale button. He would then duck underneath the bar to the small cupboard where the electric cards were kept, on the pretence that someone was purchasing one of these cards, where he would swap the cash and so get it out of the till. Again, once confronted with the evidence, he disappeared.

It isn't always cash, either. Later on in the Compton Arms I noticed that my food stocks weren't adding up, so I put a watch on that. I found that my chef, a lovely, bubbly girl, was taking home chicken breasts for her tea in her handbag, or a portion of rice and chicken curry. Every time she worked a shift, she would be picking out something nice for her supper that night, squeezing it in her bag next to her lipstick and walking out the door at the end of her day. She thought that it was ok! No matter that I have paid money out of my pocket to buy the food in the first place - it's a victimless crime, to them.

I was told by another lovely barmaid in The Compton that she used to give out an occasional free round of beers to groups of football supporters, to encourage them to come back! For fucks sake, as if my margins weren't tight enough. Although she didn't appear to profit herself from this generous gesture (although you can bet that she got "bought" one) it still meant losses for me. The fact that we served the best food and drink in the area, which were served by the best staff should really be enough to guarantee their return, without giving them the bloody stuff.

Cash temptations in a pub isn't exclusive to members of staff, either. Once in The George in Enfield, I found a bloke in the office trying to smash his way into the safe. I jumped on his back, but he was a big lad and he managed to throw me off, run down the stairs and out into the street. Another incident was in a pub I was holding called The Fulham Tup, just off The Kings Road in Chelsea, where unknown to me, the Assistant Manager had decided in his wisdom to keep his safe key in a pot on the window sill. Needless to say, one afternoon the safe was ransacked and about six grand went walkies. I have my doubts to this day whether the whole thing was a set up. I'm afraid you learn very quickly in the industry to trust absolutely no one, when cash is involved.

Stock losses are such a huge factor in a pub. As well as cash, it's so easy to lose a fortune on the booze, too. A great proportion of this, to be fair, isn't always theft, but most of it is negligent or just plain careless. Back in The Clanger, in the (good?) old days, we never had a bad stock result. The practices that went on back then were nothing short of horrendous, but were actively encouraged by the Brewery - or at the very least, they would turn a convenient blind eye, as we made them money!

If a customer ever complained about a pint, we would hold it up, check it against a light bulb and dismiss it. "Nothing wrong with that, mate." Customer service, my arse. In The Clanger, there would always be another gullible sap to replace him. That was the thought process back then, in the halcyon days of the City. We used to be provided with a giant filter bucket by the brewery, into which would be inserted a coffee type filter paper. There was a perforated rod screwed onto the bottom of this bucket, which would then be inserted into a barrel of your chosen real ale. With another metal bucket, we would go along the bar and empty all of the drip trays into it - bitters, lagers, stout (not cider, though) and go back into the cellar to pour this flavoursome mix into the filter bucket. So the pint of Charringtons IPA that this customer would be originally complaining about was, more often than not, a delicious cocktail of everything that we served on draught. Not a drop was wasted. There is an old saying in pubs - "always drink what the Landlord is drinking"...

There was even actually an official spec back in those days from the brewery, that you weren't meant to filter back into a barrel that was less than a third full. Of course, these horrible practices which were thought to be acceptable at the time, have now long since disappeared - and rightly so. Today, it would be a trade description offence, as well as a health violation. We even made a fortune flogging soda water out of the gun and selling it off as a well known sparkling water. The ladies loved it - "bit of ice and lemon with that, love?"

Pouring a pint correctly is crucial, too. In both The Compton and The Shakespeare, over 70% of my total sales was draught beer. Of that, more than half was real ale. Not spilling anything was key to the bottom line, for me, and I had to use a basic maths illustration many a time to clarify it for the errant pourer. I would sometimes watch a bar person pour a pint and see them let it slop over the side, then top it up and slop some more... I would pull them to one side, tip the excess beer from the drip tray back into a glass and show it to them.

"Ok, how much is in here?"

They'd look at it, and respond "About a quarter of a pint."

"Let's just say that was a bad one, and in reality you didn't waste 25% of my beer every time you poured a pint. What if it was only 5% - would that be accurate?"

"Probably" would be a typical response.

"Ok, so lets say that we sell this pint for four quid. And tonight, you are going to serve personally about two hundred pints." I'd have a calculator in front of us, and would be illustrating the maths as I talked. "So that's four pounds at five percent, times two hundred. That's forty quid you'll cost me tonight, and that's only if you lose five per cent per pint, which looks generous the way you're pouring it."

"Wow. Sorry." they looked amazed. But I continued...

"So you work five days a week, and I get a stock take every month. At this rate, for every stock take, I can expect you to personally cost me £40 x 5 sessions x 4 weeks which is £800 in sales loss, every month." I went on... "As this is my business, and I'm not a big company, you may as well take £800 out of my wallet, and throw it in the bin."

When you add it up like this, and illustrate it in cold, hard figures in front of them, it hopefully makes them think twice about being quite so lackadaisical about their pint pouring. If it doesn't, then you get rid of them, and quickly. A small business such as a pub can't afford people to perform at this level, as the consequences really are crippling financially.

I always found that the best way to try and combat this, was to incentivise a couple of your key members of staff, who would always be around the bar. Tell them that if you got a positive stock result, then you'd bung them £500. A fortune to them as a bonus, but a fraction of your potential losses if the pint pouring were to go unchecked for a month. I will guarantee that every time someone made a pigs ear of a pint, these incentivised people would be jumping all over them - not a drop would be wasted with these guys watching it like hawks, which as a business owner, you don't always have the time to do.

13. McDonalds On Sea

Jackson's Wharf in Brighton Marina ticked a lot of boxes for me. Again, it was a pub really undercooked and badly operated. As with the Rat and Parrot, I went in there and was able to implement changes and people very quickly which made a huge difference. It was a bit like one of those Kitchen Nightmare programmes by Gordon Ramsay, where everything is shit when you first walk in - food presentation, hygiene, a weird menu, weirder people and daft operational practices. All of a sudden, Ramsay comes in, does an egg and chips special, paints the chair legs blue, wipes the tears from the stressed and bankrupt owner and rides off into the sunset on a Harley Davidson. Put a few more facial creases on me, say fuck a thousand times and buy me a Harley - and that was me in Brighton.

What a beautiful venue. Two vast trading floors built over the sea, with stunning views of the marina and boats from all vantage points. There was a huge walkway and balconies surrounding the outside of the pub, so that the punters could dine al fresco when Mother Nature would allow. There were four separate trading bars, two on each floor and a huge kitchen upstairs capable of producing catering at great speed and volume, providing of course that the right menu and people were in operation.

Upstairs, there was a modern, clean three bedroomed flat for the managers. Very spacious, unparalleled views from all sides and no sweaty strangers lurking in the corner. We couldn't believe our luck. To compensate for the lack of perspiring nomads, I had persuaded Lee from the Rat and Parrot in Lincoln that he had a future in this industry and offered him an Assistant Manager post with us in Brighton. To ask someone to ignore what they've been studying all this time for their degree - I believe it was Sports and Leisure - and take a leap of faith to join me was a brave step indeed.

When you take on a new project, and certainly one of this potential, it's always handy to know that your assistant manager has got your back, as he is the one pulling the strings when you aren't there. To implement effective and necessary - but sometimes unpopular change, you need all of your supervisors to buy into it. Getting Lee on board to watch my back was a smart move, and he stepped up like the proverbial canard in H2O.

The previous management had very kindly left us a couple of weddings to do in the diary. As my inherited kitchen staff were up there capability wise with bus driving Barney, it was down to me to produce the goods. I actually quite enjoyed it, to be fair - it was good to dig out some of the old kitchen flair and produce something worth taking a selfie with.

The first wedding went without a hitch - it's a beautiful venue to celebrate in and they even got a cake made from that place based in Brighton that was on the telly, Choccywoccydoodah. It was a huge masterpiece about five feet tall, covered in sculpted chocolate angels, harps, bow and arrows and ornate flowers. Confident as I am when it comes to food stuffs, I was a little out of my depth once the bride and groom had stuck the ceremonial knife in the cake and delegated it to us to cut it into fifty pieces. It's not as if the thing was uniform in shape and easy to portion. I recall getting rather frustrated at one point and bit the head off a cherub.

Wedding number two was to my dismay a gypsy affair which, surprise surprise, ended up with the two families knocking seven bells out of each other. There were grown women wrestling and pulling hair with other females from the same family, and the blokes from both families just fighting whoever else fancied a fight. There was jam, snot and marmite everywhere. The beautiful bride herself pulled off one of her cinderella stilettos at one point, and tried to kebab her new mother in law. Bizarrely, once the police had separated the warring paddys and everyone was leaving, lots of them came up to me and shook my hand, and said how much they had enjoyed it.

One day, I decided that the pub needed a few bits from the local Asda and the car needed petrol. Off I went, pulled into the garage forecourt at the supermarket and filled up the car. After paying for the fuel, I went across into the superstore to leisurely browse about and managed to get all the things on my list. I came out of the shop with four heavy bags and cursed, because I couldn't remember where I had left the car. It wasn't until I mentally retraced my steps that I realised that the car was still parked at the petrol pumps. I looked across and could see members of staff surrounding the car, looking inside for clues as to the identity of the owner. I raced across to the garage, jumped in and drove away, saying "excuse me!" and "thank you!" to cover my embarrassment. Was that the first sign of dementia?

Business was going really well at Jacksons Wharf. The top line had moved from 14k a week up to 22k in just under a year. Although it wasn't an individual tenancy, I was being allowed to run it with a very free hand as there were no uniform standards across the board with Noble House, except for their brand of Thai food restaurants back then, called Jim Thompsons. Then, in late 2004, it was announced that there was to be a company restructure, with the Pioneer Pub Company being formed and a few of their assets sold off. The upshot of this was that Jackson's Wharf was being purchased by Wetherspoon.

I think everyone who frequents pubs will have been to a Wetherspoon. It is very heavily branded, the beer is sold cheaply, the food is a budget offer and this naturally attracts like minded people. I have no issue with this. My problem in this instance was that Jackson's Wharf should not have been a budget type venue. Eating and drinking here should be a relatively luxurious night out, with people coming for the ambience and stunning views, so happy to pay a little extra for a quality offer. It would be like putting a Wetherspoon on the 43rd floor of The Shard.

But they did. Like bar stools, the current payroll were included in the transfer of ownership, and I became the only non Wetherspoon trained manager in the Company at that time. We all had a crash course of a couple of weeks or so to get used to the new systems and standards, there was a massive recruitment drive and a huge refit, which took around a month. All of a sudden, my payroll of around 14 staff had shot up to 53. I was the overall manager of the establishment, which had been renamed "The West Quay", with seven assistant managers, of which Mary and Lee were two. It was a very different world. I did not get on with the new area manager from the company, as one of the first things she said to me in one of our earlier meetings was questioning why I was on such a good salary. I retorted with "Because I make good decisions" and pointed out the previous years financial performance. She informed me that it was history now, the hard work starts today and I won't have to worry about too much decision making.

I soon worked out what she was on about, as a manager of a Wetherspoon doesn't have to make any critical decision whatsoever. You want to know what to do? There's a manual for that. What goes with this burger? Here's a picture. What do I say to a customer when they walk up to the bar? Here's your checklist of questions to ask them.

Wetherspoon is a retail area for robots. You are not given points for repartee or personality when serving food or beer, but if you clean the tiny wheels that night on the glasses trolley, then you earn yourself a "green traffic light."

It is a retail space for serving value food and beer to people who just want it cheap, with no frills. A bit like a liquid Primark. And by frills I mean a personality behind the bar, or an atmosphere, or any sense of local bonding - the sort of things that pubs were originally popular for. You weren't permitted to chat around the bar as a customer and exchange banter in here anymore - the bar stools were binned. It is the perfect example of a one size fits all brand. The McDonalds of pubs. And, let's be honest, it works very well financially for that market. It just wasn't my preferred market.

Everything I love about the industry - the people, the banter, the sense of community, the chance to give a personal, quality offer and be proud of what you do - was all gone. In the six months I lasted it out, I didn't even speak to a customer more than half a dozen times. My job was in the office, wading through the (in my opinion) ridiculous amounts of daily red tape that you have to go through in order to allow the place to trade.

We now had thirteen tills, each of which had to be individually weighed on a tiny scale attached to the office computer, before we opened - 1p's first, then 2p's...all recorded on the back office. If there was a change of shift manager during the day, these tills all had to be brought upstairs and do it all again before the business could continue. There were all of the orders and deliveries to complete, a rota for 53 staff all who had different hours or days to work, and their own personal requests for time off.

Our frozen food system was a classic case in point. We had two of these vast deliveries every week, which used to arrive on a huge lorry. Our non negotiable delivery slot was 5am. In a pub! The tail was wagging the dog. It took an hour and a half to put this delivery away as we were selling 13k of food a week here - at about £3.99 selling price a pop, that's an awful lot of food. Everything was brought in pre portioned. For example, at the beginning of every session, the "Chef" would estimate how many Chicken Alfredo's he or she is likely to sell over the next two or three hours. Let's say eight. These frozen packs of Alfredo's (packaged a bit like a frozen Bird's Eye packet) are then put into a steam cupboard called a Henny Penny. When an order comes up for an Alfredo, out would come the pack, "Chef" opens it up on to a plate, and away it goes to the customer.

In this way, you are able to keep up with the hundreds of meals that you can do in a session. Just like McDonalds, it's a highly refined, speed orientated food operation that works like a conveyor belt production line system. The funny thing was, despite the fact that these people were paying just three quid to get fed, I had never had so many complaints about the food. In the preceding twelve months, I doubt I had five complaints, and I charged at least four times as much. I would be getting a dozen a day here, it was such an odd mindset - clearly successful overall, but not for me.

Once, I even got through the mail an anonymous letter from an irate punter, who had enclosed a marketing leaflet from the Wetherspoon in Brighton town centre. On this leaflet, he had circled the picture of a bottle of Newcastle Brown Ale with "£1.95!" emblazoned all over it. In the accompanying letter, he said that he was furious that we were charging £2.10 for our Newcastle Brown Ale, and that he would not step foot in The West Quay again until we stopped ripping him off. Believe me, he should be thankful that he made that letter anonymous. Before Wetherspoon took over, I was charging £3.50.

On a personal note, while we were in Brighton I lost my mother to breast cancer at just 58. She went through all of the chemotherapy agony to get an all clear, then within a further two weeks, she was gone. The glue from my immediate family had dissolved, and it has never been the same going home to Devon ever since. Before, there were homemade sausage rolls and mince pies with clotted cream whenever I would visit. Dinner would be one of her steak & kidney puddings and the house would be spotless. It's just a little soulless now. Not to put Dad down but he's a guy living on his own and he just does what he needs to do. It's just a house now, for me, and not a home. The only thing that hasn't changed is Dad's teeth in a two handled plastic cup on the bathroom sill.

Also, Mary and I got married. We had two wedding ceremonies, one in Poole, Dorset, where her grandparents originated from and one in Vancouver, Canada, where the mother in law, Theresa could ensure that we had some sort of religious blessing to our unity. We also had a wonderful honeymoon in Hawaii, where we took a bi plane trip over the volcano Kilauea, which at the time of writing is currently spewing its guts up.

Mary and I tendered our resignations in November of 2004. Neither of us were happy working in this type of pub. It was deeply unfulfilling personally and unsatisfying for both of us, which was a crying shame as it was our perfect operation before the change. I suppose it works for some people, but I was not institutionalised in the industry and there was no flexibility in this company to accommodate a manager with an opinion.

We left with the intention of taking a Christmas and New Year off for the first time together and it was wonderful. We even took in a seasonal trip to Egypt, saw the Pyramids and drank our body weight in cocktails. For me, this period of a few weeks between leaving The West Quay and moving to our next pub was the happiest of times I spent with Mary. In the New Year, I put the feelers out again to ex area managers and was offered The Oak, a one bar operation in leafy Kingston Upon Thames.

14. The Oak and a Baby

In January of 2005, I took over as a manager at The Oak in Kingston Upon Thames. This was more of a drinking pub than foodie venue which showed plenty of sport, had a pool table, dartboard and a lively regular clientele. It was a strange set up in the sense that although there were quite a few fairly regular faces, there was never a string of customers that called The Oak "home".

The pub took reasonable money when there was decent sport on the TV, as it was a good viewing venue with a sporty atmosphere. Some lads were quite regular visitors if they fancied a game of pool with their lagers, but you wouldn't see them otherwise. The Oak was never a pub with that community feel, or that place where a single man would come and sit at the bar for a couple of pints and some conversation. It was missing that homely, safe feel if you like. It certainly wasn't a place where you'd see groups of girls chatting over a bottle of Pinot.

It wasn't until I looked into the history of the pub that I found out that historically this was the place to come for all of the down and outs in the area. I found advertising in the office for Carling at £1.73, and the historical reviews for the pub were really quite unpleasant. The pub used to be called "The British Oak" and there were old pictures floating about with it adorned in Union flags. It appeared to be in recent history a meeting place for a few select organisations slightly to the right of our political spectrum.

While I was here, I had a brief dalliance with playing cricket again. I had played a lot in my youth for my village team, my school and a side in leafy Kent for a couple of seasons. I was a decent medium pace bowler and an average bat - nothing special, but I loved the game. There were a couple of random drinkers who were as daft and out of shape as I was at this time, who turned out for a nomadic team called The Wanderers. One week, they mentioned that they were a couple short for their upcoming weekend fixture, so without any thought process whatsoever, I volunteered my services. When you do that, your middle aged brain wistfully recalls you leaping and diving around the outfield, bowling searing, unplayable seamers at a fantastic pace and cover driving like David Gower when he was still curly.

In reality, of course, your body doesn't react anymore in the way that you still dream. The first ball that dared to come my way in the field went through me to the boundary as it took me a fortnight to get down to it. My searing fast - middle deliveries were now delivered as slow donkey drops, as by the time I got to the stumps from my old run up, I was wheezing like an asthmatic buffalo. To be fair, my batting wasn't too bad - not that I was ever Viv Richards in the first place, but the eye was still there. That is, until their Indian paceman got one to lift unexpectedly and smack me high on the cheekbone, sending my glasses majestically in the direction of the third man boundary.

There was blood and snot everywhere, but having found my specs and sponged myself down, I did manage to cream a boundary off the bastard in the next over. By the time I got home, my eye was as black as Newgate's knocker with an inch gash beautifully framing it underneath. I cannot tell you how many times I was asked "Who smacked you, then?" over the bar as I pulled a pint, but it was enough for me to announce my permanent retirement from the hallowed sport.

The new owners of The Oak were the Massive Pub Company, and it was one of their pubs recently purchased from the fallout of the Spirit Pub Co. A sparkle of a refit had been attempted, but the real problem was that it wasn't enough of a major refit to totally alienate the pub from its dubious past. You can put a suit on a shepherd, but he will still smell of lamb. This place needed shutting down for a month, getting rid of the pool tables, fruit machine and jukebox, create a seperate dining section, go big on real ales, a decent home cooked food range and scotch eggs sold at the bar. Renaming it the Dog and Duck wouldn't have been a terrible idea either, as by just losing "British" didn't have nearly the desired effect.

Because Massive didn't go to these lengths, the pub was always perceived still as a trouble venue and would never attract the many new markets that it was missing out on but still desired. Interestingly, I note that in the last couple of years The Oak now has a fine reputation, with excellent reviews for its culinary offer. Enough time has passed since those dubious days and no doubt enough managers and owners too, to enable them to move away and compete on a level playing field.

However, we were not back then in that position and no matter how well you dress up a pub in that situation, it will always have that natural ceiling for your financial top line, as you are only pulling trade from a certain sector of the community. As that sector generally rested on its knuckles when in passive mode, it prohibited any chance of proper growth. In real terms, I still managed to move the top line from seven to nine thousand a week, but the Massive Pub Co had budgeted for twelve.

This was not a budget based on real factors, but a budget based on what they needed. This was all too evident when the Company unfortunately went pear shaped a couple of years later, due in part to the collapse of Northern Rock and the Sports Cafe brand. In my opinion, the Company pushed too hard, too quickly, instead of trying to build their pubs and brand slowly. But hey, what did I know? I just observed these things from my blinkered view behind a ramp.

It was a very frustrating time for me in a business sense. After the freedom and success I had experienced before the Wetherspoon purchase in Brighton, I felt that I knew what I was doing at this level. I could identify what worked in certain pubs, and maybe why they wouldn't be right in others. I had listened to punters throughout my career to date and understood what turned them on in a pub, and what mattered less in their decision making on where to go for a pint or a pie. At The Oak, I was now getting stick for not pulling in 12k without any real understanding from their part on how this could happen.

Again on a personal note, Mary and I became parents together with the arrival of Ben in November of 2005. As with Jess twelve years previously, this was an extraordinarily long birth and Mary performed admirably. Instead of spending the whole labour cooped up in hospital, we went for walks around the local green spaces and burned up a lot of the labour time in that way. Bless her, she even let me knock myself up a ham, egg and chips halfway through. Having another responsibility in my world made me think even harder about going it alone in this industry. I knew what I was doing, so why was I working my ass off to make a company rich?

One day, I was introduced to my new area manager at The Oak by the outgoing one, who had found employment elsewhere. Rats and ship sprung to mind. I was rather taken aback at first, as this new chap was a good ten years my junior, with that "fresh out of Uni" look on his face - full of misplaced arrogance and smears of Ribena 'round his mouth - not dissimilar to the expression I wore myself back in '88. I wouldn't have minded the age thing too much in itself, but within 20 minutes of shaking his hand, this prick had his head in my microwave to check to see if it was clean enough. It was all I could do to hold myself back from slamming the door and defrosting him.

It was, in truth, the kick up the ass I needed to get out there and make the dream of being a self employed pub owner finally happen. After seventeen years of doing this thing as a manager for various pub company's, should I really be at the stage where an embryo with no trade experience should be critiquing my ovens? I felt I was more than ready for this challenge, so I spent most of my free time scouring trade publications and visiting pubs for sale, in the hope of finding a venue suitable for myself and my new family.

One of these visiting expeditions took me to Bristol....

15. Life at The Shakey

We embarked on the self employed dream of owning our own pub business in March of 2006. We had a four month old Ben in tow, and had just discovered that another bun was proving in Mary's pub oven. The accommodation was nothing short of disgusting and our priorities were to make the place liveable upstairs, so that the family was comfortable. I employed Alec, my elder brother, who was a dab hand with a paintbrush and his other half Pauline who was a wizz in the kitchen.

We worked all hours at first, as there was so much to do and get straight. I was almost always downstairs getting the business right, whilst Alec and Mary made a great job of making the house a home. It wasn't too long before the pub was clean, there was a fresh, new home cooked menu, the real ales were delicious and varied and the staff behind the pumps were smiling and helpful.

Within a year or so, The Shakespeare had turned into the perfect small business. It had been built up from a really underperforming site upon purchase, to one that had exceeded even my ambitious forecasts. The truth was, it was a beautiful pub with a long and intriguing history, so by getting the market right and matching it with an offer that exceeded the locals' expectations, it was always going to make a mint. An early clue that this pub could do wonders was on an early reconnaissance I undertook with my father in law, Steve, one Tuesday evening.

We had actually gone out to look at a different Bristol pub which I had been disappointed with, but as we were staying in a hotel there for the night we thought we'd check this one out as well which was also on the market. We walked in at about 8.30pm, and the place was packed. There was a quiz on, and Chloe (my future assistant manager) was the voice on the microphone asking the questions. It took an age to get served and the barman that eventually looked in our direction, had a face like a smacked arse and made it plain that we were an inconvenience.

My pint of Greene King IPA was on its last legs which I had mentioned to him, but his response was a shrug. We asked for a menu to look at, but were told that they don't do food. Even when I went to the gents, which wasn't too long after that pint, I was scared to unzip in case one of the mice crawling about bit it off. In short, this place was badly run, badly in need of a clean behind the ears and badly in need of a clear out behind the bar.

But...it was packed. On a Tuesday night. If it offered such poor fayre and could still obtain this level of business, what would it achieve when it was run properly?

And so it proved. Finally, after years of working hard to fill the pockets of the pub company's, I was getting rewarded properly for the hours of labour that you have to put in to be successful at this game. The Shakespeare was not only turning into a well oiled machine, it was genuinely a fun place to be socially, too. There was an appreciative set of locals that loved coming in to a place where they knew that the beer would be clear and the food would be tasty and wholesome. Many of the regulars lived around the harbourside on boats, so it was easier for them to pop in to us of an evening for a meal and a pint, rather than rustle something up at home.

In November of 2006, our second son Sam arrived. He was born at St Michael's hospital in the centre of Bristol, in a cleaning cupboard with a bed in it. Must have been a busy night in there. Clearly a fertile City, Bristol. Unlike the eons of time taken giving birth with my first two offspring, Sam shot out like he was coming down the Tower of Power water slide at Siam Park in Tenerife. We were back home before I even needed feeding. We now had a beautiful family of two boys in our new pub and I was incredibly proud of them and my wife. Unfortunately, we were unaware at that point how difficult this situation would turn out to be.

The new team of staff that I had assembled were treated as family and in return they looked after the pub admirably - because everyone actually cared about each other. Staff turnover was now almost non existent, as it was such a nice place to work and socialise. All who worked behind the bar were allowed to drink (as long as it was paid for!) after 9.30pm, and they could take a cigarette break at the serving hatch next to the bar whenever there was no one who needed serving. It is strange looking back that this was the norm, as the smoking ban didn't kick in until July of 2007 in the UK. There were no uniforms, deliberately, as I wanted to make this a comfortable "locals" feel without any formality of obvious rules and standards that frequent the managed house pub offer.

Even the customers wanted to contribute to the success of their "new" local. One day, Sam, a young lad in his twenties, was at the bar downing pints of Kronenbourg lager. Sam was good company, part of the set of familiar faces that surrounded our back bar on a regular basis. I was writing out one of my specials sheets next to him. I used to try and make it vaguely comedic, to attract the eye of the customer and snowball attention to the offer. Sam was observing this, and said in a slightly slurring thick tongue, that he wanted to make me a business proposal.

I gave Sam a sideways look and smiled at him. He'd had a few, but I still wanted to hear what he had to say.

"I'm listening", I said. Sam, although a little boss eyed at this stage, had a serious expression on his face.

"Pasties" he said.

"Best food ever" I said. I'm a Devonshire boy, so I was biased. "What about them?"

"If I could supply you with twenty a day at a good price, would you want to sell them in here?" Now a good pasty in the South West of England would be as popular as cake to a fat bird, so he had piqued my curiosity.

"Sure" I said, "If they were decent. Where would you get them from?"

"I'll make them myself" slurred Sam.

"Are you a chef?"

"No, but how hard is it to make a pasty?"

"Fuck off Sam, you've had too many"

"I will prove you wrong" he said. "I'll bring some in tomorrow, and we'll sit down and talk on a deal."

"Sure, Sam, you do that." I finished my signwriting, and had forgotten about the brief conversation before I even got back upstairs. Us publicans hear far more bullshit than the average man in the street.

Next day, I was downstairs in the back bar chatting to Nigel, a regular, with a cup of coffee when Sam comes around the corner, carrying a large, metallic baking tray.

"Hi Sam, how's it going?" I greeted him. Sam puts down this tray in between Nigel and I. On it were the charred remains of what used to be food. "What the fuck is that?"

"Pasties" said Sam. "Only these ones are a bit well done" Nigel's eyes were opened wide with surprise and curiosity, as he sipped his pint of Abbot.

"No shit" I observed. "Aside from the fact that they're the colour of Nelson Mandela's arse, why did you bring them here like this, instead of in a box?"

"I couldn't get them off the tray" Sam said. "I thought we could do that here". He turned the tray upside down and nothing moved. It just so happened that there was an errant chisel underneath the bar, so I reached down and passed it to Sam. I looked across at Nigel, who's by now turned a funny colour from trying to suppress laughter. Unbelievably, Sam started to attempt to free the charcoal briquettes from the tray, not realising that I was humouring him.

"I'm not buying them, Sam" I said. Sam stopped chiselling and looked at the tray, wistfully.

"Maybe I should try something else?" he said. I bought him a pint for his efforts, and I believe Nigel bought him another later on for the entertainment. Sam was always not afraid to try something new, and credit to him for that. Later that year, I remember that he had gone into self employment looking after peoples gardens. He came into the pub after work one evening, and someone asked him what he had been doing that day, and he came out with "I've been trimming old lady's bushes".

I always found that the kitchen was just a good a part of the business for a giggle as the bar. I had a lovely guy named Andrew who worked for me here at The Shakespeare. Great barman, bags of personality, lots of fun. On a quiet daytime session, we were overstaffed behind the bar, so I invited him upstairs to the kitchen to help me in there with a few jobs. He was only too willing.

"Today Andy, as it's quiet, I'm going to teach you how to make Pea and Mint Soup the old fashioned way, and we'll put it on as a special in your name this evening."

"Awesome" he responded. Keen nature, Andy.

I pointed to a large pot of simmering peas. "These are just about done", I said. I took them off the heat, refreshed them under cold water to stop them cooking, and poured them into a bowl. I don't know if you can envisage what a 10 kilo pile of peas looks like, but it's a lot. It's a pretty large mound.

"So to turn this soup from an average soup into a spectacular soup", I continued, "you have to separate the skin from the pulp, so that only the best part of the pea goes into the dish."

"Ok" says Andy.

I put a chopping board next to the giant bowl of peas. "Brown chopping board for veg" I informed him.

"Ok" he repeated, taking all of this in.

"Now, with the back of a fork" (I held up a dinner fork to show him, and took a single pea from the bowl) "You press down on it like so". I pressed the unsuspecting pea and squished the pulp out from its inside through the skin. "You then put the pulp in a pile, that's the flavour, and discard the skin to one side. You try." I handed him the fork.

Andy dutifully picked up a single pea and crudely squashed it, but with a similar result. "That ok?" he asked.

"Not bad" I said. "So eventually, you'll end up with a pile of pulp on this side of the chopping board, and a load of skins on that side. I need to nip to the Post Office, so hopefully you should be done when I get back."

"Will do" said Andy, as he enthusiastically picked up the next pea.

About half an hour later, I've got my feet up in the lounge watching Only Fools and Horses. Mary, the wife, comes in and says "What's Andy doing in the kitchen?"

"I've got him separating peas" I grinned, over my shoulder.

"For fuck's sake" she said, and went back in the kitchen to relieve him of his pointless task...

Andrew was also a victim to another old kitchen wind up a few weeks later.

"I'm making a pavlova", I told him. "I need this big bowl of heavy cream whipped into soft peaks" The bowl was ready on the work surface. Large, round and glass. I put a damp tea towel under the bowl to stop it slipping, and picked up a balloon whisk.

"Unfortunately, we don't have a machine for this, but it won't take long if you use this method." I started to whisk, under Andy's watchful, intense gaze... "If you do it this way, in a figure of eight, you incorporate all of the cream in one revolution, and it's much quicker." My hand was but a blur as I demonstrated the desired technique. "You good with that? Have a go yourself."

Andrew took the balloon whisk, and with his natural enthusiasm displayed remarkable vigour in thrashing the liquid. He was a good fifteen years younger than me, so I'm sure his wrists got a lot more exercise than mine...

"I need to go and do some work in the cellar. You should be done by the time I get back"

"Ok" he replied, still whirring his arm at a ridiculous speed.

Now depending on the amount of cream in the bowl, and the technique and staying power of the individual whipper, the soft peak stage should be achieved within five to six minutes or so. Unfortunately for the unsuspecting

Andy, the aforementioned liquid in that bowl was semi skimmed milk, and wouldn't have thickened in a thousand years, no matter how well developed his wrists.

About ten minutes later, I return to find him red faced and bent over the sink.

"What's up?" I enquired.

"I can't get it to thicken" he replied. I've been changing hands because my arms are falling off, but no luck yet. I'm just doing some dishes instead while I get some blood flow back, and I'll have another bash."

Well, I wasn't going to stop him, was I? "Are you sure you're using the right method? Remember, figure of eight, Andrew."

"Yeah, maybe I wasn't doing it right, I'll have another go." He picks up the balloon whisk again and begins another impressive thrash.

"That looks better" I say, and walk out of the kitchen into the accommodation. Mary was playing with the kids.

"What are you smirking about?" she says to me.

"I've got Andy whipping milk" I responded.

"For fuck's sake" she said, rolling her eyes, and went off to rescue him again.

The back bar in The Shakespeare was where the main regulars tended to congregate on a daily basis, and consequently where most of the socialising went on. They were a varied but entertaining bunch of characters. Mark was a daily visitor - he used to drive boats for the Bristol Ferry Boat Company around the harbour - a kind of tourist / taxi service. He also lived on a boat moored out the back of the pub, as did Alex, who was with us all through every Winter.

In the warmer months, Alex used to disappear up the Kennet and Avon canal to London, or travel up the River Severn. During these Summers, I used to go and stay with him on his boat, as he used to moor it at Limehouse docks when England were playing cricket at Lord's or the Oval. Roland was also an interesting chap who used to work on land speed cars and drink my ale, with equal enthusiasm. Gary was a proper Bristolian character with the proper accent and some bizarre hair, who lived on a wooden vessel on the other side of the harbour and spent his life fixing other boats.

I recall an eventful day out with these chaps doing the Tarka Rail Ale Trail, where we took the train down to Exeter St Davids and then embarked on a rail pub crawl, following the path of Tarka the Otter in the famous book. Basically, we would travel one stop on the branch line that wound up into North Devon and get off to grab a pint of the local tipple. Then, back on the next train to venture further onto the next stop and pub. I have no memory of the second half of this adventure, but there are a few photos flying about with me asleep in train carriages...

Nigel, Marshall and Taxi Richard were all drinking buddies, sometimes accompanied by Nigel's wife Carol. Nigel was a lazy accountant, worked hard one month a year. Good drinker and a proper cricket fan, as was Marshall, who was some sort of engineer who worked a couple of months then had about six off. Taxi Richard drove taxis. Badly. He once had a job getting Mary and I to Bristol airport for a weekend away in Dublin. It's only about six miles, but the tight prick ran out of petrol halfway. It was raining, and Mary - sporting her four inch heels - and I were pushing his bloody cab to the brow of a hill so that we could roll it down the other side. Nigel told me later that he never put more than a fivers worth of fuel in at any one time. He also had the nerve to complain that the free Kit Kat's that I used to give away with a hot drink were only two fingers...which was generally the response he got from me.

The Shakespeare as a business was on autopilot from my point of view. I had pulled together a great team - in no particular order - Big Olly, Chloe, Nick, Gay David, Andy, Sarah, Jo, Colin, James, Deb and more. These guys were my "A" team. The best crew I had ever had at one point in a pub. We were like a family, with everyone pulling together helping each other, covering each others shifts. My stocks were always good and everyone cared.

Big Olly went on to have his own tenancy in Bath some years later. At the time of writing, Gay David has a couple of pubs himself, and is trying to corner the world market with my menu, only at a quarter of the price. Chloe was an excellent assistant manager for me, both here and in The Compton Arms for a short period. She was also the boys main babysitter and is now breeding heavily herself as I write. Sarah and Jo were just great to have behind the bar - always smiling and looked after the place as if it was their own. They both helped me out at The Compton too when I first moved in. Andy has become Bristol's newest and finest postman, and Nick joined me at The Compton for extended spells and turned into another great and reliable assistant.

Colin by trade writes screenplays for TV and radio and is, by his own admission, "immensely talented". I believe he joined the team at The Shakespeare to give him a different perspective and I'm pretty sure we helped him with that. He coined the phrase "staff tequila" which cost me plenty financially, but improved morale in the workplace no end. He very kindly also paid me a visit in The Compton soon after I started there, and we had a fine drinking session. It all ended in a very loud and very public retching into the sink of the gents toilet for poor Colin, who had to crash upstairs in the pub while I got the plunger out.

James was another one who visited me in London. Bit of a ladies man, James, with disastrous luck, usually. He was like Hugh Grant but with a crap boat. Deb was a seasoned Bristolian who'd seen her share of bad men and pub kitchens. She would get the food out quickly enough, but the kitchen would look like an explosion in a custard factory when she'd finished. She was also the subject of quite an unusual occurrence at The Shakespeare.

Very sadly, Debs brother had passed away. She had been to his funeral, then at some point a few days later been to pick up his ashes. On her way back from this she had dropped into the pub for a nice glass of wine to socialise. This particular Friday lunchtime, I was getting my butt kicked in the kitchen - there were orders everywhere, so I was racing around trying to keep up. I recall having three sausage and mash tickets to do along with a load of other meals, so I'd put the sausages on the grill, the kettle on for the gravy, spooned the granules into a jug - not sure why Deb has decanted that into a jar, but it looked good - put some mash and peas on to heat up, rescued a fish from the deep fat fryer - you get the picture. Anyone who has cooked in a busy pub kitchen will know this feeling.

I've mixed the boiling water with the granules and it looked awful - it just wasn't mixing into a paste like it normally would, so I tipped it down the sink and started again. Same thing happened. Tipped that mixture away too. I looked at the granules and decided that as I was in the shit, I'd just get a new box opened to save time, which did the trick. Next day, Debs comes into the kitchen and you could tell that she was suffering from yesterday's "social" visit. Not unusual for Debs.

"There it is!" she exclaimed, reaching for the decanted granules.

I was doing some pots in the sink, as I looked over to see what she was on about.

"Whatever brand that is, it's shit" I said. "Didn't mix at all"

"That's my brother" said Debs. "Left him here yesterday and forgot about him when I got pissed."

My stomach just dropped to the floor. "You have to be kidding me. I thought that was the gravy. I wondered why it was in a jar. I made about a legs worth trying to get it to mix!"

In fairness, Debs took it better than I thought she would. I know it was a stupid place to leave him, but I felt just dreadful. The thought of almost pouring a dead guy onto somebody's lunch....

When my son Ben was around eighteen months old, we got a diagnosis from the paediatrician that he had autism. In truth, we knew that something wasn't quite right as there were no responses, speech or any development that you would normally expect from a small toddler. We were very ignorant of the causes, symptoms or traits associated with being on the spectrum but then, as we were to find out so was everyone else - including the National Health. We saw little difference in the development of Sam to his elder sibling and sure enough, about six months later our youngest lad also got the same diagnosis.

What was odd about this is that both our boys were completely different in character, showing different personalities and enjoying opposing types of toys and games, yet they both got a one serves all umbrella diagnosis. There is so much to be learned about this condition even today, but back then Mary and I were on our own. We were told what the verdict was but not how to handle it, or taught what was the best way for us to adapt as their parents in order to give our boys the best possible support. There was no information given to us to assist with bringing them up - no do's and don'ts, no handy tips, no medical answers - just "Here is your diagnosis, now you're on your own".

We were lost, blind and panicking. We poured our hearts and efforts into bringing them up, not knowing if we were doing it rightly or wrongly. In the end, in truth, the boys showed us the way. We got to know them as small individuals, got to know their traits, what disturbed them, what they liked to taste, to feel, to smell. We realised that they were just viewing the world in a different way to the rest of us and it was our job to make that acceptable. Once we got the hang of this, once we knew what to do day in, day out then it was easier to cope with and understand. Routines became so important, teaching them patterns that they understood so that they knew what was about to happen, or signs that food, a walk, bath or bedtime was to be next on their agendas.

They do say that when you become parents for the first time you are walking into the unknown, not knowing how it is done. You have a great desire to do the absolute best for them, so you buy the biggest and fanciest child carrier worth £500, nappy disposal units, fancy cots, top of the range car seats, every item of clothing in every size and colour. In reality, the only thing that really matters to a young person when starting out on this planet is the love, closeness and understanding of their parents. Get everything second hand - they don't care and they won't remember anyway, as long as you get to know them and you're there for them when they need you.

16. Pub Diaries, Part 3

Saturday 1ˢᵗ December 2007

It is the first of the festive month and our thoughts here at The Shakespeare Tavern turn to decorations. Tomorrow evening we (a chosen, browbeaten group of volunteers) are going to attempt to put up lights and wreaths in an effort to turn our establishment from a normal pub into a normal pub with lights and wreaths.

We are all of the same opinion that Christmas can't come late enough. Apparently, there used to be a tradition here that anyone who mentions the "C" word before the fifteenth of December, had to put ten pence into the lifeboat collection box on the bar as a forfeit. Rumour has it that we are personally responsible for a new kettle in the Mousehole branch of the R.N.L.I.

Unfortunately, times have moved on and the office crowds that gather here for their annual glug of mulled wine during the yuletide season, do additionally expect a bit of Bing Crosby, lights and wreaths. Money talks, so I'm putting them up. As practice, I erected our personal tree in the flat upstairs, all ready for the kids to pull it down again when they wake up tomorrow morning.

Thoughts of drawing pins, pine needles and sellotape aside, today was a very normal Saturday here. Steady trade, a chef was late, it pissed own all day, Arsenal won and I had a curry for supper.

Sunday 2ⁿᵈ December

Now I don't want to put you off ever visiting The Shakespeare Tavern - I'm happy to take anyone's money - but I am beginning to question the catering training of Chef Nick.

Every Sunday I print off a "Sunday menu" which I position in a holder on both bars, so that the punters are aware of the choice of a roast or the normal fayre for the day. I also have a copy on a blackboard outside the pub front door, as well as one for the kitchen upstairs. As usual, I printed them off and put them all up in their appropriate positions this morning. Chef Nick starts his shift, has a look at the menu and calls me into the kitchen.

"You have made a mistake - it's pork, not turkey today."

"You have cooked the joint off, haven't you?"

"Yes."

"And sliced it up, ready for service?"

"Yes."

"And you still think it's pork?"

Nick investigates. He unwraps the slices and peers inside. "It might be turkey, you know."

"Of course it's bloody turkey, you goon. I paid for it. Would you like me to ask them to leave the bloody feathers on it next time so you can recognise it?"

"I can't believe that - I wondered why there was no crackling." Nick is still staring at the meat.

"Nice applesauce" I remarked as I walked out of the kitchen, leaving him to stew in a morass of his own embarrassment.

To be fair, when you receive meat after a butcher has butchered it, the appearance does not bear much resemblance to that of the living version when they were running around their pen / coop / kennel (for our Korean readers). However, it is probably true to say that your chef should be able to recognise the difference. I am sure Bernard Matthews would have noticed if Porky Pig was having a stroll on his land...

The weather is fowl (nice link) today. It is hammering down with rain, literally bouncing off the road. There will be a limited number of folk braving these elements today in order to fill my coffers, I'm afraid. Mary has said that she would like to go to a supermarket to get out of the building, as it will be quiet. Hooray. Packed aisles, long queues, two squirming kids, gale force winds, howling rain, nowhere to park. Today's British Sunday supermarket experience. Wish me luck.

Monday 3rd December

The decorations are up! We look like a traditional pub with lights and wreaths. To complement the new look, I have relented on the music front and put a Christmas CD in one of the slots of the music carousel (there are five slots, so every fifth song played is a festive one).

This evening was a "penguin night". About five times per year the large hotel next door hold a gala boxing evening, where about two hundred big nobs from Bristol local business and the council, converge for a night of pugilism and a five course meal. The dress code is dinner jackets and dicky bows - it looks a grand affair. The great bit for us is that the bar attached to the hotel is complete pants, so they all tend to pile in The Shakespeare at about six thirty and leave for the event at around eight o'clock.

We get an hour and a half of a hundred or so mutton dressed as lamb trade, as they have three or four pints each and then go - superb for a Monday. By nine o'clock, there were two blokes playing chess and an old guy talking to himself in the corner, with a half of Speckled Hen and two packets of dry roasted. However, we had taken double what we had the previous Monday - happy days.

Tuesday 4th December

Spent three hours compiling, costing and writing a new food menu today. I have changed one or two dishes for seasonal purposes - no more ploughman's, a couple more hot dishes - but it would be unwise to tweak too much as we have a very successful food operation at present. With any luck, the menus should be back from the printers soon so that we can move the business forward. I have already written a new wine list for Christmas, so things are progressing nicely at present.

Disaster! I have just spent a couple of hours trying to fix our front bar till which Mary has decided to maim. Basically, the till roll ran out and gave a message "PE18" which means "the till roll has run out, please change me". Unfortunately, Mary read it as "PE18, keep hitting all of my buttons in a random sequence until I break". So she did.

This is not the time of year to only have one till downstairs, as we are careering into festive silly season, so I need to act pretty fast. I have decided to bite the bullet and get a new one - similar design, but about fifty years younger. You remember the one from "Open All Hours" with Ronnie Barker as Arkwright and David Jason as Granville? Their till was newer. We are here for at least another three and a half years, so I may as well do it now. I found a supplier who does next working day delivery, so I have ordered it online. I will have to program it on Thursday night in time for Friday, when we will definitely be requiring two tills. Best part of five hundred quid - ouch.

Early hours of tomorrow morning, I have a flight to Newcastle to see Jessica and the Arsenal. I can't wait to see her - it's been far too long. Olly is working all hours to cover the business and Mary is staying behind with the boys. She is also looking at another nursery so we can give ourselves a break for one day per week - hope it's good.

I will catch up upon my return…

Broccoli and Cheese Potato Bake
The Shakespeare has always prided itself on its vegetarian option. We opt out.
Just to show there's no hard feelings, here is a dish that makes me want to stop licking raw bacon. Served with a wonderful mixed salad and coleslaw.
£5.95

Chef Nick's Cottage Pie
In the past, this man has burned Weetabix. Today however, he gives you undoubtedly his finest ever creation, with seasonal vegetables and gravy.
Enjoy.
£5.50

Friday 7th December

So much to say. Firstly, my trip in the main was excellent. I picked up Jess from her school on the Wednesday and took her to have something to eat. It is the simple pleasures such as this that I particularly miss, not being there for her physically every day. This was the first time I have seen her school, so it was good for me in the sense that I can now picture her daily routines a little better when talking on the phone. She is so mature for her young years and I take great pride in being able to converse as an adult with her.

However, she is still a teenager at heart as it proved with her dining preference, McDonald's. My burger was very passable - although not in the same league as our homemade ones - but my side dish of "cheese melts" came with a dip of caramelised onion, which appeared to have the consistency of melted seals. I will be sticking to my previous side dish preference of Chicken McNuggets, when I next patronise one of these restaurants.

After dropping Jess back home, I made my way (via my hotel) to St James Park, home of the mighty Newcastle United for the Arsenal game. All of the Arsenal fans were seated right at the top of the biggest stand, which was about four miles up in the air. You could see right across the city towards Gateshead and Sunderland, which was lit up with a million lights - quite spectacular. I have been to hundreds of matches at dozens of different stadiums all across Europe following the Arsenal, but I don't think I have ever been as far away from the pitch as on this occasion.

The match itself was quite a nail - biter, with us taking the lead with a great goal from Emmanuel Adebayor, our striker from Togo. In the second half, Newcastle equalised with a scrappy, scrubber of a goal which dribbled in off the post. Final score was a one all draw, which was about right. Fabulous ground, great atmosphere - Newcastle has always been a good place to go and see a game - their fans are amazingly passionate. Of course we usually win, but we are four points clear at the top of the league, so one can't be too downhearted about the situation.

Next morning, Jessica had a "dentist appointment" so that she could spend the morning with her Dad. We went Christmas shopping at the Metro Centre, an out of town shopping mall about the size of Greenland. It was good to do normal stuff with her - shopping for the family Xmas presents, a gingerbread latte at Starbucks and just chatting about school, work, life etc. I had her back for the post lunch session at school at one thirty, so that I could make my way to the airport for my afternoon flight home.

So, on to airports. I'll tell you, September 11th has influenced all of our lives - and not for the better. Security checks, understandably, are as water tight as a frigid ducks arse, going to extreme lengths on the exclusion of various liquids on hand luggage and the inspection of shoes, etc. I found this out to my cost at Bristol Airport on my outward journey early Wednesday morning.

I deliberately did not take a suitcase in order to avoid the pain of having hold luggage - I am always the last person to receive their case from the carousel after a flight. Every time, hundreds of people disappear through the "nothing to declare" passage with their ten bags on a trolley, while I still wait for my one. In the end, it is just me, the bloke sweeping up and some tumbleweed remaining in the baggage reclaim room when my battered case finally enters the arena. So as the trip was for one night only, I just took a kit bag as hand luggage.

Mary had bought me these little travel packs for such trips - shampoo, deodorant, body wash etc. When I went through the scanner at security, this jobsworth emptied them all out and said that they should be in a clear plastic bag to take them on the plane.

"OK", I said - "do you have one?"

"No, you have go out into departures and buy one and then queue up again through security. You can buy the bags from a vending machine for a pound."

It had just taken me twenty minutes to get through this queue, which was growing by the second. I would have missed my flight. "I don't have time - can you not just give me a plastic bag?"

"Not my rules, you need to go back."

"Well, I can't. In other airports, there is a desk where they give you plastic bags - it's just here that we are fleeced to buy them. Also, it is only liquids over 100ml that are confiscated - these are just 25 ml each. Your rules are ridiculous. You can keep the toiletries. The shampoo is really good - it will give your hair a real sheen."

"We just put it all in a skip, actually."

"Sure you do, enjoy them, won't you."

It really pisses me off when you have idiot jobsworth such as this bloke who is doing it just for spite. I am sure that he is following the rules set by an even more powerful jobsworth at Bristol Airport, which makes that person an even bigger bully. Surely the rules concerning what is safe to carry on a plane in hand luggage should be universally agreed and adhered to. Everyone should know what is permissible and what is not. I would have been allowed my toiletry bag if I had flown from Newcastle to Bristol - why is this? As for ripping the customers off with the plastic bag vending machine - just taking the piss. No common sense. Bristol Airport - you suck.

Having said all of that, my experience at Newcastle Airport coming home was nothing short of hair raising. When I dropped Jessica off at her house on the Wednesday, Lara (ex - wife) kindly gave me some Christmas presents for Ben, Sam, Mary and myself to take home. When I went through security and my kit bag was scanned, I suddenly had three burly blokes with high pitched squeaky Geordie voices asking me daft questions in threatening, high pitched squeaky Geordie voices. When I admitted to owning my bag, I was physically lifted off my feet and pinned to the far wall.

Lara's thoughtful Christmas present for Mary and I was a quite exquisite

Viner's carvery set, with a huge two pronged fork, sharpening steel and a seven inch bladed knife. It was beautifully presented in a wooden case with a red velvet lining. To the Geordie security three, however, I was the Bin Laden of Bristol. Of course, I had no idea what was going on, so I was at a loss to explain the situation until I saw the gift. Naturally, they wouldn't let me on board with that, so Mary and I are a Christmas present down. Lara was pretty pissed off too - but she did apologise, although it was a genuine mistake.

Anyway, I got back to the pub to find out that Olly has had to go home to Birmingham as his father is in a pretty bad way. He has cancer of the everything and had taken a turn for the worse. Unsure when he will be back - but he should take all the time he needs. It puts us in the mire a tad, but some things are more important than work.

Tried to program the new till, but the instruction manual for it may as well have been written in high pitched squeaky Geordie for all I could understand of it. Have bitten yet another bullet and couriered it back to the supplier so that they can program it for me - at great cost - but I am too pushed for time at the moment to do it myself, plus I would probably cock it up anyway. I have a spare till to put on the back bar which is rather small and limited. It just has numbers on it as opposed to our other tills which have itemised keys for all of our products. One of the bar staff - James, I suspect - wrote "Fisher Price" on a bit of paper and blu tacked it to the top. Tosser.

Saturday 8th December

Olly's father died yesterday. It was expected and mercifully short, but no less painful for someone of Olly's age - he needs to be with his mother as he is the only child, so he has other responsibilities to think about as well as his own feelings. The shock of losing a parent can never be underestimated, however expected it is. I find myself daydreaming sometimes about my mother and what she has missed out on, or how much she would have loved my two boys. After more than three years, I still feel amazed sometimes that she is not around. Olly has all of his grieving to go through, which I do not envy, but he is a switched on young man who will cope with the differing stages of mourning. The funeral is next Monday, (17th) in Birmingham, which is when it will really hit him, from personal experience.

There is a top boxing match tonight, between Britain's Ricky Hatton and Floyd Mayweather in Las Vegas. The sentimental vote goes to our Ricky, but my head tells me that Mayweather will win - he is a boxing great who has beaten everyone there is to beat. I am having a nap during the evening so that I will be able to watch it in the early morning hours - usually about a 4am start. Mary says that she wants to watch it, but she likes her bed far too much to be interrupted at that ungodly hour, so I will be supping my Horlicks solo.

Poor Ben is very unwell. He is usually bouncing off all four walls of the lounge at one hundred miles per hour from about 7.30 am every day, until he runs out of gas at about eight in the evening, when he just falls asleep for the night. This morning, I woke him up just before ten o'clock and he has just been lying on the couch, with red, running eyes and twin rivers of snot linking his nose to his chin. He looks so pitiful and mournful - it just breaks your heart to see him this way. I suppose we should count our blessings - he has just turned two years old and this is his first significant illness. Ironically, we have spent the whole of the twenty four months trying to get him not to climb on the dining table, or slam the living room door and now we are bemoaning the fact that he is physically incapable of doing it. Some people are never happy...

Sunday 9th December

'Twas a veritable ghost town in The Shakespeare Tavern this lunchtime - methinks that the public at large are Christmas shopping and foregoing the traditional pleasure that is our Sunday roast. Santa, you have a lot to answer for.

Ben is on the mend to the extent that he is wandering around at half speed. Full speed is defined as him haring around as fast as his small legs will whirr, until he smashes into a wall or desk to halt the momentum. Half speed can be described as an almost melancholy stutter - a tad unsure on the feet - until he staggers into the same wall or desk in order to stop. You feel that there is a problem with brakes on a two year old, as they are plainly not relative to the momentum in which the toddler moves. Perhaps it can be likened to an oil tanker, where a standard hand brake would be ineffective and, like Ben, it takes them a mile and a half to turn.

Ricky Hatton was outclassed against Floyd Mayweather in the boxing ring last night. It was an effort that cannot be criticised for heart, application and will but when it came down to it, the American's ring craft, know how and superior pugilistic skills were the telling factor. It is significant the guy has fought about forty times in the ring against the best there is in this generation, has never been defeated or knocked down and has the complexion of a baby's bum. Hatton looks like he has been pummelled by a steak tenderiser before being finished off with a cheese grater to the face. Also on the sporting front, Arsenal lost today for the first time in the league since April - but that's just boring, so we'll skip that.

Monday 10th December

Tonight is the staff Christmas party. Mary decided to organise a civilised drink for all of the staff and regulars for the yuletide season, with a local charity to benefit from the occasion. The criteria is that every guest who attends - staff member or customer - should bring a brand new toy of varying description, to be given to a local charity who distributes them to poor or homeless families in and around Bristol so that their children can open something on the day. It is a great idea and one with winners all 'round - we promote a sense of staff and regular bonding, eat and drink until we fall over or throw up and the local disadvantaged children come up trumps into the bargain. I have a special t-shirt for this festive occasion, which has three comic reindeer faces emblazoned across the chest, with the slogan "Santa Has Aides".

The back bar roof is leaking like a bad political cabinet. Almost every time it rains, I have to have four strategically placed buckets catching the drips - it is not a selling point for my business. I have placed numerous calls to the maintenance department of the brewery, but all we have had so far in terms of response is a bloke in builders wellies standing next to these buckets, stroking his chin and proclaiming "It's definitely a leak, we'll be back in the morning to fix it". Obviously, the term "morning" does not refer to the morning which follows the statement - it could be a morning from the following week, month, decade or generation - who knows for sure? We will have to rely on the roof actually caving in on someone before a proper response is warranted.

Tuesday 11th December

As luck would have it, the Regional Manager for the brewery popped in this lunchtime to spread his yuletide cheer. The chap likes the Shakespeare Tavern, because it causes him no excess grief in his working life. There are no hassles for him here, like his tenants not paying their exorbitant liquor bills or buying in products from elsewhere to save a few quid. The temptation must be really strong for those publicans who need to scrape together every penny to try and make a living - I heard of one guy who was so desperate he robbed his own fruit machine to get the pound coins out. When you go to the cash and carry and see a barrel of your lager on sale for a hundred pounds less than you are paying for it, there must be a great temptation for a quick win - but it is never worth it when you consider the penalty of ultimately losing your pub for such an insignificant sum, in relative terms.

As this is such a solid business, I do not have those concerns consuming my waking moments. However, I was at pains to point out to the Regional Manager - we'll call him Tony - that my ceiling did not possess that solidity and would be travelling South quite quickly should any more rain get through. Tony phones up the maintenance department - as I had done numerous times with regard to this matter - and a short bloke with one of those lumberjack type shirts was here within half an hour. He has put a quote in for new guttering and erected a tarpaulin over the offending area to stop the leaking in the interim. How come I didn't get the same response? It's not what you know...

Wednesday 12th December

We are getting hammered in the bar at present - the office party season is in full swing, so we are getting lots of new faces who do not normally frequent pubs. Typically, a whole workplace will converge on the pub for a drink before going on to the local Tapas bar or Thai restaurant for their Christmas beano. Within the thirty or so who come in, there will always be half a dozen pub wallflowers who are uncomfortable in this environment and have absolutely no idea what they want to drink.

They tend to make drinks up when they are asked by the chap who is ordering the round - in the past, I have been asked for a bitter lemon shandy, a lemonade top, a whisky and fruit juice, some beer please and a vodka and wine. These once-a-year drinkers must listen to other people ordering and then just mix them all up. If asked for my advice - and many do - I will always direct them to that bottle of liqueur at the back of the display which has the same dust on it from the previous Christmas.

It is also the time of year when the regulars of this establishment get a little shirty as their favourite stool may have been taken, or it takes them two minutes longer to get served. If you impose on the habits of a pub regular, they get most indignant as they regard the place as their own. The office riff raff who pile in every December are far too loud and can't take their drink - the pub just isn't the same. It is true that the character of the place does change for silly season, but it is also financially a crucial period for a publican - and one which he or she must maximise. You will be grateful that the money is banked when all you have is the solitary regular in the back bar in January who is in a much happier state of mind now that he has his favourite stool back.

Thursday 13th December

I have just finished the rotas for the next three weeks, so that all of the staff can plot their personal exploits over the Christmas and New Year periods. Inevitably, most prefer to be with their families on the day, so it is important that they can now all make their respective plans for the big occasion. Within ten minutes of me pinning the sheets to the staff notice board behind the bar flap, one of the barmen said "I can't do those shifts", pointing to the week of the new year. This despite the fact that I have put up rota request sheets for the last month, which all and sundry have filled in. So, I rejig the offending week to hopefully everyone's satisfaction.

The bloody till is still being re-programmed. They have had it for three "working" days now, but I bet it is still in its couriered packaging. I chased it up twice today, to show them that I wasn't going to take this delay pleasantly. It amazes me that some business owners do not try to exceed customer expectations, but just do the bare minimum in order to earn a living. Have that attitude in this trade and it won't take long before you are with the down and outs under Waterloo Bridge. Actually, Waterloo Bridge is quite nice now - cardboard city is a thing of the past, as they have cleaned it all up and moved the homeless to The Strand.

Apparently, the quickest that they can send me the completed till back is Monday, because - and I quote - the courier is unreliable. This is the boss of the business that was talking - who plainly can't see wood through trees. I imagine that he is an incredibly talented chap when it comes to machinery such as squeaky Geordie programmed tills and the like, but is perhaps not as switched on when it comes to the business world as a whole. He needs a figure such as Gordon Ramsey in the catering world to shake up his operation - I am unsure who the "till guru" equivalent would be - I was thinking Sir Clive Sinclair, but he cocked his electric tricycle business up too, as I recall.

Friday 14th December

The new menus have arrived! They look rather pristine on the tables in comparison to their well thumbed predecessors. On the back, at the bottom of the page in small print, I have a section which I am obliged to complete that is supposed to inform our customers of the legalities of the food offer - stuff like VAT included, allergies, certain dishes take longer as they are cooked to order etc. This is my latest text:

"Subject to availability of dishes and the assumption that the chef has
turned up. If your meal does not arrive within an acceptable time,
there is a kebab van parked behind the pub on a Friday night."

Believe me, nobody ever reads this section on a menu. In the eighteen months or more that we have had menus here, I have not once been pulled up about the text or even had it commented upon. The previous menu read:

"On occasion, the chef ignites certain foods or equipment in the course
of her duties. We will try to ensure that this does not affect
your dining experience with us too adversely."

The menu before that one proclaimed:

"On wetter days, your meal may be delayed slightly more than
usual, due to the Chef's arthritis. We ask you to check the
forecast before dining with us, if this may turn out to be an issue."

As a manager for larger breweries before I took the plunge with my own business, I can tell you that you would never get away with trying humour within the operation. This is one of the key differences between a branded business and one with the freedom to express some individuality with their offer. In many cases, the product served - whether it be a pint or a pudding - may be exactly the same as their chained counterpart, but if it is delivered with a touch of personality as opposed to branded blandness, then the customer will, in most cases, return to the individual - even if it means paying a little more for the product. Mind you, get a chap who thinks he's funny and gets it consistently wrong, then he will just annoy the crap out of your customer, who will then be delighted to pay less...

Homemade Vegetable Soup
'Tis the season to be bloody cold outside. So combat the onset of frostbite
with this warming number from the larder of Chef David.
Comes with a crusty baguette and butter.
£4.25

Warm Salmon Salad
These fish have swam halfway around the World just
to be on your plate, so be grateful.
Served with a large mixed salad and homemade coleslaw
£5.95

Saturday 15th December

From my childhood, I remember the 15th of December as the day that I first went on a school trip to see the England football team play at Wembley. It would have been around 1982 and the opposition was Luxembourg - hardly a footballing superpower, as we trounced them 9 - 0. An up and coming forward named Luther Blissett scored a hat trick that evening and I remember telling myself that he was a fantastic prospect who will be adorning an England shirt for many years to come. It turned out that this particular evening was pretty much the career highlight for this young man, who earned the nickname "Luther Missit" in our school playground. He is around the game still, in a coaching capacity somewhere, so I don't suppose he was that bad after all.

Going to a place like Wembley as a child was just awe inspiring. The sheer size of the stadium took my breath away - but when your normal standing view is generally that of the knee caps of the bloke next to you, then I suppose it would. In truth, Wembley was beginning to get a little ramshackle by then, but the thought of being in a place that I had only read about, or seen on TV was huge for me at that time and blinkered the lack of cosmetics.

The main downside of the evening for me was getting my hat pinched during a goal celebration. Some streetwise kid - not in our school party - who was older and bigger, swiped it as I jumped up and down following a fluky Phil Neal strike. When I complained to the supervising teacher, he told me to sit down. Obviously the kids Dad was bigger than him. If that kid is reading this today and recalls the incident, I hope my hat gave you head lice.

Chef Nick phoned in sick today. As Chef David is camping it up around his hometown patch of the Isle of Wight, I am left with no alternative but to cover the kitchen myself. There has been a cold / flu bug (I really do not know the difference between the two - headaches and snot seem to be a common theme) going around the workplace, started by Ben and contracted by most here - none more so than myself. Having to tie yourself up in the kitchen on the penultimate weekend before Christmas is not ideal for a publican, so our Nick better have something wrong with him, or I will make sure that he does...

Another busy day on the bar. The festive spirit is beginning to take a murderous grip on Bristol, as everyone seems hell bent on consuming as much ethanol as the body can take - and then a tad more. Both ladies and gents washrooms were re-decorated within the course of the nights frivolities, with varying shades of vomit. I would suggest that the female guilty party would have been drinking varying vintages of red from our extensive wine list, whereas the gentleman was on the lager with what looked like a penchant for dry roasted nuts.

Sunday 16th December

A relatively quiet Sunday - as was last week, which is probably explained by the insatiable British desire to shop until you can carry no more. At this time of year, shopping on a weekend is not to be advised unless you enjoy queuing, crowds and queuing in crowds. Thankfully, Mary has taught me the value of getting Christmas shopping finished by the end of November, so I can view the wild eyed, fanatical mayhem within the boundaries of Broadmead shopping centre with a smug, distant disdain. Since I have learned to purchase my needs online, I can complete the arduous annual task of fulfilling my Christmas list in a not so arduous fashion.

On to the not so side issue of an Arsenal v Chelsea fixture, which was played this afternoon. I always believe that you should be gracious in defeat, yet rather humble when you are fortunate enough to taste victory - but when it comes to Chelsea, I unashamedly rip up the manual of good manners and humility. This was a club that for a century had a respectable, if not a little showbiz, reputation. They won the occasional cup here and there, but were never what you would call a footballing heavyweight.

That is until a rather suspect Soviet billionaire decided that he was bored wiping his arse with one hundred rouble bills, and required something a little more high profile and absorbent with which to soak up his finances. He decided to buy a Premiership football club. He had no allegiances to any - he is a Rusky, after all - so after all of the big clubs told him that they didn't want to be the washing machines for his laundering, Chairman Ken Bates bowed under the substantial pressure of being offered millions for his club - Chelsea - and sold out.

Today, Chelski operate at staggering losses of anything approaching 100 million pounds per annum. They buy all of the most talented players from around the globe at vastly inflated prices, in order to stop other clubs who have financial structures and commitments in place from having them. The majority of these footballers then spend the bulk of their time with the club playing for their reserves, as you can only physically field eleven players at one time. The support for Chelski has pretty much doubled since the injection of finance, simply because they have won some silverware on the back of this policy.

There is a familiar cry from opposing terraces of "Where were you when you were shit?" for which their fans have no credible response. I really feel for the true Chelsea supporters, who followed their team through the dark days of the old second division, who now find the club they once knew is an immoral, bullying business hiding behind the Chelsea badge. They must be ashamed at what has evolved there, as their once beloved team is now, in truth, a plaything for their owner which he will no doubt drop when he starts to get bored - and when that day comes, their fair weathered support will also disappear as quickly as it came. If he was serious about the club, then it would be run as a legitimate business, which would not be allowed to haemorrhage money at the rate it does.

Anyway, gingerly dismounting from my box on the scenic side of Speakers Corner, I can smugly say that we thrashed the Soviets one nil today. A magnificent, towering header from our captain fantastic, William Gallas (an ex Chelsea player who obviously feels the same way I do about the goings on in West London) was enough to send the zillionaires packing.

We are back on top of the league, having spent probably about a tenth on players as they have over the last five years. As luck would have it, Chef Nick - who bravely crawled into work today from his festering sickbed - is one of the glory hunting Chelski so-called "fans". I was able to vent some serious stick in his direction to make up for calling in sick yesterday.

Monday 17th December

Today is Olly's fathers funeral. Hope it all goes well for him up in Birmingham, as it not the easiest of things to go through. He is back at work on Wednesday, which I imagine will be a positive thing for all concerned. We are desperately short here at such a critical time of year, so his return will definitely be a boost for us. I recall feeling much more together upon my return to working life after my mothers funeral - I suppose it just takes your mind off it.

I am still one till down at the moment in my back bar. It has been a week since the courier collected my new investment in order to get it programmed. The till itself was returned today, minus the keys and manual. Apparently, they are on the boss' desk, who is unavailable for comment. As he is in charge, the rest of the company will only work to his level anyway, which is turning out to be as useful as a fart in a wind tunnel. I have been promised the keys by courier by midday tomorrow, which will enable me to turn the bloody thing on.

Tuesday 18th December

Am feeling more than a little worse for wear today. The bug that Ben had, he has most generously passed around the family - which is unusual as he has never been noted for sharing anything in his short life to date. The last thing I need right now is to go down with anything significant, as it is when us publicans need to be at their sharpest. The offices are emptying out for their annual beanos on a daily basis, so there is unlikely to be a quiet session between now and Christmas Day.

Tonight is the final quiz of 2007, as both Christmas and New Year both fall on a Tuesday. We have been most generously been donated a "Christmas themed" quiz by one of the regulars from the Youth Hostel (who won't be there on the night) so that saves a job of having to compile one. The way my poor noggin is throbbing at the moment, I think that too long in front of this screen will kill me off anyway…so I'm off to the kitchen to try and organise Chef Nick into compiling a decent looking spread of sandwiches for the aforementioned quiz.

Wednesday 19th December

I am at death's door. It's big, black and forbidding with a huge brass knocker containing the face of Jacob Marley on it.   My sinuses seem to be plugged with superglue and my head feels like I have completed ten rounds with Muhammad Ali *before* the Parkinson's took hold.

Last night, Chloe - our official pub quiz mistress - phoned in sick. She said that she had been suffering from some sort of flu bug and had been in bed for two days. Now our Chloe is not the type to just pull a sicky willy nilly, so I am sure that her reasons for pulling out were completely justified - but taking into account both the time of year and the state that I was in, then you could understand that I was less than enamoured with her for bailing. As it turned out, we were getting absolutely slaughtered from around four o'clock in the afternoon - so the quiz was cancelled and the remaining bar staff just took a ton of cash instead.

Unfortunately, Chef Nick was neglected in his kitchen a floor above, so he was happily plodding on making these sandwiches for the masses, until I spotted him when he was just about done. I informed him that the quiz was no more and we would not be requiring his freshly prepared efforts - he gave me a look like I had just pissed on his sister. I munched on a quarter of egg mayo in front of him to further cement him being miffed and retreated back to the lounge.

Thursday 20th December

So this is what death feels like. I have been to the doctors (which is as about a common occurrence for me as a visit to the opera / church / brothel - pick your funniest) and was told that whatever is eating me is viral. "Take paracetamol and ibuprofen at regular intervals and wait for it to take its course."   I pointed out that we could put man on the moon, but there was nothing they could give me for this? We need to re-assess our priorities here - I have a pub to run.

Meanwhile, without my interference, the pub is getting absolutely tonked. It is my one salvation.

Friday 21st December

Today will be one of the top taking days of the year. All of the surrounding offices finish for the festive break today and will pour into The Shakespeare at around noon, some of them not leaving until we tell them to about eleven hours later, or until they roll dribbling incoherently down our front steps.

All hands are required at the pumps today, so what happens to the number one guy? (That's me, by the way) His untreatable virus has taken hold over his bloody eyeball and is oozing puss out of it. I cannot now utter a sound, as the voice has disappeared completely. The sinus is so swollen that it feels like I have a tennis ball stuffed behind my eyeballs and the head is pounding, pounding, pounding - why do people talk so loudly? I am consigned to fetching change, cleaning, changing barrels etc. I am akin to the phantom of the opera - always in the building, rarely seen and hideous in appearance.

Monday 24th December

It is Christmas Eve. I have been a recluse for days now, for fear of frightening my customers, children and staff. I work in the mornings before anyone is around, cleaning the pub, organising the cellar, doing all of the ordering, office work etc. I find that by the time we open the doors I am spent, exhausted and in dire need of sleep - but I cannot, as every time I am horizontal, I begin to cough which keeps me awake as well as Mary, who has been most understanding of late.

I know how much Mary wants to celebrate the arrival of Christmas Day in the bar this evening, so I have resolved to join her for a swift half. The eye has receded a tad, but I still only have half of a voice. The drugs most certainly don't work, so I don't think a small celebratory shandy will hit me too hard.

Christmas Day

Big mistake, drinking. I'll tell you tomorrow. Merry Christmas.

Wednesday 26th December

I went down to the bar with Mary on Christmas Eve after we had completely sorted out the preparations for the big day. The presents for all and sundry had been organised and were in good order under the tree. The vegetables had been peeled for Christmas day and I had made a rather excellent (even if I do say so myself) marinade for the rib of beef (we are usually more traditional with a turkey, but there was only two adults this year).

So my intentions were to have a celebratory quick drink and then progress to coffee, tea or lemsip for the rest of the evening. I decided on a shot of Jameson's Irish Whiskey to warm the breastbone, as nothing else had got through that region in recent times. It was nice - neat, no ice and Mary had her traditional vodka with diet coke. It went down rather well, so I thought another would do no harm.

Moving on until about three in the morning and I have to rely on accounts from the others involved in our session - my memory got a tad patchy by this time. I have consumed three quarters of a bottle of the said Jameson's, played darts with a picture of Posh Spice and hollered "Five Hundred Miles" by the Proclaimers on the pub quiz microphone. Obviously, I was not the only one who got medically pickled at this social gathering - all who were present picked their own tunes to murder - but I was probably the one to suffer most in the aftermath.

Christmas Day was initially a day of great suffering. I had the mother of all hangovers and was still in poor health from the virus, so I was in no state to face our potentially wonderful lunch. So lunch turned into dinner and then supper. We finally had our feast at around nine in the evening and it was quite excellent. Bt that time, I had been ill a couple of times and had an afternoon nap, so it was hardly your traditional Christmas card scene type day. Today, I actually feel that I have physically turned a corner. I have two pretty good eyes and a voice that you can hear more than three feet away. Mary, however, is feeling under the weather...

Thursday 27th December

We had a surprisingly busy lunch. Although there were no offices open, we got quite busy from plenty of tourists wandering around the waterfront, looking to escape the confines of their family homes. I was cooking, so I was kept busy up until about half past two with about forty lunches - and not a single request for a turkey dinner.

Last night, I picked up Jessica - my daughter - from Bristol airport. She is staying for ten days or so before she has to go back to school, so it is a chance to spend a little quality time with her. She also enjoys seeing her brothers, of course and was amazed at the size of both of them. When you live with your children, you do not notice things like how quickly they grow, as you are in constant contact with them on a daily basis. The last time Jess saw the boys - which was only late Summer - Sam could only crawl backwards and Ben was seemingly half his current height. We had a great time opening all of Jessica's presents, as well as the few Mary and I had kept back for ourselves. Poor Mary is not feeling at her best - this bout of colds and flu seem to be doing the rounds again.

Friday 28th December

Another steady lunchtime, although not to the degree of yesterday, as it was peeing down with rain. No tourist in his right mind wants to brave Bristol's waterfront in this weather. It is just as well, really as one or two members of staff have cried off with various ailments - flu or cold related. Mary is feeling a little better today, but poor Ben looks like he is going to cop yet another dose. He has not been sick for the whole of his life, yet gets two bouts in the space of a fortnight. Tomorrow we have planned to go to my Fathers for a Christmas celebration and to swap presents - I hope we are all well enough to do so.

Potato and Chicken Balti
As voted for by Brummie bus conductors.
Potatoes, chicken and peppers in a
traditional Balti curry sauce.
Served with pilau rice and naan bread.
£5.75

Profiterole Mousse Cake
If you feel that you haven't sufficiently stuffed yourself
this Christmas, then here's an ideal way to make
up those final, nagging pounds.
We'll even pile on cream and ice cream for you.
£3.50

Saturday 29th December

Poor Ben looked absolutely desperate this morning - his little face was forlorn, red eyed and covered in running snot. He stayed behind with doting mother Mary as Jessica, Sam and myself drove to Dartmoor to see Dad, Granny Audrey and Vie.

Jess has been visiting the house where I grew up from birth, but since we lost my Mum, her visits are far more sporadic. As she is now in her mid teens, her priorities in life begin to change as well, so my Father and Gran tend to see her much more infrequently these days - as do I, I suppose. It is odd when you look at her with her brothers to think that they are all of the same generation, but I imagine that we are far from unique when you consider the fractured nature of today's family compositions.

The visit itself was very pleasant - we had an excellent roast lamb cooked by Vie, although Dad was constantly trying to claim credit - and we had yet another bout of present swapping. I received a great gift of two framed photographs of my parents the year they got married - they will command a view of the living room when I get the chance to rearrange a few shelves.

Mary's gift of some sort of lazy susan device has us scratching our heads, somewhat. We are all unsure as to what it is for - my guess is stationery, perhaps on a desk - but it could well be useful in a kitchen environment. We all await with baited breath as to where Mary decides to have it. Currently Ben is getting the most use out of it, putting it on its side and vigorously spinning the base. All of the bloody money that his relatives have spent on him this year and he is playing with that.

It was a very pleasant journey home this evening, listening on the car radio to Manchester United getting thrashed at West Ham and then Arsenal pounding Everton. We always seem to pound Everton. We begin 2008 at the top of the league, hurrah!

Sunday 30th December

Olly is beginning to appreciate a little more what is expected of him in his role as the no.2 at The Shakespeare. In his previous position, he was basically a very hands on bar supervisor who served at one hundred miles an hour and monitored change, barrels, complaints and blocked toilets. Here, I am asking him to be the one who is able to take a step back from the mayhem and try to have a broader perspective of the business. Service is generally not as aggressive or panic stricken as one would find in a nightclub and the customer base is also a generation older. Therefore, our standards here need to be second to none - sticky floors, bar tops and tables are not acceptable. Litter on the floor or in the toilets need to be immediately removed, the music has to be of a certain quality, at the right level and the food service must be prompt and of immaculate presentation.

Olly's abilities and areas of responsibilities are being stretched and, hopefully, will soon become second nature. We had yet another member of staff phone in sick today and Olly immediately volunteered to cover - even though he is salaried. That attitude will stand him in very good stead when it comes to looking after the pub for a week in January, when we go on our holidays. Big up to the big guy.

I got a message on my mobile phone yesterday from my Granny Audrey. Over the previous week or two, my voice has resembled - at best - Lee Marvin with laryngitis. It is little better today. When Audrey called last night I was elsewhere, so the call went to my recorded answer phone message. She remarked that my voice was sounding much better and could I give her a call back when I have the time. Classic.

Monday 31st December

As I write this, it is already 2008 in Auckland, New Zealand. They don't hang about, do they?

Tonight, we expect to get leathered in the bar, so we have three of our finest working - none of whom will be phoning in sick, might I add. This leaves Mary, Jess and myself to enjoy the evening - and I am mightily looking forward to it. Already we have had a couple of regulars leave ten pounds each as a thank you to my staff for serving them in 2007, so that they can have a drink to see in 2008. We intend to be putting together a few sandwiches for those seeing in the new year with us and we'll crank up the Power Ballads album at full whack. Oh yes.

Mary has organised for the boys to have their baths and be in bed by nine o'clock at the latest this evening, which will leave her just enough time to shower and do her makeup and hair before Big Ben tolls twelve, methinks. I'll just splash my face, bit of Brylcreem, a touch of Molton Brown Black Pepper and my best Ben Sherman Shirt. Pure girl bait. Jess has bought herself some new clobber in the sales, which she will no doubt be parading tonight...

Tuesday 1st January 2008

...and a very happy New Year to all.

Last night was rather sociable. It was perfect for the staff really, as it was absolutely rammed from around four in the afternoon until ten in the evening, at which point it thinned out somewhat. This left us plenty of opportunity to see in 2008 in a proper manner, with a glass of champagne and a rowdy chorus of Auld Lang Syne. Jessica had burned a version of the song on to a CD, along with a recording of the Big Ben chimes so that we could play it at an annoyingly loud volume cometh the hour. It was an excellent idea as the dregs that were left all joined in with some enthusiastic vocals and the traditional cross - armed dance.

Being the old fashioned venue that we are, most of the punters departed soon after the big moment to stagger home and put their teeth in a glass for the night. We shut the pub at one in the morning and had a swift half or seven with the staff. Evenings like this are so important for morale and team bonding - I would much rather have taken a couple of hundred pounds less like last night, than be absolutely rammed and no-one get a chance to celebrate personally. It was good to have Jess join in the fun, too - she loves to be accepted as an adult in these situations, so her glass of champagne was turned into a very orange bucks fizz, which she loved.

Today, the pub is closed, so we plan to take a trip to Wells in Somerset, to see my brother Alec and Pauline at their new jobs in a restaurant near the cathedral. It is very unusual to be able to take a day out of this nature when you are in this industry with the whole family, so the food better be bloody good.

Wednesday 2nd January

Food was bloody good yesterday. Unfortunately, the rest of the business is an incredibly disorganised toilet. Every room you walk into behind the scenes (we got a tour, naturally) was piled high with junk that should have been discarded a decade ago. Apparently, the chef has been there very long term and has been in charge overall since the General Manager (who was also her lover) left the business. It is rather obvious that this particular chef has considerable talents in the cooking side of things, but has little skill in how to run a business.

Alec and Pauline were employed to redress this imbalance and add a touch of calm and direction to the proceedings, but apparently this chef has viewed their appointment as a bit of a threat and is pulling rank to keep them firmly in her sights. I hope that the situation resolves itself, as Alec has plenty of good ideas for the place and it would be a shame to see such a lovely site falter on the ego of one person. She should be welcoming them with open arms really, as their presence can only make her life much easier.

Naturally, business was quieter than a mute guy in a soundproof room today as virtually none of the surrounding offices are back at work yet. Despite it not being a public holiday, the vast majority of the British workforce annually stick two fingers up to the thought of going back on January 2nd. Might as well make it a public holiday.

Thursday 3rd January

Having problems with my rubbish collectors. They are rubbish, which is ironic, but as I am paying through the nose to have them collect my waste, I want it collected. My normal pick up days for my wheelie bin are Tuesdays and Fridays, but as both Christmas and New Year fell on a Tuesday, they haven't bothered collecting on either of these days, or made a contingency plan to pick up on the Monday or Wednesday instead.

Needless to say, I have a rubbish mountain which the EEC would be proud of. The chances of these idiot drivers picking up the excess are nil, as they refuse to move overstuffed bins (because of health and safety) or any bags lying beside the bin that would make it overstuffed (because they are lazy tossers). It is getting to the stage where I will be calling rival companies for quotes, as I am getting such crap service. If the guys don't want to collect rubbish, do something else - no one forces them to do the job - if you do it, do it well, like any job.

At the absence of any inspiration on "what shall we have for dinner?" I drove through a KFC drive - through for the third time in a week. We all love it - the new "boneless box" is the current favourite - but I am unsure how much my bathroom scales will appreciate such an indulgence come the end of the week…

Friday 4th January

In theory, the first week in January should be the quietest financial week of the year. No one has any money left from the indulgences of the yuletide season and their thoughts are turning to the ominous heavy thudding sound in early January, as the credit card statement hits the front mat. This annual mindset is reflected in business' such as this, where people tend to look at the frequenting of their local as an excess. Last year, I found that the first seven days of the New Year was a really quiet period, but by the time of the second week the men of the house were back in here, choosing not to feed their kids as an alternative way of saving the pennies instead.

Today however was exceptionally quiet for a Friday - principally I suppose because the offices are not yet filled. After the one hundred mile an hour efforts of December, it is maybe a good thing for my staff to have an easy shift or two. Hope it doesn't last mind - I want to see them sweat again real soon.

Tomorrow, Jess flies back to Newcastle. I hope that she has enjoyed her stay here - I know that she thinks that Dad having a pub is a cool thing, but it also tends to limit the quality time I can give her when she visits. Being the age she is however, she seems to want to spend most of her time chatting on messenger with her friends from school, so having broadband in the office is a real plus for her. While she has been here, we have been to the cinema, gone out for dinner, had every kind of takeaway or delivery that exists (thank you, Colonel Sanders) and taken advantage of the January sales. When I look back at this, we have had some excellent bonding times, doing cool things that teenagers would want to do - but you never get too much feedback from young ladies of that age as parents, so I really hope that she feels the same way.

Our last meal (her choice) was a delivered Chinese of crispy duck pancakes, chilli beef and Singapore noodles which hit many a good spot. I have always wondered about when you order from an oriental menu and you select random dishes, do the Chinese staff roll their eyes and think "How can you be combining dish number 29 with a 54?" Or "This idiot is having the 13 (extra spicy) with the 42A - how revolting is that?" With English food, you would never ask for the Cumberland sausages in onion gravy to come with spaghetti and apple pie, or a breast of pheasant with battered haddock and custard sauce. It just occurs to me that there are either not enough rules for ordering Chinese food, or we are just very ignorant of them. Still tastes good, though.

Saturday 5th January

Up at six this morning in order to take Jess to Bristol airport for her early morning flight back to her Mum in Newcastle. Had a very welcome double latte at departures after checking her bags in, with Jess opting for a hot chocolate. I asked for the option of a "flake and whipped cream for an extra 30p" but the young Eastern European lady behind the counter snapped "We don't have cream" without looking up or pausing in her stride. How do people with such bad public personas get jobs such as this? If you don't have a product that is advertised, the minimum you should do is smile, apologise, make eye contact etc. No one will hold the absence of the product personally against you - but please don't be rude about it and make the customer feel like he was an idiot for asking. I really hate bad service such as this - and I am more inclined to blame the moron line manager who hired her, or the manager who hired the line manager, etc etc.

It is the third round of the FA cup this weekend, one of the more intriguing days of the British sporting calendar, where the little team gets a shot at playing one of the prima donna big boys. There are one or two potential upsets on the cards over the next couple of days, none more so than the mighty Arsenal's trip to the frozen Northern wastelands of Burnley. This particular game is to be played tomorrow, as the BBC have marked it down as their live game, hoping to show the nation a "great cup shock." I sincerely hope that this policy backfires big time. I don't pay my unjustified licence fee to watch my team get humiliated, you know.

Chef Nick has told me that he feels he deserves more money and that he has been offered a job elsewhere. I told him that I feel he works hard and has a great will to succeed in the position, but I don't think he deserves more pay as he can't actually cook, which I feel is an integral part of his position as Head Chef here. I don't think he took it too well, so I expect him to be handing his notice in sooner rather than later. Mary's response was "Good, he's crap". She has a knack for summarising, but I am glad that I personally deal with the employees face to face.

Sunday 6th January

The bloody roof in the back bar has been pissing rain into half a dozen buckets all day. This is by far the rainiest place I have ever lived - and that is saying something, having been brought up on Dartmoor. How are my customers meant to enjoy their Sunday lunches when three feet from their feet there is a plopping sound every two seconds, as yet another ice or champagne bucket gets filled up. Since I first complained about this problem - about eighteen months ago - I have had maybe a dozen separate visits from all knowing builders about how the rain is penetrating my eighteenth century ceiling and what magic shortcut they can take in order to relieve my indoor waterfall feature. Nothing short of ripping the ceiling down and finding the hole will solve this, but the brewery seem loath to spend the money. Meanwhile, my business is taking a trip down the river (or at the very least, a small stream).

Monday 7th January

It is so quiet...although today is the day when it can safely be assumed that everyone should be back in their offices, so at least we should be banging out a few more lunchtime meals to the suits this week.

Tuesday 8th January

It is Mary's birthday tomorrow - and I am still waiting on a couple of bits to be delivered. God help me if they don't arrive…

Tonight is the first quiz of the new year, so I am hoping for a decent turnout. I was contemplating serving the mountain of mince pies that we have, in addition to the free sandwiches for all of the contestants, but I think that it may come across as more of a negative than a positive gesture, as: 1/ Everyone is sick of mince pies. 2/ We leave ourselves open to "How come we're getting your bloody leftovers?" and 3/ It's more work for Chef Nick, who struggles with more work. So I'll throw them in the bin.

Lamb Madras
Chunks of tender lamb in a sauce hot enough to set fire to your teeth.
Rather pleasant cuisine from our colonial cousins.
Served with pilau rice and naan bread
£5.95

Homemade Cottage Pie
Makes you feel like you're eating at home,
unless you are divorced /
sad & lonely, in which case your mother's home.
Served with mixed vegetables and gravy
£5.75

Wednesday 9th January

It's the wife's birthday…and there is just one gift that has not made it in time. I would like to state that she has been thoroughly spoiled today in the gift department, even without the absentee, so I am firmly not in the doghouse. In fact, I am so far away from the doghouse, that I couldn't even tell you where it is. I would need a London cabbie who was full of the knowledge of all doghouses in order to get me in one. Anyway, to cut it short, she's opened her presents and she's happy. Tonight we are going to our favourite Italian restaurant to celebrate whilst Olly looks after the pub. With any luck, we'll also make it to the casino.

Thursday 10th January

A good night was had by all yesterday. Mary and I had a very nice meal, a few relaxing beers and, to top off the evening, won a few pennies at the casino. The pub was reasonably busy too, so whilst uneventful it was rather pleasing. On the down side, the leak in the roof is becoming decidedly bad - it needs some serious work doing to it.

Friday 11th January

Mary's final gift arrived today, which puts me swimming in brownie points. I wonder where "brownie points" come from? Is it a scouting thing? Answers on a postcard, please.

Things are getting back to normal on the sales front, with a very decent lunchtime session. All coped well - no-one waited more than fifteen minutes for their meals, the standards were good on the floor and the place was pretty full, with one or two of the punters electing to eat standing up as there was no seating. Fridays are good to me. In theory, we are still in one of the quietest weeks of the year, so my expectations are relatively low. It is an excellent time to be giving Olly more responsibility as the service times have less pressure on them due to lack of numbers. With this in mind, Mary, myself and the ankle - biters are off on a weeks break to the Lake District on Monday. Olly will be doing his first "relief", being in total charge for the period of our absence. As you can imagine, he is shitting himself. With this in mind (and for my own entertainment, naturally) I am taking him to see the mighty Arsenal play his lowly team, Birmingham City tomorrow at the Emirates stadium.

Saturday 12th January

I am writing this in the small, wee hours after driving back from London, dropping Olly off at his home and getting accidentally plastered in my pub. I say accidentally because it was not my intention to get plastered, although the rhythmical purchasing of alcoholic drinks was quite deliberate. It was just one of those evenings where you walk into a place and the atmosphere is just right, the company is spot on and the beer is quite excellent. It is also a bonus when the pub happens to be yours.

For the record, the game at The Emirates finished in a one - one draw. A disappointment for myself, but elation for Olly. He was also blown away by the sheer majesty of the stadium - its facilities, atmosphere and opulence for a sporting venue are second to none in this country (possibly the new Wembley aside, although I am yet to experience it). The time spent in the car there and back was also productive, as I believe Olly is in the right frame of mind to do a good job during our absence next week.

Monday 21st January

What a drive back from the Lake District that was. For the first two and a half hours, the visibility on the M6 was not much further than the thickness of the windscreen, as we were completely bombarded by driving, sheeting rain. My God, how do people "up North" survive in this desperate climate? It pretty much pissed down all week - but then, when you book a holiday in January in the UK, you don't expect a bloody tan, I suppose.

Our lodge in the forest was more than comfortable - it was a real escape. Looking out through the French doors at the back of the accommodation was forestation as far as you could see, with towering pines, thick, lush green undergrowth and a variety of scampering wildlife. We had a regular morning visitor to our doors in the form of a rather curious pheasant. Occasionally, he would bring a pal, too - much to the straight faced entertainment of Ben, who would just sit on the mat in his sleep suit and have a staring contest with the bird - they would be literally twelve inches separating them, with just the glass pane in between. There are numerous photos on my camera phone to celebrate the event of Ben caught in shot without his legs being a blur.

A feature of the site which Mary and I appreciated in spades was the "Time Out Club". This was essentially a crèche, which allowed you to purchase a session for your children so that you could swan off elsewhere and do adult stuff. This we took advantage of when we booked some treatments at the Aqua Sana, the on site spa centre. On one afternoon we had a "couples special" which involved a back, shoulder and neck massage - which I was fully looking forward to - and a facial treatment - which I was a little more dubious. It turned out to be a rather pleasant hour, however (and my t-zone has never felt better).

A second visit to the spa saw us drop off our two ankle biters into the "bumblebees club" so that Mary could have a hair do and I participate in a reflexology session. I tried to appreciate the intricacies of the treatment, but I really wished that she had just rubbed my feet harder. I am lying on my back with my cheesy plates of meat in Svetlana's hands, goading her into giving them a good squeeze. She was far more set on unblocking one of the six energy channels either side of my tortured body, by barely applying pressure on various points such as a middle toe here, or the side of a heel there. The room had a slight, warming breeze and soft "babbling brook" type music wafting in the air to promote total relaxation, but I am lying there with my eyes closed thinking "Come on, love - give my bunion a good squeeze". But she never did.

Tuesday 22nd January

So back to work. Apparently Chef Nick did a tearful walk out before service on Sunday lunch. At five to twelve midday, he just had a breakdown of sorts and went home, leaving Olly to get through potentially our busiest food session with one chef. Luckily, Olly's other half stepped up to the plate, put on her rubber gloves and washed it. Between her and Chef David they got through it - luckily it was not our busiest Sunday ever, but that no way excuses Chef Nick for letting down the team. I have arranged a meeting with him tomorrow morning, at which I will be taking appropriate action after I have listened to his side of things.

That incident aside, the week away posed few problems for Olly, who appears to have coped rather well. There have been issues, of course, as there are in every week, but he appears to have dealt with them in a professional and appropriate manner, so thumbs up for him. In short, we now have a hole in the ceiling of the back bar where the rain has finally worn it away and I have sacked our refuse collectors because they are crap at doing the one thing that I want them to do well - collect our refuse. Contractually, I have to give two months notice, so I am now looking at eight weeks of extra bad rubbish service (excuse the pun).

Wednesday 23rd January

Last night, Arsenal got slaughtered 5-1 by Tottenham Hotspur. It was a nightmare performance and absolutely mortifying for Gooners everywhere, as they are our fiercest rivals. You have to take the odd defeat on the chin occasionally, but a scoreline like that against them is about as bad as it can get. My local newsagent who has his shop a couple of doors down the road is a Spurs fan. He photocopied the back sports pages of the national newspapers and blu-tacked them to the front door of the pub at six in the morning. It was not what I wanted to see first thing, I can tell you. All day, every sports mad regular that frequents The Shakespeare Tavern has been reminding me of the score. I have received countless texts and calls on my mobile and even the staff have been less than sympathetic. When the worm turns and Arsenal get back to winning ways, I will let everyone know, believe me.

In our meeting today, Chef Nick has given in his notice. He seems genuinely apologetic for his behaviour on Sunday and appreciates how much he let everyone down, but this is a business and I cannot risk having someone in such an important position as his who is clearly not up to speed. Shame, because he is a nice guy. I now have until Sunday week to try to find someone to replace him.

Thursday 24th January

Had a very productive meeting with an alternative refuse collector today. Not only does the rep want my business, but he has offered a ridiculously low collection charge to get it. I am saving over three pounds per pick up, twice a week against my current fees, as well as getting new drivers. If I had not had such appalling service from my present company, I would not have been looking to change in the first place, so not realising that I could get better value for my business. Funny how things turn out - those idiot bin men have done me a favour.

Gammon and Eggs
Compulsory attire for any self respecting swine should be a well placed fried egg
or two. Gammon, fried eggs, chips and peas. Yum.
£6.25

Homemade Pea Soup
A fine Winter Warmer, sourced from the fields of this fine land, then

lovingly
pureed by the men in white coats upstairs.
Served with a warm, crusty baguette and butter.
£4.25

Friday 25th January

An advert has gone on the web for a new chef. Fingers crossed for a positive response from a keen wannabe Gordon Ramsay. The likelihood is, however, that we are more likely to end up with a Gordon Bennett.

It was another decent lunch session today. It is incredible how well Chef Nick is performing now that he has given in his notice. He seems like a new person - happier in himself and far more competent and willing than he ever has been. He has either had the World's problems lifted from his shoulders, or he's getting laid.

Mary and I are thinking of asking one of the new members of our bar team, Beth, if she fancies having a go at a spot of childminding. She is a qualified nurse, part time University student and pretty switched on. She is also begging me for as many hours as possible, which I do not have on the bar rota, so this could solve a few problems.

Saturday 26th January

Today the Arsenal play Newcastle United in the F.A. Cup fourth round. They have just had a managerial change, having re-appointed Kevin Keegan as their boss. Let's hope that he does not have too much of a positive influence on them...

We have had such a busy day in the pub. It started off with a coach load of blue rinses from Wales on a day trip to Bristol, for a pub lunch and to see "Mamma Mia", the stage show featuring the music of Abba. They all poured in about half past midday and stayed for a couple of pints and a sausage and mash. Nice crowd, good atmosphere.

Early evening saw the arrival of a slightly more upbeat set of clientele - a retirement party for some poor sap who would probably end the night strapped to a lamp post in the city centre or face to arse with a stripper in some seedy nude bar. There was about thirty of these gentlemen celebrating this guy leaving, who all had a preference for a pint of Fosters. Although they were not the most cultured bunch that ever walked through my doors, they spent an awful lot of money before they spilled out into the night.

One of the things that I love about my pub, is the fact that we seem to be the place where everyone comes to get tanked up before moving on to their intended destination. It's like we are the warm up comedian for the main act, but it means that they spend a lot of money with me before they get drunk and throw up elsewhere - so we get the revenue without the hassle.

Tuesday 29th January

Quiz night tonight sees our new potential childminder, Beth, trying out as the quizmaster (or is it quiz mistress?). She has a pair of lungs on her, so we may have to turn down the microphone...I have doctored one or two of the questions for the amusement of the punters - we will have to see if she falls for it.

We had another walk in audit from Cask Marque today, who monitor the quality of real ales throughout the beer drinking community. Those that pass their stringent tests qualify for a certificate and plaque guaranteeing the perfect pint to all and sundry - so it is an extremely good thing to be able to shout about. Our real ales are a massive selling point here and an integral part of my offer to our discerning public. The auditor requests a half pint of all real ales on show (five, in our case) and checks temperature - must be between 11 and 14 degrees, clarity - must be brilliant in appearance, not hazy or dull, and taste - should not taste like a bottle of Sarsons, Domestos or Reggae Reggae sauce. Thankfully (although expected) we got 100% on all categories for all five beers, so we are entitled to show our achievements for another six months or so.

For the second time in four days, the magnificent Arsenal beat Newcastle United three nil. Can we play them every week?

Wednesday 30th January

I have to admit, our Beth was quite excellent on the microphone last night. She will make a very entertaining quiz host in the long term. There is an art in being able to shut people up while the questions are being read out, or deal with the occasional cretinous heckler / wannabe comedian. Beth managed to put them all firmly in their place and added some personality to the delivery of the quiz. Out of the three bombs which I planted, she fell for only one (What was the frequency of Radio Luxembourg? The real answer is "208 longwave". The answer I put down for her to read out was "Once a week"). I confess that I took advantage of her blondness, but she did take it in good spirit.

Today, Beth worked the lunch shift on the bar until 3pm and then spent the afternoon with Mary and our two boys. The plan is to integrate her for a session or two so that they are familiar with her, before starting in earnest next week. Everything seemed to go smoothly enough and Mary was pleased at the end of the day, which is the clincher, to be honest. I do hope that this will work for us.

17. Parting is Such Sweet Sorrow

Having such a great team with a decent smattering of leaders within it, I was able to be much more of a supervisor and delegate most of the practical stuff within the pub, as opposed to being quite so hands on which I had needed to be for the first couple of years. Because of this, I was able to help out Mary a lot more with our boys which she very much needed. Unfortunately for us, the damage was already done in our relationship by this time, as we were just effectively ships in the night with each other.

It's a crying shame that we weren't able to get to this stage in our business before our marital flame went out. With the boys' autism, it had proved too much of an obstacle I suppose, and Mary was living a nightmare existence trapped upstairs in crappy pub accommodation with two unresponsive full time toddlers. I guess I was seen as someone who to be with you had to live in this world, and it just wasn't fun for her.

It didn't help our situation that we had virtually no support from our families principally due to geography, so we really were on our own save for a babysitter once a week. I was desperate to save my marriage as Mary and the boys meant everything to me, but I could very well sense that I was increasingly on my own with regard to this. One evening over dinner, Mary told me quite bluntly that she'd had enough and wanted out of the marriage. I was empty inside.

I had shaken hands with Clive, the Regional Manager for Greene King, on another deal to extend our current contract for another five years. I would have been mad to give this place up financially, and my thoughts were that if we continued to make enough money then maybe Mary, the boys and I could move out to see if that could help our personal situation. When you live above a pub, there is no privacy - everyone knows your business and it's a real goldfish bowl at times.

It had been an extraordinarily long time waiting for the renewal contracts to arrive, so I started chasing them with the Area Manager. It was usually such a routine procedure. After a while, my calls were not being returned. One day, I got a call from Sim, who introduced himself as our new Area Manager, wanting to make an appointment with Mary and I. In this meeting, we were informed that Greene King had changed their minds and they wanted to buy the lease back off us.

Basically, their accountants had looked at the number of barrels that we were now buying from them and thought "We wouldn't mind this ourselves", so their plan was to get the pub back and convert it into a managed house. As it was the end of our contract, we had no say in the matter - we were out. In fairness, the terms were generous, so we planned to take six months off to recuperate and decide what the next step was.

The Shakespeare was taken over by a nice enough couple on a salary, and the pub itself was converted into a managed house with its uniform menus, decor, tills and beer range. It was now just the same as the Red Lion or the Dog and Duck - and that's what the Pub Co's just don't get. All of the character, history, personality and individuality was eradicated in one fell swoop of an accountants nib and along with it - unsurprisingly - half of the sales.

My family and I moved into a fresh, clean two bed apartment in South Bristol while we cleared our heads. Nice, new, open plan - it even had a running track on top of the complex. This was I thought, just what we needed - but if anything Mary pulled even further away. With me now having nothing else to do, I was more than keen to take the pressure off Mary and get more involved with the boys. I had a great time getting up with them when they woke up, breakfast, taking them out to the park, feeding them dinner. It was a really nice period between myself and the boys, without the daily grind of the pub.

Unfortunately, Mary stayed in bed late almost every day. Don't get me wrong, I wanted to be up with the boys, so I didn't complain. Then she started to go clubbing, coming in at three or four in the morning, two or three times a week. At first, I thought it was just her getting it out of her system, but it wasn't. At that point in time, I was doing most of the work with the boys, and Mary was just retreating. It was painfully evident that she was really unhappy. Mentioning it would cause arguments, so I tried to reason, but I suppose she had got to that stage because of the last five years, not the weeks or months since we got out of the pub.

Things didn't help when we had to start school for Ben. Due to our location, Ben was to start at the Holy Cross Primary School and we interviewed with the headmaster, as we had concerns about the support offered for autistic children. The answer that came back, in short, was none. It was shocking, as if he had never heard of it. To him, it was all about how much extra it would cost the school, rather than how they could best support Ben in the classroom.

When I mentioned that Ben was still using a nappy, he said bluntly that there were no facilities for changing kids, and he wouldn't expect his staff to have to undertake that. He said it would be essential that we got Ben trained up, as if it was our fault that he wasn't out of them yet, or Ben's fault for being a late developer. This basic denial of a condition which is now so commonplace in the Western world was short sighted and amateurish, even back then. Taking your child into their first school is a huge step for any parent, and you want to feel confident when you walk away from the gate - but neither Mary nor myself were happy with Ben schooling here.

It all came to a head quite quickly at home. Mary and I had argued again, and I suggested that she might be happier back home in Canada. She needed no second bidding. With the advice and support of her father, she had arranged flights and asked me to sign a solicitors release to enable the boys to travel without me. In truth, she was making me so miserable at home, with her current attitude to our marriage and her late night clubbing. In return, I was damn sure that I made her miserable, too - no matter how hard I tried, or what I did. The damage was permanent, and it was time to face up to it.

Mary and my boys left in July of 2011. I drove them to Heathrow terminal 3, and dropped them at security. Whenever I go through there these days, it always brings a lump to my throat. I drove home in tears and let myself back in to my empty flat. And that's all I did for three months - have breakfast on my own, go for a run on the roof, make a nice dinner, eat it on my own and finally go to bed alone. I could go days without talking to another soul in real life. Of course, I would facetime the boys on a daily basis, as I still do to this day, but I really missed my family - all of them.

The support you get in Canada for autistic children is nothing short of outstanding. Physical, financial, emotional - everything that this country should aspire to in this regard. With time to grow and with incredible support from the now immediate family and society, our two boys have evolved into lovely, well mannered young men. Indeed, if you did not know it, you would be hard pressed to realise that there was anything amiss at all.

They are both great company, but very different kids. Ben is a practical, outgoing young man, and can look at something and fix it or build it. Sam is a little more reserved and is currently into his supercars. Sam has also memorised every King of England in sequence, as well as the entire London

Underground map. They both play "soccer" for their local boy's team and both support Arsenal. Funny coincidence, that. Oddly enough, Ben also likes Real Madrid, while Sam follows Barcelona.

I manage to pop over three or four times a year, and usually we hop on a flight to Vegas for a week - it's only a two hour flight from their home in Vancouver. While we are there, I can play at being Dad, as we rent a condo where I can cook for them, and we jump in a pool every day or go ten pin bowling. In addition, they both spend six weeks of the Summer holidays living over here in the UK with me. For the great distance that we live apart, I suppose we don't do too badly. It's not enough for me, but I do know that they are in the best place where they can prosper.

Mary herself has morphed into some kind of SuperMom. She has done an incredible job with the boys and is thriving in her life. We are now officially divorced, and have both moved on privately. She has been a great Mom and role model since she went back home, and I couldn't wish for my kids to be in better hands. Ironically, we get on really well these days - gone are the arguments, distrust and dislike of the final months of our marriage. In spite of everything, we have always had the best interests of our boys at the forefront of every decision, so by sticking to that, we have come through any personal beef that we had with each other. Mary has my complete respect, trust and admiration and long may that continue.

In September of 2011, I got a call from Clive, the same Regional Manager of Greene King that I had shaken on a contract exchange with. Clive, like myself, has a season ticket at Arsenal. He explained that he had a pub in trouble near Highbury and Islington, about a ten minute walk from the Emirates stadium. Could I check it out, and if I liked it, then we'd work out a deal.

Tired of living an empty life and in need of personal motivation, I drove to London...

18. My Little Corner of Canonbury

I met David, the business manager for Greene King's central London tenanted pubs, in a small coffee shop in Victoria Station. The meeting had been set up by Clive, his regional manager and I viewed it as an interview situation. I had done many visits to The Compton Arms at various points of the day and week at this point, and reckoned I could make a good go of it. I turned up to the meeting armed to the teeth with a business plan, sales forecasts, marketing strategies, new menu and the like. I was quite proud of the background work I had done for this and was determined to give David a positive show.

We chatted for a bit about personal stuff, as a loose introduction. We both hailed from the West Country, both football fans - he is a season ticket holder at Brighton, the poor sod - and then the conversation started to turn to the Compton. As I'm about to wow him with my impressive collection of numbers (I had even bought a new plastic pouch in green to keep it all in from WHSmith before the meeting) he told me that this get together was essentially just to get to know each other. He had been told that the pub was mine if I wanted it, on the strength of what I achieved at The Shakespeare, so this wasn't a formal interview.

I thought about claiming expenses for the green plastic pouch, but realised that I was actually on to a good thing and it was best if I didn't cock it up while I was in front. I told him that I thought I could do a job there, and promised to get back to him with an appropriate date to take over the pub. I went home, organised my life, and agreed to start in October of 2011. The first week there I closed down for 4 days and with my old friend Martin's assistance along with his son Will, Chloe from The Shakespeare, and all of the new staff, the pub got a splash of paint, some new speakers and a damn good clean.

The accommodation was less important in this situation, principally because it was just me on my own. It was a good job, too, as it was totally unsuitable for a family. No security - not even a front door - rotting windows, leaking roof - it was pretty rubbish, but as it was just me I covered it in band aids and moved in my stuff. In reality, I was going to spend most of my life downstairs anyway and the flat was just a place to put my head at night.

I inherited just four staff. Three of them local to Islington and a Welsh girl, who had just won "The World's Most Miserable Barmaid" award for the fifth year running. She was a very capable worker when she chose to be, but just never could reconcile that when you hand over a pint, you have to smile at the same time. If you got a grunt and a scowl off this girl you were doing well. I later found out that she and the outgoing manager were bonking for Britain, so maybe his exit had something to do with the look on her face.

Donna and Grainne were two local girls who had great personalities and were very popular with the locals. Grainne was a young student and eventually went travelling. Donna was similar in age to myself and worked with me a little longer over lunchtimes, before finding a nice position for herself at Marks & Spencer, which suited her better. Before she left, she got married to a local bloke called Ronnie and we all had a lovely time at their wedding.

Then there was Lee. Where do you start with this guy? He reminded me very much of an old employee I had back in The Sutton Arms in that everything he touched, shattered. He was the most accident prone human being I have ever come across. Every session he worked, I would lose four or five glasses - dropped, tipped over, accidentally nudged with his arse or just exploded randomly while he was near it.

Most of his family were regulars in the pub which didn't make handling his situation the easiest thing, but the truth was that there wasn't a malicious bone in the guys body - he was just shockingly unlucky, or clumsy. I recall having a conversation about him with his Uncle Gary, with whom he was living at the time. He was telling me that Lee had decided to do a nice thing and wash his living room net curtains, but when he took them out of the machine they had drastically shrunk. Of course, Lee still put them back up and waited for Gary to notice. Wouldn't have covered a Wendy House window, apparently. I asked Gary why Lee was living with him. He told me that Lee used to live with his Gran, but she threw him out when he flooded her house. I'm sure he didn't mean to….

Once, Lee tried to deliver a tray of coffee to a punter who was sat in our back garden area. This rear patio could be accessed through a side door from the bar, or through a stable type door with two flaps via the trade kitchen. The top half of the stable door I always kept open, so that I could both keep an eye on outside while I was cooking and to get some fresh air. Lee didn't even check to see if the bottom half was bolted or not. He just ploughed through it. Splinters everywhere, the lock hanging off, wooden shards all over the floor. He didn't even pause, just carried on to the customer without spilling a drop. When Lee finally moved on, he nearly hacked his hand off cutting up a cabbage for the Sunday roast on his last day. Didn't even finish his last shift because he was in accident and emergency up at the Whittington hospital. Probably an appropriate finish, really.

The regulars at The Compton Arms were many. It is a proper locals kind of pub, a real centre of the community. Everyone used to meet around the bar and talk shit for their "shift", before being replaced by the next wave of familiar faces once the first batch couldn't fit any more beer in. All they required was fresh, varied, well kept ales, a bit of food to keep them going and a little personality from the person pulling the pints. Emily, a most entertaining daytime real ale sponge, wanted the heating turned up a bit too much, but I wasn't taking enough over the bar at that point to accommodate her daily goosebumps. It isn't rocket science, running a pub. It's all about people, understanding what they want from your pub and accommodating them. Look after your regulars, don't serve the idiots and you'll have a happy and profitable environment in no time.

When I first became the landlord here, there was an unusual spate of deaths of regulars. Being a proper, traditional pub the average age of my punter was a tad higher than your normal high street hostilery, so maybe one should have expected the odd fatality - but we had eight in the first six months. I got fed up of smart arses telling me I should clean my pipes out. Buying into their black humour, I started a sweepstake for the next regular to die. Favourites in the betting were Fabien, because the French notoriously are good at surrender, and Heart Attack Dave, because he had managed three heart attacks already and still drank for Hackney. Oddly enough, the next bloke to snuff it was indeed Dave who didn't get past number four, but thankfully that was a good six years later.

Daytimes were slow during the week. Gone were the days when all of the offices emptied out at midday and poured into the nearest pub for refreshment. These times of alcoholic abstinence that companies now insist upon has killed the luncheon gravy train. I created a deal between midday and three pm where you could get anything from the menu for just a fiver, to try and create some sort of daytime boost. I was never too happy about flogging my home cooked wares at that price, but needs dictated my strategy.

It got me a little extra top line sales, so just about made it worthwhile opening before five in the afternoon.

One lunchtime, Emily was returning from a regular trip to Bristol to see her extended family. I believe her train to Paddington was delayed a little, so instead of taking the tube from the train station which I guess would have cost her about four pounds to Highbury & Islington, she opted for a black cab to race across London in time for three o'clock, so that she would get to the pub to get the fiver meal deal. I would imagine the cab would have set her back about twenty five quid....and this learned lady holds down a position in the Houses of Parliament!

My daylight regulars were mainly Kevin (and Ned, his dog), Dennis (who fancied Emily), Emily (who fancied Fabien), Fabien (who fancied another beer), Gary (who fancied his mad bird, Trish), Trish (who fancied her dog, Ted) and Andy the Hat (who'd have been grateful for a shot at any of them). There were plenty of others who used to flit in and out of this mad ensemble, but that was the core. A normal afternoon would start off civilly enough, but generally disintegrated after a couple of barrels had been changed and more often than not, ended up with one or all of them shouting at each other. Next day, they would all come in, fresh as daisies and start all over again.

Fabien used to drink for France. All day, every day. Many a time the poor chap would nod off at the bar, mid conversation. Actually, that's not fair. Fabien rarely participated in conversation as it was pretty much one way traffic from Emily. He did a lot of listening, but had a fantastic ability to zone out when necessary. It's a male trait, zoning out. It's a scientific fact that females speak around seven thousand words a day, whereas us men make do with just two thousand. Consequently, we learn to filter out what isn't relevant to us, ie zoning out. Like white noise, if you will. If a woman wants us to actually listen to what she is saying, she needs to throw in some key words or phrases in order for us to pay attention. These words are many and varied, but include "football", "meat", "beer", "blow job" and "tits". You're welcome. Anyway, as it wasn't a good look for my business having a Frenchman fall asleep face down on my bar counter, I used to wake him up by smashing a metal ladle onto a frying pan right above his head.

Wednesdays and Fridays were significant for me because that's when the Compton Arms darts team would come in. About a dozen or so splendid chaps from the surveying or planning departments at Islington Council - most of them now retired - frequented my humble business twice weekly and used to consume impressive quantities of ale. About twenty five years previously, they were looking for a place to call home and convinced their wives that they had started a darts team - practise on Wednesdays, matches on Fridays. So they've been doing this for a quarter of a century. The Compton doesn't even have a dartboard. If one of the spouses popped in, we always told them that the board was kept behind the big TV...

The darts team always had their functions with me in the pub, too. These were usually a traditional Christmas dinner and Burns Night. They only had one Jock amongst them, but if there's an excuse for a celebration they would embrace it. I used to do a bit of Scottish Smoked Salmon to start, Haggis, Neeps & Tatties for the main (with a shot of a Scottish Malt Whisky in the middle) and a cranachan to finish. Robbie, the token Scotsman of the group, used to do this ceremony with the haggis which involved a ritual stabbing and quoting Robbie Burns at full volume. Odd bunch, the Picts.

The Christmas dinner was always good fun, so I put a lot of groundwork into getting it right. They usually opted for beef over turkey, principally because it tastes better, or so they said. I used to do a parsnip soup to warm them up, and a Christmas pud with brandy sauce. It was generally an all day drinking fest, with some splendid reds and ports to help while the afternoon away. It was always a lovely event, incredibly civilised and they always gave my staff very generous tips on the day.

Louise started off working for me as a glass and plate clearer, food deliverer and runner. She was 16, so too young to serve alcohol, but help like hers was invaluable during a match day, when The Arsenal were at home. Her mother, Tina, also worked in the pub. Both were purebred Islington girls, completely at home in the environment, ducks in water. Tina would go on to manage a pub of her own locally, so she was pretty switched on.

Louise, however, despite the inherited decent work ethic, was still young enough to be gullible, so it was only natural that she ended up doing amusing things. During a quieter session one weekend, I managed to convince her that the floor mats located behind the bar and in the private areas needed beating. Her mother found her in the garden area knocking the dust out of these carpets with a small spoon.

Another of my favourites with Louise was a day that we were putting up the pub Christmas decorations. Louise wanted to be in charge of the tree. It was a real one, which we were situating in the rear dining area of the pub. In all fairness, she did a cracking job - far better than I would have done with my limited creative abilities, but she was having trouble finishing it off with the star at the tree's peak...

"The very top of the tree won't stand up straight. Every time I try to put the star on it, it flops over."

"Have you used the blue pill?"

"The what?"

"Have you given the tree the blue pill that comes with it, to keep the top bit erect for the star?"

"Er, no..."

"Ok, well I gave it to your mother when I put the tree on the stand - go ask her for it."

You have to deliver lines like that with a poker face.

So Tina was busy behind the bar serving the lunchtime punters, when in front of everyone, her daughter asks her for a blue pill to keep the top of the Christmas tree erect.

Absolutely priceless.

On one rare occasion I managed to dupe Tina, too. Arsenal had just beaten Hull City in the F.A, Cup final of 2014 and I had got this quite magnificent panoramic framed photograph of the Wembley crowd, which was taken at the match and put up on the pub wall. I offered her £50 if she could spot my face in the crowd, as I of course was at the game. Give the girl her dues, it took her three days of perseverance and bad guesses before she admitted defeat, only to be told that I was seated behind the camera at the ground...in my defence, I was paying her for her time.

The busiest time at The Compton was evenings during the week and footballing occasions. It was important for me to expand the pubs horizons when it came to attracting new trade. Traditionally, The Compton had been branded an old man's pub - a term Emily would object to, as she could hold her own at the bar, round for round with any man. I was keen to try and glean new avenues of trade, so relative innovations for this pub was a proper wine list, varied real ales, refurbished toilets, appropriate background music and a menu that was homemade and affordable. By introducing these basics, The Compton would attract more female groups, office workers, lads starting their night out and single men looking for a little banter over the bar.

Many locals who loved the pub had begun to frequent our geographical rivals due to the poor standards from the previous owners, so it was nice to "win" these guys and girls back. By showing the football on the TV's in the pub ensured that we were a go to place to see the big match. There was a lovely little patio area to the rear of the pub, which I got redecked and painted, which was a nice place to drink al fresco and also made it smoker friendly.

A regular family were the Howe's, Andy and Lynne, plus their daughter Kirsty who were related to Lee and Gary, along with their friends Dave, Danielle and Scary Dave. (It was the eyebrows, in case you're wondering. If you saw them, you'd understand. He wasn't really that Scary, unless you offended him....) One night soon after I took over, we had a little bit of a lock in as we all had got the taste for it. As the pub was down a couple of side streets you could kind of get away with that sort of thing, which you wouldn't be likely to if the pub was on a main road. No-one walked past the front door unless you knew it was there, which made it hard to build up the business very quickly, but good for an illegal lock in situation...

Anyway, I had vague recollections of doing "Gangnam Style" behind the bar that night with Roxy, a lively barmaid of ours. She also had quite a history with the pub, as her parents had met in there. I don't remember too much of it while it was going on but the bad dancing was caught on Andy Howe's phone and can be found on YouTube today, if you so desired. Even later on during that evening's proceedings at about three in the morning, I recall that we were all in a long line stretched across the bar floor, doing the Time Warp at full volume...

As we all "jumped to the left," two people in coloured macs walked in the front door. In my drunken state, I tried to usher them out, saying that we were closed. "And then a step to the riiiiight" bellowed the rest of them. The macs informed me that they were from Islington Council's noise abatement department, and that they have had complaints about the late night music. "With your hands on your hips" screamed the others.... I raced around the bar and turned it down, sharpish. I told the council guys that we weren't still serving drinks at this hour, which must have sounded ridiculous as the bar and tables were covered with empties and everyone's pint was still nicely fizzy. The two of them smiled and left us to it, with a warning about the volume button.

Other mainstays of the regular Compton evening scene were Guinness Terry, West Ham John, Mick the Shoe, Sid the Trumpet, Gas Fire Brian, Builder Brian, Arsenal Brian, Colin, Dave the Bus, Taxi Ian, Taxi John, Comedy Derek and Diver Sam. There are dozens more, of course, but I've been fortunate enough to share many a pint talking absolute nonsense with all of these people, and to me, that's what pubs are for.

Colin was a particular favourite of mine. Very dry sense of humour but brutal in his opinions, which made for quality banter over the bar. His latest employment was on the ticket barriers at St Pancras station, where he would like nothing more than to catch someone travelling with the wrong or no ticket on them. There was a rumour that he once jammed a broom handle in a wheelchair wheel to stop a disabled chap escaping without paying the proper fare. Former jobs included monitoring speed cameras, so I think you get the theme...Traffic wardens or passport control would have also been a perfect fit for Colin. He was kind enough during one Summer when I had my boys over, to organise us a cab ride in the front of a high speed train. I probably enjoyed it more than my kids, which would eventually lead me on to a different path in the years that followed.

Later on, the evenings guests were the guys that used to come in for a couple just before close - Guinness Gary and Lou. Both were interesting characters in their own ways.

Guinness Gary was very particular about his place setting at the bar. Clean bar towel, dry bar top, immaculate Guinness, 80's background music. Get these ingredients right, and you've a customer for life. Cock any of it up, and you were toast. He used to bring in the most stunning of women, different ones every time. All of them liked being spoiled and, according to Gary, all enjoyed a good spanking.

Lou was in the army as a younger man, something to do with radios and electronics, I believe. Spent most of his youth in the desert eating sand and getting pissed on the back of land rovers and camels. Big white beard like Santa, got an annual haircut whether he needed it or not. (Sid the Trumpet was another infrequent barnet pruner). In recent times, Lou had taken up sailing on charity ships around the globe. In his seventies, he phoned the pub once from Rio to wish us all a merry Christmas, the sentimental sod. I think he was about to set sail from there to South Africa, or somewhere equally mad.

Whenever he walked into the pub, I would change the music to the Captain Pugwash theme tune, as a kind of ring walk entrance for him. He pretended to hate it, but we all know he didn't. He always complained at the price of my beer and used to give me humbugs every Christmas. When I left the pub, I got a whole tin of them from Harrods as a gift from him. The pub music used to be on my spotify account on an old iPod behind the bar. As it was my personal account I was able to control the music from my mobile phone, so knowing that Lou would always come in at 10.20 of an evening, I could be on a sun lounger in Vegas with my kids and change the music to Captain Pugwash at 2.20 in the afternoon, as there is an eight hour time difference, knowing that I've just put it on back home in the pub as he's walking in.

Christmas time was always a little melancholy for me personally, in The Compton. My family had disappeared to Vancouver, so I was very much on my own at the beginning of my tenure here. I always opened the pub from twelve to two on the day, just for drinks. It was always very well attended, with many regulars popping in while their respective turkeys were cooking. I used to get bought many a festive pint and rarely turned them down on this day.

At two o'clock, the pub naturally emptied out and everyone disappeared to have their family Christmas dinner. I would then clear up, get the pub set ready for Boxing Day, then rescue my own seasonal food which had been in the oven while I was serving. I would generally have done something smaller for myself, like a bit of roasted duck. I would take it upstairs and eat it on my lap whilst watching The Queen. After a festive facetime with my boys from Canada, when they would excitedly show off their gifts to me, I would generally fall asleep full of a quality whisky in front of Only Fools and Horses.

These were the times that hurt the most. Spending birthdays and Christmas away from my family made me realise how much alone personally I was. Everybody else my age had their partners and kids around them at these times of the year and here was I having failed twice at marriage, eating a slice of Christmas Cake on my own and saying good night to no-one. I remember once getting a Christmas package in the post from the boys. I waited until Christmas morning to open it. It was a starbucks mug from Canada, which had shattered in the mail. It was a tough period.

In later years, things were a little better and I had certainly come to terms more with my situation. I had my girlfriend, Jenny, who was always around and we had started to do a Christmas Day lunch for single guys. It was an excellent idea, as there was half a dozen or so of us Comptonites who now didn't have to sit alone on Christmas Day. Kevin hosted one year and did a magnificent turkey, although his parsnips turned out a bit darker and crunchier than intended.   When it was my turn I put together a beef wellington, which turned out rather better than I'd hoped - didn't even have a soggy bottom. I had to do a separate turkey crown for West Ham John that year, because he was a peasant who only ate beige coloured foods.

19. An Arsenal Connection

I had met Rob through Mo and James, from The Clanger, who were at that time sharing a Greene King tenancy on Fleet Street called The Tipperary. This is quite a famous pub, as it was the first one outside of Ireland ever to serve draught Guinness, or so the legend goes. It is situated directly across the road from Ye Olde Cheshire Cheese, of Samuel Johnson fame. Mary and I had helped out there once holding the pub, while James and Patti went off to one of their boat shows. Stunning place to have a tenancy.

Rob used to work close by trying to write five thousand words a day on a treadmill in Fleet Street, so productively spent his lunch hours propped up against the bar chatting with Mo or James, whilst inhaling their quality refreshment. Rob is a quick drinker. He is also an Arsenal man, so it was inevitable that we would cross paths at some point. At that time, I was in Bristol running The Shakespeare and had given up my Arsenal season ticket for a short period for logistical reasons, so Rob and his circle of chaps became an excellent source for the occasional match ticket when I could get up to London for a game.

I used to leave Bristol early in the morning on a matchday and drive along the M4 to Hatton Cross tube station where there was a car park, hop on to the Piccadilly line and get to the Arsenal from there. Paul, Jeremy, Dallas, Ross, Aash and his son Jack are the other mainstays of this group, and between us we pretty much go to every game. Personally, I enjoy the away trips better in this company, because the way The Arsenal work their ticket system we tend to be spread all over the Emirates, with Rob and I having seats away from the others.

When I got back to London via The Compton, I got my season ticket back. I had a magnificent view right behind the goal of the North Bank, on the top shelf. I loved that seat, but the reality was I would have to leave games early in order to get back to my pub before the crowds got there, as The Compton got rammed with punters before and after the matches. In between seasons, The Arsenal very kindly took pity on my unique situation, and moved my seat to the corner of the ground closest to my pub.

Before I knew these chaps, they used to frequent The Compton in previous years before the standards there went pear shaped, so when they heard that I was taking over this pub they naturally all came back and made it their pre match ritual. I'm unsure whether they did this out of blind loyalty to the friendship or whether they actually enjoyed their sausage and mash, but I don't really care as I managed to get six and a half years worth of trade out of them.

We were on an awayday trip to Nottingham Forest once. I think all of us were there, but my girlfriend Jenny and I had made our way up separately so that we could include a little romance to go with the football on this trip (the lucky lady!) and stay in a Nottingham hotel for the night. We had arranged to meet up at Ye Olde Trip to Jerusalem, reputedly Britain's oldest pub, situated under Nottingham Castle. I had texted Paul that we had been shopping as Jenny was after a "pearl necklace", and would meet in the pub shortly. This was a private text, man to man. As any bloke knows, there are unwritten rules in these situations.

Over my inadequate fish and chips in the Nottingham pub, Paul blurts out in front of all and sundry "Did you get your pearl necklace?" Couldn't believe it, dropped me right in it

from a great height. Naturally, Jenny got the raving hump over that, and went and sat in the pregnancy chair in the pub for revenge (look it up). Paul may be the go to man for a match ticket, but never trust him to keep a joke going whilst following the code of conduct. I guess being married for so long he's forgotten the rules of the game...

In the Compton, pretty much everyone is an Arsenal fan. It's ten to twelve minutes walk to the ground, so is perfect for the pre match couple of beers before getting in your seat. It is one of those pubs that the normal football fan loves to go to. Out of all the boozers on the Arsenal Pubwatch, we were the only one that didn't have door staff to control the fans - it's just not a trouble spot.

You came to the Compton pre match for some great real ale and a homemade chilli burger, or a home cooked lasagne. This wasn't the place for knuckle dragging morons looking for ten pints of fizzy lager and a punch up. That's what the cheaper branded pubs on Upper Street and the Holloway Road were for. Being tucked down a back street served us well in these situations, as the trouble seeking hooligan can't operate google maps on his phone without opposable thumbs.

There was a lovely man called Ray who frequented the pub on weekend lunchtimes, who still works for Arsenal in the Community. He would do anything to promote the club, and always used to look after my boys when they visited with tickets for games or signed shirts. He used to sup a beer with Gerry and Bill Greaves, and collectively they used to cock up the Sun crossword. Gerry is a staunch Northern Irish Gooner who had certain opinions in the later years on where Arsene Wenger should be going. Bill Greaves was an amazing old chap, a Huddersfield Town supporter who in his pomp was a reporter on Fleet Street for the Daily Mail.

Bill was famous in pub circles for establishing a set of etiquette guidelines for buying rounds of drinks in British pubs. They were first published as an essay in the now defunct Today newspaper, and reprinted in the Daily Telegraph in 1993 and are known internationally as "Greaves' Rules". They define a set of do's and don'ts governing whose turn it is to buy a round of drinks, and many copies of this fine "document" can be found hanging on pub walls throughout the land. Bill died recently, at age 79. We all attended his funeral at St Bride's in Fleet Street, a church famous for having the shaped spire that wedding cakes are based on today.

Match days were amazing in the pub. If it was a traditional Saturday three o'clock kick off (how rare are they for Arsenal now?) then we would start getting busy at around midday. By one, the pub would be packed, with overspills into the back garden and the road outside. If you weren't consuming your beverage inside the premises, then there was a police rule that you had to serve the pint in a plastic glass which I was never a fan of, but I could see the logic. Greene King once did an advert for their IPA bitter and filmed it at the Compton, complete with my voice over and smiling, handsome face walking to the stadium. This can also be found on YouTube.

At around 2.30, most of the supporters would be on their way to the stadium. All of the staff would run around and clear up the glassware, crockery and assorted debris, grab something to eat, sit down, breathe a little and then prepare themselves for the second onslaught at full time. By ten past five, the pub would be packed again. The match result decreed how packed, because if the Arsenal lost it would be less so, and a tad more melancholic. If we had just won, then there would be a celebratory feel to the evening and more fans tended to come back to the pub afterwards to enjoy a victory tipple.

Match days from a business point of view were so important. For the first couple of years at The Compton, I made a financial loss as it was so difficult to turn around a bad reputation, especially when nobody naturally walks past your front door. A home game was a fabulous opportunity of guaranteed footfall, which helped bridge the gap concerning the constant issue of cash flow. There were 26 of these opportunities (the number of home games on an Arsenal season ticket) to try and maximise these sales gifts, so the systems were put in place to ensure that we could take the most money possible during these occasions.

We always had plenty of people serving at all times, that was a basic. There was also a spare person collecting glasses and crockery, someone delivering the food from the kitchen, someone changing the barrels and looking after the cellar, someone doing till drops and making sure you don't run out of change. You can never over staff these situations. Always make sure that the punters are served quickly and efficiently on these days, and that you don't run out of stuff. It was my job to ensure that my staff had the various tools that they required to do their jobs properly, and that there was enough of them. If it's quieter than you anticipated you can always send someone home, but if you're understaffed then it can all fall apart pretty rapidly. A match day was not the day to be understaffed.

We were fortunate during my tenure at The Compton that Arsenal won the FA Cup three times in four years (are you watching Tottenham?). For the magic day, I used to decorate the pub with scarves, banners, red and white bunting and a load of my old Arsenal shirts pinned to the ceiling. There was a fabulous atmosphere in the pub on all three occasions - it was a proper go to place for Gooners to watch the match. They were the best days for me personally as I would be at Wembley for the game, we always won the cup, I'd have one or two shandies in celebration and come staggering home to find the mortgage had been paid.

My staff had bought into the system and methods of doing things at the Compton so well, that they used to cope with these days admirably. Just as at The Shakespeare, it was so well organised beforehand that it was difficult for much to go wrong on the day - but it still needed a terrific amount of hard work and dedication while they were getting their butts kicked to carry it off. Generally, I would return from a cup final with most of them on their knees. They would always get rewarded, so I guess everyone was happy in the end.

I always enjoyed chatting all things Arsenal in the pub. As I previously mentioned, most regulars were Gooners and there was always a healthy range of opinions spread right across the board, when it came to dissecting Arsenal's fortunes. Mick the Shoe was legendary for regurgitating theories and tactics that he picked up from Charles Buchan's Football Monthly. It was hard for him to accept that the ball didn't have a lace in it anymore, so we used to leave him to talk to himself in the corner.

Guinness Terry was always very critical of Arsenal whilst watching a game, and used to struggle to describe proceedings in words of more than one syllable or four letters. He was a Viking in a previous life, and had his hair generally styled in the way that his great great grandfather, Olaf the Hairy had done in order to provide padding for his wonky helmet. Terry even married a Dane and produced a baby viking between them. Loved his bacon, too.

West Ham John didn't support The Arsenal. He was the odd one out when it came to club allegiance, but still used to join in the footballing discussions although he naturally had a very different viewpoint on the subject. He was a skilled carpenter, although you'd never guess that looking at him. Could drink for the East End, West Ham John. Still can't remember who he supported.

I was fortunate during my time at The Compton that I always seemed to have one or two key staff that would help carry the others through. It is so difficult to get good staff in Central London, so to get an assistant capable of ensuring that the standards are always adhered to in my absence was a real godsend. It was tough at first, as I couldn't get a decent deputy for love nor money.

After a year or so of being at The Compton, this gorgeous young lady called Jenny, a Lithuanian girl, applied for a job. She was separated from her husband and wanted a few hours to help pay for stuff and to get her out of the house. We became an item very quickly, which lasted pretty much up to the end of my tenure at the pub, five years later. In addition, she learned the ropes of the business very quickly, from never having poured a beer to be compiling orders, counting tills and balancing the end of week paperwork in the office. She was our quickest server towards the end, and would have been the assistant manager if it wasn't for the fact that we always took our holidays together.

Nick from The Shakespeare joined me after a year or two. He was with me on and off for most of the time I was at the pub. He would work for eight or nine months, and then disappear to coach tennis in Italy for the Summer.

Then, when he had run out of cash he'd be back again for another stint. As he was Shakespeare Tavern trained, Nick already knew how I wanted things done, so slotted in very nicely. He and I became great friends, too, and when he left in early 2017, I missed his camaraderie.

Bill was another assistant who we had christened "the dolphin". Not that he was a super intelligent mammal - far from it, despite the degrees. No, it was just that he had the silhouette of a dolphin. He was a decent chap as in he would be able to follow the systems well enough, but didn't really have the capacity to think on his feet like a Jenny or a Nick. He was always looking for love, was Bill, and he brought some right dodgy sorts back to the pub on his quests. I remember him telling Roxy, a barmaid with locally famous assets, that she had no chance with him because he was her boss. Like Danny DeVito telling Scarlett Johansson she hasn't got a shot. Not much made Roxy speechless, I can tell you…

He once almost killed me by cocking up in the cellar. When you change a real ale, the sediment from the bottom of the barrel gets dragged through the pipe with the last pint or two, which is why you get a murky pint sometimes - it's just the end of the tub. Before the next ale is connected up, you either flush the beerline through with fresh, cold water, or you can clean the line with a food bleach, which removes the yeast particles attached to the inside of the pipe. To do this, you fill the line with the bleach solution, let it soak for 20 to 30 minutes and then thoroughly flush it through with the cold water.

Bill had filled this particular beer pipe with bleach, left it soaking and then stolen the bucket of water intended for that pipe and used it to flush a different barrel - he was too lazy to fill up a different bucket. The first pipe then got attached to a new barrel by someone else, assuming that it had been flushed as there was no bucket present, and the fresh beer pulled through. Fortunately (not for me) I decided to check the new ale when it was deemed to be ready and got a gob full of bleach. Some went down my throat but I managed to vomit the rest back up. Burned like a bitch. If that had been a customer, the pub would have been toast, as might the poor punter.

Bill eventually got suckered in by this rubber faced bird from Bolivia who tried to marry him for his passport. It was sickening how you'd see posts on Facebook of them together, showing balloons and cake for their "twelve week" anniversary. He was gutted when he discovered what we could already see from a safe distance. When he left, he began sending love messages in Google translated Lithuanian to Jenny, demanding that she bear her true feelings for him. I don't think anything more than sign language would have been needed for that.

Later on, towards the end of my life at The Compton, Zsolt and Jason were the mainstays along with Jenny at the pub. Zsolt is over here from Hungary and joined to learn the bar trade, as he had already been a cook in other Central London pubs. It wasn't long before he, like Jenny before him, had picked up pretty much everything required to hold the pub in my absence, which was to prove invaluable later on. If Zsolt liked people, he would be the perfect publican - but he doesn't. He has a shorter fuse for bullshit than most, so being surrounded by punters soaked in our products wasn't a great recipe for him. Fortunately, when you're in charge of an establishment such as this, there are always plenty of opportunities and necessities which give you a reason to escape the front line.

Jason was a fresh faced young lad from the haddock smelling world of Peterhead, somewhere in North East Scotland, when he moved in with his Dad who lived down here on the same street as the pub. He joined us part time at first and learned the ropes behind the bar, then went full time and was trained up in the kitchen and cellar, too. Not bad for a bloke with two left hands and English as a second language. He too used to try and chase skirt all over London. At one point he had this voluptuous Aussie cornered, and she had to catch a flight back to Sydney to escape him. He also had his go to bird, Holly, who has worked in various bars around Islington, but she got the hump with him when he started to fancy her mum more than her. He's now settled with this slightly older German girl who keeps him organised, in check and makes him follow orders. Just what he needs, really.

20. Betting With Gary's

When you're in your local pub's social scene - which a helpless Landlord is by default most evenings - you tend to discuss the matters of the hour in depth with the assortment of clientele you have at your disposal at that particular time. This clientele varies from day to day, session to session, even hour by hour; but after a while, you can more or less set your watch by a few of them. These are known as your "regulars". Your bread and butter, those who pay the bills, those whose lives and habits are deeply entwined with your own, whether you like it or not. If they aren't, then you ain't doing it right.

Having these people visit your home (the pub itself) at such set patterns creates your personal social circle. You spend extraordinary amounts of time chewing the cud and setting the World to rights. If you and these educated folk had the reigns of this country, there wouldn't be any issues to chat about - the planet would be perfectly run..... But of course these magical ideas and opinions were principally formed once the learned participants and contributors had consumed a certain substantial amount of the product that I was there to flog. Funnily enough, the more booze that was sold, the more that these solutions spouted forth, and the more holes in these solutions appeared.

It was generally around this point that pride in their opinions, bias' and beliefs shouted down the logic in their systems. It was at this delicate balance in time that the quality Landlord would step in and make a bet.

Because, naturally, the vast majority of "regular" is of the male gender, a great proportion of debate and conversation will be linked to sport. Within this territory, great tribal instincts will surface in these individuals, in defence of their particular team - no matter if the bare facts outweigh their blustering - these chaps will defend their positions with their dying breath. It is this illogical vulnerability that the aforementioned Landlord seeks to exploit.

Back in the Shakespeare, there was a fine social regular who used to pop in on a Tuesday and a Friday. Very nice chap, great fun, good banter - one of the lads - indeed, I still meet up with him occasionally to this day to watch cricket, despite us living at opposite widths of our fine land.

So this excellent fellow, Nigel, was not only regular in his appearances, but in his habits of consumption. Two pints of Abbot Ale to start, then on to large vodka and cokes for the rest of the session. The man was a machine. He would be in the Shakey from around 6pm until closing and then off to Urban Tiger for a few late ones and a lapdance. In my establishment alone it was not an unusual occurrence to note that he had polished off a bottle of Smirnoff single handedly. Incredible capacity. How he functioned on a Wednesday and Saturday is anyone's guess - maybe he didn't. But then he was an accountant, so he probably didn't need to. They only work in January.

Nigel's downfall was that he was a Spurs fan. The negatives of this are obvious (at the time of writing, they haven't won the league in 57 years, or any major trophy for 27) but being an Arsenal man, I won't labour this point.... Back in 2007, we made a bet when Nigel was post Abbot and halfway up a bottle of Smirnoff (I say up, in case you are questioning, because the bottles are on optics and so upside down) of £50, who would finish higher in the league, Spurs or Arsenal.

Of course I won. Arsenal were an excellent team still at that point, although getting worse annually. I was more fortunate that Spurs were an absolute pile of shite at that same stage, and continued to avoid competence for many years following. This particular bet became an annual occurrence, giving me an additional income of £50 per annum, as Nigels ill judged confidence in his side would resurface every August, or certainly enough to renew the wager, after a couple of hours into a Tuesday or Friday session at my establishment. Being a Gentleman, I always bought him his next vodka after the handshake, probably more out of guilt than anything else.

After moving to The Compton Arms, a chap of similar allegiance (we'll call him Gary 1) continued the bet for me, and conveniently kept it at a nice, round £50. He was similar to Nigel in the way that his inebriated self shouted louder than the logical part of his cranium after a certain point in the evenings proceedings, and it was usually around this point that the annual bet would be struck.

After a few years of this merciless fleecing, Gary1 would refuse to renew the wager unless his team was gifted a set number of points head start. I thought this immoral and cowardly, but I would go along with it after negotiation, as I was beginning to feel a little guilty about always winning, to be honest. As well as betting adversaries, these chaps were also mates and good customers, so it was important to keep it competitive and friendly.

Realistically, if Nigel or Gary1 would ever have won these bets, where do you think they would have spent their gains?

It had got to the stage where I purchased a giant presentation cheque, so when it came around to St Totteringham's day (the point every year when the mighty Arsenal couldn't be overtaken by the upstarts from Middlesex) we would have a presentation evening. I would subtly get dressed in an Arsenal shirt and have Gary1 hand over the dosh during this photo opportunity with a handshake and the aforementioned giant cheque. The cheques date was filled in "every May".

This lack of confidence in Gary1's conviction about his own team exposed a flaw in the man, which he was mercilessly ribbed about in the bar on many an occasion. If you are a dye hard fan, you wouldn't back down under any provocation or slur against your team. The relationship you have with your team allegiance is unmovable, unbreakable and sacred. Unfortunately, it turns out that our Gary1 has changed his team on numerous occasions. The poor sap has supported West Brom and Southampton in previous times and those are only the ones I know about. You can't change your bloody team. Unforgivable.

I myself was tested a few decades back by my first wife, Lara. I was considering my first tattoo and was contemplating the options on what to have permanently scarred on my body. I eventually settled on the Arsenal cannon on my calf (the real one, not the current cartoon). She tried to helpfully suggest:

"Why don't you have "Lara" tattooed on your leg?"

"A tattoo is for life, you know. You can't change your team" was my ill thought response.

It turned out that she changed me, eventually. I couldn't blame her, in fairness. Far too good for me.

As time drew towards the final years of my tenure at The Compton, Gary1 got very ill. He was diagnosed with a kind of blood cancer, and it all got very hairy and emotional. The poor chap was only 4 weeks older than myself (although my boyish, flawless skin always belied my advanced years!). Like me at that point, he had kids living away, but he was still a Dad to them. When an illness like this is contracted, it affects all those around them - he had both parents still going, two boys, an ex wife, a dog named Ted and a girlfriend. All right, his bird was as mad as a box of frogs, but she was still otherwise deeply affected.

Not only are his blood relatives on the back foot, but Gary1's implied family are also in shock. That implied family was us. The regulars, staff and myself saw more of him on a daily basis than anyone (except for the girlfriend) and we would have done anything we could have to see him through.

It really brings home to you the fragility of life when this stuff happens to people at an age when it shouldn't. It was Gary1's brush with death and the passing of my younger brother around the same time, that got me to thinking about my occupation and whether there were other things in life that I wouldn't mind achieving. Happily, after a year or so of heavy chemotherapy, Gary1 was given an all clear of sorts. Because of the type of cancer that he contracted, it's unlikely he'll emulate Methuselah, but he is grabbing life by the balls as we speak, and long may it continue. He looked really funny without eyebrows, mind you...

Gary2 was one of my favourite regulars of all time. He was naturally good natured, jolly and down to earth. A proper, old school product of Islington and its environment who was a prolific drinker, in the same league as Nigel from the Shakespeare. He would arrive on a Saturday around lunchtime and stagger out, the last to leave, after kicking out time in the early hours.

The difference in their two habits, although similar in volume, was the variety that Gary2 had. He would always start with a light and bitter. Or three. Once that was done, it was anyone's guess. There wasn't a bottle of spirits, wine or liqueur that Gary2 hadn't sampled on my shelves. When it came to the latter half of his Saturday session, you wouldn't glance over to the end of the bar at his perch and see less than three different drinks in front of him. Loved a scotch and coke, a nice rum or a sambuca (the black one).

Because of this, and also because he was the most entertainingly opinionated man the World has ever known, Gary2 would always be up for a bet. For some reason, our chosen field would be boxing. Now I love the noble art of pugilism. Love its history, studied the greats. Gary2 knew squat. But unfortunately for him, the variety of drink by a certain point in the proceedings had rendered logic and reasoning null and void, so he was always keen to shout the odds when it came to predictions.

Our bets had a strange evolution. I won the first half a dozen or so. When the next big fight was on the horizon, we would debate in a drunken fashion and shake on the outcome. I would always manage to maneuver him to back the loser, so ending up flush - the bet was friendly, always a tenner.

As I have mentioned earlier, I was always a little uncomfortable with winning every time as these guys are my bread and butter - and friends. So after the first half a dozen or so of these bets, I'd lay off the knowledge and let him choose. It got to the stage where Gary2 would have first dibs without any interference from me, because I actually wanted him to win one. Remarkably, the bloke couldn't pick his own nose, and proceeded to lose time after time after time. It was extraordinary. I believe I won around 16 - against my will - before he finally got one.

Talking of winning stuff, I somehow managed to get to the final of the World Pasty Championships in 2015, which are held annually at the Eden Project, near St Austell in Cornwall. I had won a competition held by the West Cornwall Pasty Company, who have kiosks in many railway stations (they are yellow coloured with a bearded pirates face logo). I was entered in the "Open Savoury" category, with my homemade meatball and mozzarella recipe. Jenny and I were treated to a lovely weekend away in a luxury hotel in Cornwall as a prize, to attend the finals. I didn't win, but my pasty sold over 10,000 units in the kiosks up and down the land, plus it gave some great publicity for the pub, as it was named "The Compton Pasty".

21. Painting the Beams

Creating the best environment to suit your chosen clientele is sometimes taken out of your hands. In many pubs, especially in the historical City of London or the West End, you'll find such stunning examples of Victorian architecture that the building itself or internally in part or whole, will be listed. This is a great thing, as then centuries of history can't be eradicated on the whim of an over enthusiastic pub decorating company.

One of my favourite places in the World to go for a pint is around the old Docklands areas of East London. Wapping boasts three or four seriously famous pubs hanging over the Thames, where Charles Dickens and Samuel Pepys supposedly used to drink. Close by is The Grapes in Narrow Street, currently owned by the actor Sir Ian McKellen and across the water in Rotherhithe is The Mayflower, which took its name from the ship which was constructed and launched from that spot to carry the Pilgrim Fathers over to America. If they'd have known that Donald Trump would eventually be pulling the strings there, I would think they'd have just stayed on in the pub that lunchtime.

The Mayflower and The Grapes are particular favourites. Unchanged, unspoilt and magical because of it. When you walk into either establishment you get a real sense of history, you can see where these famous figures of times past used to sit and because it still looks like it did back then, you can feel that atmosphere, their presence, that age. Dickens himself wrote about The Grapes (he called it the Six Jolly Fellowship Porters, in Our Mutual Friend) and his descriptions of it still resonate to this day as you explore inside.

The most famous pub of the area is probably The Prospect of Whitby, beautifully situated with Wapping Wall displaying its frontage and the Thames itself to the rear. They say that this is the oldest watering hole on the water, with a history dating back to 1520. When I first moved to London, a mere 468 years later, it was one of the first places I wanted to see - and it didn't disappoint. There was a gorgeous pewter topped bar, original flagstone floors, a creaky wooden interior and knick knacks of all description hanging from the ceilings. Go in there today, and it looks like any identikit bar you'll find on any identikit high street. Modern, polished tables, the latest in computer tills, a frozen menu and chrome, hideous bar pumps. What a waste.

My local county of Devon and indeed all over the South West boasts some extraordinary buildings that have been pubs for centuries. Nooks and crannies, flagstone floors, bars modelled from a ships hull and ceiling beams constructed from a mast. Fishermen, smugglers, thieves, writers and politicians once sat on that stool by the window, so, in my book, if it was good enough for them....

Fast forward to The Compton Arms, four centuries later.... It took a long while for sales to pick up at The Compton, for two main reasons. Firstly, the awful reputation that I inherited. It had been run pretty haphazardly previously by an inexperienced manager. Standards were well below average, and one or two of the staff cared even less. Secondly, The Compton is situated well hidden down a couple of side streets from the hustle and bustle of Upper Street, near Highbury & Islington tube station. You had to know it was there to find it - nobody walked past the front door by chance.

It was agreed with the brewery that a mini decoration and refit scheme would be a decent thing to do to support my business and help boost the trade. They could see that we were going in the right direction, so they knew that by throwing some cash at The Compton now would reap benefits in the future. Their proposal was a franchise type of agreement. In short, they wanted a small percentage of my gross in exchange for £180k worth of investment, where it would be transformed into one of their brands.

This involved all manner of tie ups and branding which would have, in my opinion, made my pub feel like every other branded box along Upper Street. From the menus, to chalk boards, to the computerised Greene King tills, to even a glass floor area where the punters could look down into the real ale cellar - this was everything that The Compton Arms didn't need. The Compton is a unique and historical place that had boasted an ale house on the same site since the sixteenth century, and it's attraction is that you can't get that experience elsewhere.

After much negotiation, it was agreed that the brewery would spend just £40k redoing the toilets, repairing and sanding the wooden bar floor, changing carpets and a lick of paint. By doing this, the character and feel of The Compton was preserved for another generation to come, and its uniqueness was not banished to history under the brushes of corporate pubcos. Well done Greene King.

A footnote to this though. The Compton's low ceiling boasted some very characterful black beams. They looked original, but they weren't (one of Hitler's V1 flying bombs in 1944 saw to that). The decorators in their wisdom painted them all white, to match the new paint on the ceiling itself. When they left, I got them painted them black again and covered them with all of the real ale pump clip badges that I had served in the venue.

Not long ago, I revisited my old haunt The Shakespeare Tavern on a visit to Bristol. I was dismayed to see that their latest refit had glossed and varnished over the originality and character of this beautiful pub. Although the building dates from 1729, inside it could now be mistaken for another identikit brand. When will these guys learn that the beauty and history of an original pub is a, or the, prime reason to visit? Once you change that, it's lost forever. Mind you, I still turn up for every game at The Emirates stadium to watch The Arsenal, yet yearn for the spiritual home of Highbury.

Maybe I'm the relic, and it's me who needs to change....

22. The Loss of Larry

It's June 17th 2016, and the pub phone is going off. It's early, and I open my eyes just enough to see that the Arsenal clock on my bedroom wall shows it's five to seven in the morning. The pub phone is programmed to kick in with an answerphone after six rings, so it's stopped now. Bit of a fluffy head, as last night England beat Wales in the European Championships, so I'd had a couple in celebration with the regulars. What idiot calls a pub at seven in the morning? I turn over to see that Jenny hasn't moved, so I put a pillow over my head and try to nod off again.

Fifteen minutes later, and my mobile is going off. I instinctively stretch out my arm, pull it off the bedside table and squint at it. It's my older brother, Alec. Ok, that's weird. We talk infrequently, like four or five times a year. And never at stupid o'clock. He has my attention, and I answer.

"Malc, you awake?"

"I am now, what's up?"

"Got some really bad news." A pause. "It's Larry. He's been found dead."

I'm sat upright. I'm pulling on some jogging pants, but I don't know why. "Malc, are you there?"

"Yes," I croaked. My voice was weird. "What happened?"

"He was found in his caravan, the police are with Dad, but they won't tell me any more. Dad just got hold of me, he said he was trying to get hold of you, and he wants you to call."

"Ok. I'll call him now. I'll chat in a bit."

I ring off and get out of the bedroom, grabbing a t shirt. I can't breathe. I walk into the upstairs kitchen, and then out again. I still have my phone in my hand. I sit on the couch for maybe two seconds, and get up again. Dad never calls my mobile, even though he has my number. When we chat, he always uses the pub landline. Doesn't believe in mobiles, never has. "I've survived seventy odd years without one, why would I need it now?" Well, you bloody do.

I call home, and Dad picks up before the second ring. He is gabbling, breathless. The police are with him, he doesn't know what to do. I ask to speak to the police, Dad introduces me as his son, and a lady comes onto the line.

"Larry's body was found this morning, in his caravan in Langport in Somerset. He has been taken for an autopsy. There are no suspicious circumstances, but we believe he died of health reasons"

"What does that mean, health reasons?"

"We cannot tell you that at the moment, I'm afraid. Also, his dog was killed near the scene."

"Right, OK. Thank you." His dog? Can't take this in. I was passed back to Dad. We chatted, there was nothing anyone could do at this moment, and I promised to come as soon as I could. The poor guy sounded very old and confused, and I guess he was. I can't imagine the pain of being told your youngest son is dead.

I'm stood in the trade kitchen downstairs, leaning against a worktop. I don't remember going downstairs. I realise my face is streaming and I'm really short of breath. I take my time, and wash my face in cold water. I'm awake now, but I want this day to restart. My mind is racing, there is so much to do, but actually there isn't. Nothing I can do is going to change this, but there's a part of me that doesn't actually believe that it's final.

I go back upstairs to the bedroom where Jenny is now sat up. "What's happened?"

"Larry is dead, I croak" and by saying it, it makes my face melt again.

Later that day, Alec and I chat. He has been in touch with Larry's landlord where his caravan was kept, and has arranged to visit to collect any personal items. We both agree to meet there, before I would head on down to see Dad at home in Devon. Alec has his own cake making business with his better half, Pauline, and is up to his eyeballs in work. As there is nothing he can do, he doesn't want to go to Devon. He and Dad aren't too close anyway - at least I can chat about cricket with him.

A couple of days later, we arrive at the site. Now Larry had virtually disappeared over the previous couple of years, no contact, no address. He was withdrawing from us and society. He had a part time job delivering eggs around Somerset and Dorset for a local farmer, but that was his only source of income. Once, I managed to pin him down and met him at a local service station for a coffee, about eighteen months previously. He had refused to meet at his "home". Before I met up, I had done this giant shop at Tesco's and filled his boot up with foodstuffs and goodies. I remember I had even included a bottle of Teachers scotch whisky, for good measure.

Larry had worked for me countless times in various pubs before. He was always in between jobs, a bit of a nomad. Usually when I got into a new pub, he was the perfect person to have around - pulling pints, fixing stuff, helping to move, looking after my cellar. He was generally a loner, but when things were going well for him, he was an absolute pleasure to be in company with. When things were tough, he was aloof, rude and arrogant.

We shared a room for fifteen years growing up, until Alec joined the RAF, then Larry moved into his room. We are (were) just thirteen months apart, so were always fighting and playing as kids. As my world went to London, he stayed closer to home as he was always a proper West Country boy. He was also really close to Mum, so when she died in 2004, Larry's world probably started to disintegrate.

She was his glue, his go to point when things were going pear shaped in his life. Now that she was gone, he was on his own and couldn't cope with the world. I now realise that Larry was on the spectrum, to some degree. Having been through experiences with my two boys, it is clear to me that Larry has always shown these signs, but of course, Autism or Aspergers wasn't "invented" when we were kids, so Larry had never received any appropriate help. In life, Larry never forged any relationships with anyone outside family or a workplace. Conversation with a stranger was tough and embarrassing for him and he certainly never had a girlfriend, ever.

Conversely, I spent some of the best and funniest evenings of my life with him. When he was in the mood, Larry's wit was wonderfully dry and to the point. Once, Larry, myself and Martin (from Sutton Arms fame) were out on a bit of a pub crawl. We walked (stumbled) into this pub called The Lord Nelson near the Old Street roundabout, on the edge of the City. Ropey place, sticky, dark. "We'll have one then move on."

We're leant against the bar and after about a third of the way into our one pint, this music pipes up and a load of spotlights come on in the darkest far corner of the pub. There was a pole now illuminated. From behind a filthy curtain came this old sort, creaking with arthritis, wearing a feather in her head and some strategically placed Bacofoil. Within five minutes, the poor cow had lost all of her Bacofoil whilst trying to wrap herself around this still dry pole, at which point the music faded away.

She then approached the still shocked punters in the pub clutching a pint pot with a handle - I think there were seven of us in there, of which we were three.   As she creaked towards us, tripping over her tits, Martin and I dutifully got out a couple of pounds from our pockets, presumably so that she could go to Tesco next door for some more foil to replace what she'd just lost.   As we donated, Larry leans across and drops a 2p coin into the jug, and says

"And I want change."

We were out of there so fast we took some varnish off the front door.

Another time, it was just Larry and myself, a long way into a pleasant day on the beer.   We found ourselves in The Coal Hole, a rather famous pub on The Strand, next to the Savoy Hotel.   We had got to that stage in the proceedings where we were full, but had not yet accepted that fact.   We were both propped up on tall stools in the rear bar, when this good looking mid to late thirties lady arrived at the counter next to Larry to order a gin and tonic.   In our unacceptable state, we looked at each other approvingly, as you do when you don't realise how far out of your depth you are.   Larry turned to her...

"So" he slurs. "How old are you, then?"

The lady benefits Larry with a rightly disgusted sideways look, and responds,

"You never ask a woman her age."   Quick as a flash, Larry comes back with,

"Alright then - how much do you weigh?"

Alec and I enter the site.   It was small, surrounded by an old metal fence and barbed wire. It had been raining, and there was a lot of standing water on the uneven gravel.   You couldn't walk to Larry's car or caravan without getting ankle deep.   We jumped across as best we could.   The caravan itself was one of those small, bubble shaped vans from the 70's that you hitched onto the back of your car.   It was in a horrible state of disrepair and was caked in muddy streaks.   A couple of the windows were cracked and one of the tyres was flat.

We opened the unlocked door and went inside.   I have never seen such squalor and filth in all of my life, and I've been to games at White Hart Lane.   Everything was caked in grime.   There were empty cans of food everywhere - both human and dog varieties, a sink and worktops full of dirty crockery and utensils.   To the side of the caravan, the bathroom area was foul smelling and there were flies buzzing around, oblivious of the aroma.   Dirty, unwashed clothes were littered everywhere you looked. On the small table next to the bed, there was a stack of bills, reminders, warning letters and lottery tickets. The bed itself, where Larry was found, was adorned with a beige coloured bed sheet and duvet set that had never been washed. It was covered in years old stains. Worse, there were large, pooled patches of dried blood where Larry had bled, from both ends.

Finally, the overriding and dominating feature of the caravan were the empty whisky bottles. Litre and a halves of "Blended Scotch Whisky 3 years old" from the local Tesco Metro supermarket. They were everywhere, covering every flat surface, the floor, in the sink, under the bed. In that caravan, there would have been over a hundred alone. It was too much for me and as I felt vomit coming, I backed out off the caravan and went around the side.

I threw up into the overgrown wasteland behind the van. As I turned to go back in, I looked to my right and caught my breath. In front of me was a pile of the same branded bottles, all 1.5 litres, in the region of two hundred or more. When the police woman said it was health reasons, she was spot on. Larry had drank himself to death. Looking at the way he lived, he had spent every spare penny trying to escape this world. It explained his withdrawal and eventual disappearance, and the reluctance to let me or anyone else find him.

When Larry passed in his sleep, when his body finally gave up, his dog ran for help. He somehow climbed the wire fence and got run over by a passing lorry. The lorry driver went for help about the dying dog, who was recognised as Larry's. A friend came to tell Larry about his dog, and found Larry in bed. The local council classified Larry as a vagrant, and volunteered to cremate him as one. It was a simple ceremony, which Alec and I attended, along with a few of Larry's local acquaintances and his egg boss. Dad did not attend, he just couldn't.

There were many people chasing money that Larry died owing, including the local vet who still had a German shepherd ice lolly taking up room in his freezer. Phone contracts, bank overdrafts, credit cards and the landlord of the hovel that Larry lived in. This was all paid off with the sale of his car. It must have been an absolutely miserable existence for Larry at the end, and I pray he's at rest now. As the closest person left in his life after Mum, I continue to question to this day what more I could and should have done to help him, and curse myself for not properly stepping up.

23. Last Orders at the Bar

In June of 2015, Greene King spent seven hundred odd million pounds on buying the Spirit Pub Company. In one fell swoop, they became the largest managed pub company in the UK and further added hundreds of pubs to their tenanted and leased division. The upshot of this was, after all of the initial mayhem from the deal had settled down, that a hit list was created for pubs that were to be sold off, to help with a bit of cash flow and to ease the monopoly and congestion of their owned pubs that this purchase had created.

On this departures list was The Compton Arms. I didn't find out about this until at least a year after the big merger was completed, but as a mere tenant you're pretty much on a need to know basis. The rationale for this decision was that my pub is too small to turn into a managed house (it wouldn't have fitted into any of their managed profiles) and they would realise a lot of ready cash from it because of the value of its proximity to Central London.

Initially, there was a big hoo ha about the pub being sold off and turned into accommodation, because land is so valuable in London that it would make a developer a mint, should they be able to do so. In reality though, The Compton was always too valuable as an asset to the local people for them to allow this to happen, plus there was always the historical connection to George Orwell to add weight to the reasons for keeping it on as a pub. A petition was raised by the locals and regulars which quickly turned the pub into an Asset of Community Value, so sealing it's future as a pub for some years to come.

Despite the fact that it was now to stay as a pub, which I was delighted with, I was informed that when Greene King found a buyer then it was to be sold with vacant possession, ie without me in it. Again, they were fair with negotiations, so the pub was put up for sale and I agreed as part of the deal to carry on owning the business until the sale date. Naturally, being put in this position created a very different set of priorities on how the pub was to be run, and I struggled with that.

I have always taken a mindset that I would action decisions in my pubs for the greater benefit of long term gain. My pubs have always shown a steady upward curve when it comes to profit and loss, because of my insistence that the right thing is done for the good of long term benefit in all situations, rather than trying to chase the immediate quick buck. For example, I've turned down many a function which would have made me a fortune on a Friday night, because they had wanted to take over the whole pub. What do I then say to the regulars that come to me seven days a week - go somewhere else, I don't need your money tonight? Bad for long term gain - your locals may never come back. You might take an extra couple of thousand with the function, but lose half a dozen permanent customers by doing so.

Even something as trivial as a group of locals that have had one too many and want to choose their own music and have it turned up, because they want to sing badly and have a boogie - they may individually spend a few more quid over the next hour, but they also might put off anyone new who walks in the door, or piss off the group of girls in the corner with a bottle of plonk, who only came in for a quiet natter.

So I now found myself in the position of knowing that there was a finish line to my occupancy of The Compton Arms, but without knowing the exact date. This meant that critical decisions about how the pub was to be operated always had to be made with the mindset that we could all be out of here in a few months. When my Sky and BT contracts were up for renewal to show football in the pub, I had to take the tough decision to stop broadcasting sport. They both sign you up with a twelve month minimum, so if I was suddenly told that the pub is to go in six months, then I was told I would find myself liable for the remainder of those contracts.

By the end of my tenure in the pub, I only had three or four chairs that weren't broken in the back garden. What was the point in replacing them, as I wouldn't get paid for them when the pub was sold? If I was staying on, I would have been carrying on a programme of maintenance like reflooring the toilets, replacing the oven, installing an eye level grill, repainting the outside of the pub - there was an endless list of jobs that I wanted to action, but it would have been financially daft to do them. As the sale date of the pub dragged on and on, the business unfortunately started looking tattier and tattier.

It was a frustrating period, because the visual standards being shown in the pub at this time were not acceptable to me, so why would they be okay for my customers? The quality of food and drink were unaffected, of course, but I was very proud of the community pub that we had become and didn't want that tarnished with the impression that some may have got with what it was starting to display. It was also difficult to recruit quality people to work for me too, as I felt it unfair not to mention that we were being sold at the point of interview.

Finally, in the late Spring of 2017, we got the word that a buyer had been found, a price agreed and the sale date would be October of 2017. That gave us a few months to get ready to hand over. It's so much easier to have an exact date, because then you can make more precise decisions around it like finishing up contracts and giving more accurate notice, plus you can also make better decisions on what is worth repairing or replacing if something breaks down.

It was always my intention to take a couple months off and then go and find another pub to run. After all, this is all I'd ever done - what else could I possibly consider as I have mortgages and kids to pay for still, like anyone else of my age. I was also aware in a strange twist of fate that the new buyer of the Compton Arms' freehold may even want me to stay on as a tenant, so I kept my powder dry and intended to sit back and see what happened.

One evening, as I was winding down to go to bed after the pub had closed, I was chilling out and messing about online when I came across an advert saying that London Underground were looking for tube drivers. I recall rolling my eyes, as they had recently been in the news because one of the lines had just gone on strike for some reason. It had been revealed how much money the drivers all got paid and how pissed off the commuters were that they had the cheek to down tools. I'd had a couple of beers, so I naturally thought to myself "I can do that - I've had a cab ride in a high speed train and it looked straight forward enough to me!" Anyway, it seemed like an easy life compared to the eighty odd hours a week I was doing, so I clicked on the button, filled in the form, moved on to twitter and forgot about it.

Next day, I got an email saying that they liked my form and sent a link directing me to a question and answer exercise. I filled that in and forgot all about it. Meanwhile David, who was still my Business Manager for Greene King, told me that the date had changed for the sale and it was now November of 2017. Not a massive difference I thought, as it would be pretty easy to stretch the staff for a few more weeks. Very quickly after that, I was told that it was then going to be January of 2018. I was beginning to get a little irritated with this, as it meant reorganising termination dates for lots of utilities and insurances, plus I now had to persuade my staff to work through the Christmas period.

While this was going on, I was invited to an assessment day by Transport for London in one of their offices in North Greenwich. The job was for a Train Operator for the newly formed night tube, which runs on a Friday and Saturday night. Sixteen hours per week, for decent money. I started to think seriously about this. I had always assumed that I would be a publican until I either won the pools or, more likely, it killed me. It would be impossible to jump career ladders after thirty years and still earn enough money to pay for mortgages and kids - I had done nothing else but run pubs.

I decided that I was going to give this my best shot, and researched what was likely to be asked of me or tested. I studied hard and did my best on the day. If I failed, then it would be because I didn't possess what they were looking for, rather than my poor preparation or application. Unbelievably, I found out the very next day via email that I had got through.

The next and final stage was to be a morning of a number of specific exercises geared to the requirements of the job, plus a two on one interview. Having been self employed for so long and been offered managed pub positions on reputation alone before that, I hadn't been properly formally interviewed since 1988. I was so far out of my own comfort zone that when I turned around to look for it in the interviewing chair, I couldn't even see it. It was a small shadow in the distance somewhere. More of a dot than a zone. Rather strange when you consider how many interviews I have given from the other chair in my career. The morning was a blur of coffee, sweaty palms and trying to remember a script. I thought I did ok in the circumstances, and got back to the pub in time to serve a few late lunches.

I was in Vancouver with my boys in August of 2017 when I got the call from London Underground offering me a position. To say I was shocked was an understatement. They said that they would get back to me regarding a start date, after they knew when the new intake for induction courses were happening. The training was to be sixteen weeks full time before you actually qualified to drive a train. Now my thoughts turned to how I was going to work this, with still having a pub and committing to my new job.

24. Regrets? I've Had a Few...

As I've previously alluded to, we poor Guv'nors work long hours, long days and are pretty much glued to the lifestyle. Your time off is rare and sacred, yet is also conditional on the fact that everyone turns up when they are supposed to turn up, and nothing goes wrong which needs your immediate attention.

The mindset we breed have is that no one else can solve it. The glasswasher seizes up and you get a phone call from the barman. He can't get it going and you think to yourself that if it just had your magic touch then all would be solved. Same with the card machine packing up, or the Carlsberg isn't coming out right. The oven won't light and the ice cubes are coming out in triangles. Could be anything.

There is no logic to this theory that I, of all people, have a golden pair of healing hands. I am to DIY what Donald Trump is to world harmony - indeed, I am famous for it. What can't be fixed with blu tack isn't fixable in my book, and it is at this point you have to call someone out. But it's the mentality that we Publicans have (especially when it's our money) that we need to have a shot at giving the piece of equipment in question our own personal version of the kiss of life, before accepting defeat.

The only thing I really avoided trying to repair was electrics. Even with my own misplaced sense of bravado and competence, I knew that I could die with an ill advised application of blu tack here, so I generally gave this a swerve. When I first took over The Compton, if you put both microwaves on at the same time in the kitchen, the TV's used to trip in the bar. My punters once missed a penalty in a Man Utd v Liverpool game because some selfish customer had ordered a chilli con carne and a chicken soup at the same time.

There have been countless times that a date has been called off with a wife or girlfriend because of one of these last minute emergencies. I look back with a little embarrassment at times over this, especially in the earlier years when a little perspective would have been better employed. As I got longer in the tooth, better trained and just plain smarter, I learned to filter what was really important in the scheme of things, and what was better prioritised.

Unfortunately for me, all of my romantic relationships have suffered and died over the years largely because of this pub life. A couple of wives and a few girlfriends have come and gone, and I often wonder where I'd be if I had attached as much importance to them as I did my work.

I recall years ago, back around 1993 in the Sutton Arms in London's Barbican, when I was a young manager with a newborn baby, Jess. I remember lecturing my first wife Lara about how important it was that I was allowed to sleep all night, as "the pub came first". What an ass. I look back on stuff like that and am shocked at my immaturity and ignorance.

Later on, when Mary and I took on The Shakespeare back in 2006, it was my first stab at doing this with our own money. The pressure was on to get it right, as the days of receiving a salary and having that security were over. I really put my heart, soul and industry in to getting the pub going and it turned out to be a success. Unfortunately, with my head down and ass up with the business, I couldn't see that who I was working for - my wife and children - were being seriously neglected.

So we have a new pub, self employed for the first time, a newborn baby, another pregnancy and the worst, dirtiest, shittiest accommodation above to move in to. It wasn't that it structurally wasn't comprehensive enough - it was a massive Georgian building - but the state of it was just disgusting. Filthy, run down, leaking, mouldy. Nothing was salvageable. I recall (again with some embarrassment) pregnant Mary on her hands and knees scrubbing the bathroom floor with a scourer to make it habitable for us. At the time, my mindset was that this was her doing her bit, as I was concentrating on the business downstairs. How short sighted.

Of course, with hindsight, it should have been the Brewery who handed over the pub in an acceptable state. Later on, when I bought the tenancy of The Compton, I made sure that everything was acceptable in that regard. It was my own naivety that led to Mary getting on her hands and knees.

It's not until you sit down on your own in an empty flat, with your family gone, that you realise how differently you could have managed certain situations. Only little things, every now and then, but they add up over time. I was blind to the fact that Mary, who was a young mother to begin with, was under a tremendous amount of pressure without the extra burden of the pub.

This was compounded when both Ben and Sam were diagnosed with autism at an early stage of life. In addition to the extraordinary strain that Mary was already under, we now had two kids that had no speech, in nappies until they were four or five, no eye contact and no responses. No matter that these boys had both our unconditional love and support, the extra pressure that this brought to our marriage was unbearable. We would hand over the baton of parental responsibility to each other when we ran out of gas, and it became more of a brother and sister type of relationship. We would put aside a date night every week, but we'd just go to a different restaurant and talk about the boys, or the pub… or just eat in silence.

The moment I knew that deep down that Mary and I were over, was an innocuous one over a domestic dinner one evening. It had been a particularly trying day with the boys and the business, which wasn't unusual, and Mary was not hiding her dissatisfaction (who could blame her!) We had one of those Bernard Matthews packs of Mini Kievs - delicious, along with mash and peas, probably. Of course, as it was being served, a barrel goes in the pub, so I race down, change it, and race back up again. Mary had almost finished hers, and mine was on the table. On my plate, was the mash, peas and six Kiev balls. There are fifteen in a packet, as everyone knows. She had taken nine for herself. NINE!

No coming back from that.

Even at that stage, the majority of my thoughts were concerned with my business. My intentions were always good ones, my heart was always in the right place, but my views on the work and life balance were so blinkered and skewed, that I ended up losing the people that I should have been prioritising - first Jess, then Mary and the Boys.

The harsh truth is that this pub industry by nature is so full on, so time consuming and so lacking in any quality downtime, that it is a ticking time bomb for any relationship. Chuck in my obvious naivety and you get to where I am today - a divorced, distant parent.

Whenever I hear people looking back on their lives and saying that they wouldn't have changed anything, I never believe them. Nobody has gone through their lives regret free, however smart they think they've been.

25. My Moon Under Water

I like real pubs. Proper pubs.

Call me old fashioned, but I think the good, old fashioned classic, stereotypical English boozer has an esteemed place in our history - and also the present. Whether it'll still be living and breathing in the future remains to be seen, but for my generation, it's an essential part of every decent community in this fine land.

The Compton Arms was one of a triumvirate of local pubs thought to be referred to by George Orwell back in 1946 for his essay used in the Evening Standard entitled "The Moon Under Water." In it, Orwell stipulated ten key points that he believed a London pub should have, in order for it to be the ideal drinking hole. He stipulated things such as Victorian architecture, no pianos, the selling of aspirins and even biscuits with caraway seeds. One or two of these in today's pub climate you could possibly raise an eyebrow at, but other principles he mentioned such as "barmaids knowing customers by name" and the "availability of a good, solid lunch" still ring true today.

In my experience….

A pub should be a cornerstone of every village square, like a post office, church and chip shop. It's a place where a community knits and socialises. It's a second front room, where you go to meet your neighbours, vent your woes, network your small business or join a darts team. You can have a bite to eat, watch the football if the wife refuses to miss Corrie, and is the perfect place to take the in laws when the conversation at home has dried up.

The two (non managed) pubs that I have run, that were my business - The Shakespeare Tavern and The Compton Arms - have been fine examples of a quality local. In both cases, the majority of the trade comes from a six hundred yard radius of the building. Of course one would be unwise to exclude or discourage the outsider, but the guarantee of the regular who walks to you (and staggers home) is where the bread and butter is. In both cases, I gave punters from all walks of life and geography good reasons to give us a visit - but without a quality set of regulars, it's not a real pub.

A pub is so much more than the building. The real attraction is its people - on both sides of the bar. I used to sell Carlsberg in The Compton at £4.35 per pint. A couple of hundred yards away, there was a certain brand of pub flogging exactly the same beer at £1.99. Now why would anyone pay me more than double? Atmosphere.

No decent minded fellow wants to be supping their immaculate real ale at the bar, and have to duck every five minutes as a bar stool whistles past his ears. You wouldn't want to be treating the wife or girlfriend to a gin and tonic or a glass of rose', whilst surrounded by high volume, limited colourful vocabulary. You'd be unwise to have the Sunday afternoon neighbourhood watch in, while the local dealer of talc substitute does a quick line off the window sill.

Creating the correct atmosphere for the right pub is everything. Appeal to your chosen market. My market was always judged on what I personally wanted to feel / see / drink / eat and listen to while I was socialising. Because of this, it was essential that when I ploughed my hard earned pennies into buying a pub, I already knew that it had the potential to be a place that I'd love to drink in myself. Being of a certain generation and probably a little old school in this respect, I knew that if my offer was what I personally enjoyed, there were plenty more like minded people out there who would love to empty their pockets in my direction, in exchange for these familiar sensations.

Both of these pubs followed a very similar blueprint. This system had been learned and refined over seventeen years of being a manager for various Pub Company's or breweries. Always steal the best ideas. Always make your mistakes with somebody else's money. Always be true to your own feelings.

One of my employees from The Shakespeare, David, has heeded this advice to the letter. The lad could serve behind the bar, cook a Sunday roast and was great with the customers. Let's call it a "flamboyant" personality. He made plenty of mistakes (nothing serious) whilst on my payroll, but had the kind of ethic and application to learn from them. He now owns a few pubs himself around the Bristol and Bath area, all boasting an uncanny resemblance if not actual replica of my menu that he cut his teeth on. Well done David, you cheeky robbing bastard.

You can't cheat yourself running your own business, least of all in a pub. You live and breathe it and it consumes your every waking moment - so if you've bought yourself a loud music venue and you hate music, or a big boozer next to Wembley Stadium, yet you don't like football, then you are going to spend most of your life being miserable. It just so happens that I enjoy a quality food and beverage offer and serious amounts of local banter while I'm consuming it.

My TV's will only ever be on if there's live sport. The music that's playing has to be at a low volume, so that you can have a conversation at normal speaking levels over it. Music should be there just to assist an empty atmosphere. It's not even needed when the pub is flowing, as there is no better sound than the hum of conversation and the clink of glasses in a pub. It also has to be of a certain vintage, which would reflect the generation that all of these things appeal to. Nobody of my age needs to listen to Pusha T, Lil Peep or Waka Flocka Flame at deafening decibels.

When I was first offered The Compton Arms I visited the pub on many occasions, so that I could get a feel for what the pub was, and its possibilities for the future. Different times of the day or week, having a bar snack or dinner, during a match day and on a dead Monday lunch. One of the things that stuck out on these visits during the weekday lunch periods was the feeling of uncomfortableness when I'd walk in alone. There were the regulars chatting at the bar, but their conversations dominated proceedings - I don't know if you've ever seen the film American Werewolf in London? It was like walking into the Slaughtered Lamb…

By putting in speakers and having the background silence broken - albeit at a low level, that feeling of exclusion was removed. During the first week of my trade I was accosted rather aggressively by a lady who was swiftly approaching a middle aged vintage, Emily. She was clearly a regular of the establishment and seemed keen to preserve the "old order". She thrust a business card into my hand, which identified her as "Against Music in Pubs". I wasn't aware there was such a club (!) Fast forward a couple of years, and the now rejuvenated Emily could be found off her bar stool in the pub, throwing shapes across the pub floor whilst being serenaded by Suggs, of Madness fame. She would always request "The Snake", by Al Wilson after a few too many IPA's.

My food menus have always followed the theme of "Old Fashioned Pub Grub." Of course tastes and trends change, but you need to adapt these days to make it local, or organic. In my opinion, any valid pub menu without Ham Egg & Chips or Sausage & Mash on it needs to be thrown in the bin. I always felt that we needed to be a little better than the managed house food offer with their standard frozen fayre, so it was important to me that we kept our menu manageable, fresh and home cooked.

My drinks offer reflected both the heritage of the pub and diversity of my target market. In both cases of establishment at the time of my purchase, the wine offer was "red or white". This immediately would exclude half of the World's population from wanting to visit. The fairer sex are a lot more discerning in their tastes for the noble grape these days, so a proper wine list was put together offering a decent range in all varieties of colour, grape and geography.

The female market is so important these days. Gone are the times when the pub was a sticky haven for blokes eager to escape their families. In this age of relative equality, without a decent drinks range, healthier food and clean toilet facilities, you won't move forward with the times. It's also essential that the pub comes across as safe, so that women feel comfortable. I was always quite proud that neither of my own business pubs ever had a security door person obligation on their liquor license. Indeed, The Compton was the only establishment on the Arsenal pubwatch scheme without door staff on a match day.

The beers themselves were a big draw. Get a pint of real ale right, and keep it right. Every time. The number of times I've had a manky beer in other establishments, managed or otherwise is shocking. If you get a bad pint of milk from Tesco, you take it back and get a replacement, no bother. You'll still frequent that Tesco's, because it sells a thousand other things you want, and it's probably the closest to where you live. If you get a dodgy pint in a pub, then the guest NEVER comes back. Lost them for good. They'll also tell their mates, too. The poor person only came in for a pint - and if it's shit, you don't offer them or sell them any other reason to see you again. There are probably a dozen other boozers who could be arsed to clean their lines properly within spitting distance. When it's your own money, who can afford that?

Like wine, a decent variety of ales on offer is also a great thing to do. Strong ones, session ones, light ones, stouts, local ones, standards or guests. Make it interesting. But whatever you serve, make sure that every pint you draw up is perfection. If you don't have the turnover for a range of five, then don't have five on. Serve three. If those three varieties are perfect every time, then I guarantee that after a short while, you'll be able to manage four, as the word spreads.

I've always felt that a proper variety of spirits and liqueurs added a certain something to my pub. The legal wording for weights and measures being served in 25, 35 or 50 ml measures (one third or one sixth of a gill, when I first started!) only stipulates "gin, rum, vodka or whisky". Nowadays, there are literally thousands of different types of short or shot available. When I was a very young man, there were no such things available such as sambuca or tequila in a pub. Even when I joined The Clanger in the City of London back in '88, the shorter drink of choice for the City boys was a large vodka and orange.

In my day, as a student type, we used to go out to have a few beers and have a great time. As a consequence of this, we'd get pissed in the process. Nowadays, the younger lot want to go out to get pissed. That's the actual goal. They'll be knocking back vodka at home getting ready, so they'll be drunk by the time they get to their pub or club of choice. I don't really get that. However, partly due to this, the spirits market has grown in sales volume and diversity beyond belief in the past decade or three. I'm happy to stock a decent range to accommodate this, but in my Pub Utopia, a great range of Malt Whiskies will always be centre stage on my top shelf.

These days soft drinks are a huge and necessary part of a pub. Gone are the days of drinking and driving. I have an early memory of the Old Man screeching home in his car, singing at full volume with the window wound (!) down around midnight. It was Buddy Holly, if I remember correctly. Funny thing was, that was the only time. I never knew Dad as a regular drinker by any means, although he did tell me that drinking and driving was the norm back in the 50's, around the watering holes of Plymouth.

It's not enough these days to have the prim rows of tiny Britvic bottles of juices and mixers sat on a warm shelf. Now there is a veritable assortment of fruit punch and trendy lemonades for the discerning Des. In addition, in many more family friendly (not mine) establishments, you'd probably expect a Capri Sun or Fruit Shoot to be on display.

Kids in my pubs were excluded from 6pm. My profile punter would come to the pub to escape the ankle biter, not to immerse himself with somebody else's. Generally, they were accepted when the parents were having a lunch in the pub, usually on a Sunday with the family. We would expect the parents to be responsible and look after their own, which was usually the case, but unfortunately in this day and age, not all of the time.

My Moon Under Water could possibly be considered an updated list of niceties of Orwell's, from seventy odd years previously. I don't think that George and I have greatly differing tastes or principles in this regard -

perhaps mine is just a modern version. Many folks may have other things they believe should be included or omitted, but then this isn't their book, is it?

26. Time, Gentlemen Please.

Zsolt and Jason had come along in leaps and bounds over the preceding few months. This was really timely, as Jenny had gone back to being very part time by this stage for personal reasons, so they had taken up the slack which had been created by her reduced hours. Both were turning into excellent day to day duty managers, and Zsolt even had the capability now of being able to complete pretty much all of the office duties that were required to run the business on a weekly basis.

One morning, we had a long sit down and discussed the impending closure together. We only had a few months left, so the parameters for operating the pub were set out clearly between us so that we were all singing from the same hymn sheet. We were to be strict with the ordering, we had to run down wet and dry stocks and begin to reduce the range of our food offer, we were not permitted to employ new people by request of Greene King, plus repairs and cash expenditure all had to be authorised through myself. This was a similar set of parameters that I had to work with through the Spirit Pub Co, at my Kew Gardens site some years back.

I also offered both Zsolt and Jason incentives to stay on until the bitter end, as they too were concerned about their own futures. Uncertainty in this situation is not an easy thing to live with, but I assured them both that they would have no problems finding decent employment in this industry. They are both very switched on chaps, although Jason can be a complete fruit loop after one too many. The other staff were naturally all going their own ways, so they were less of an issue for me. It was established that I had to go full time during my training with London Underground, so I made plans to move out of the pub accommodation in December, and Zsolt move in to be full time and on site with Jason until the sale went through.

I had a flat in the Docklands area of London near City Airport, that Guinness Terry and West Ham John did up for me. It's amazing how people who can drink their own body weight in one session can be so talented at anything, but they both did a fine job. I moved in around mid December time and drove to work, instead of my commute being a slide down the bannisters. I got notice from the Underground that I was to start on February 16th, which was perfect. That gave me three weeks off after the sale of the pub as rest before I started training in my new job.

Meanwhile, Jenny was not handling me living alone and away from the pub at all. According to her, I was having different women over every other night, and she was too far away to keep an eye on me. I learned some harsh life lessons regarding that kind of behaviour with my first wife in that respect twenty years before, and I wasn't ever going to make those mistakes again, so this began to piss me off more than a little. Apart from that, Jenny was twenty years younger than me (thank you) and smoking hot. Where would I get the time, energy or inclination to even look for another woman elsewhere, let alone do anything about it? We began to see each other less from this point, through time constraints, arguments, inconvenience etc.

Then, Greene King dropped a bombshell by informing us that the prospective purchaser now didn't want to complete until May 25th of 2018. This seriously threw a spanner in all of the plans, as I was virtually out of the business from February 16th with my new job. It took a lot of persuading and reorganising to be able to make this new date viable from the trading point of view. The ban on new staff that had been imposed by Greene King was now lifted, which was a good thing as Jenny walked out on New Years Eve because of another row. Zsolt and Jason were excellent in accepting the situation, and I thanked them by increasing their golden handshakes at the end of it.

As I anticipated, I got a call from the purchaser of the pub offering me a lease option on The Compton after the sale. By this time, I had done an awful lot of soul searching about what my future should be. Up until I fell into the tube employment position I had never considered leaving this industry, but here was a chance from nowhere to try something new. I figured that not too many lifetime publicans end up getting a telegram from the Queen, so maybe this was an opportunity to give a different and perhaps more health friendly path a try. Aside from that, I felt that one can be a position for too long, where you can subconsciously take your eye off the ball through habits and routine. I thanked the man for his offer, but turned it down.

My training with London Underground was now pretty full on. Learning something different and opening yourself up to a new industry is actually quite refreshing at middle age. I would never have said that I was in a professional rut, but when you've done the same job for thirty years your skills, thought processes, comfort zones and experiences are naturally both similar and predictable. Learning about how trains and railways operate was, to me, fascinating and inspirational - I'm sure it's rather mundane to many but I was new to this - new to anything but catering - and I lapped it up.

Back at the pub, everything wound down to the big day. Stocks were reduced to a minimum, the accommodation was vacated and cleaned, the staff were laid off and all of the relevant people involved with the sale converged on the date to cross the t's and dot the i's. I took the new owner around with my bunch of keys, showing him which ones locked each door, but he didn't really seem too interested. I suppose he wasn't going to be the poor sap actually running it anyway.

The stocktakers and brokers for both sides were doing their thing in the back room of the pub, when the new owner said he was happy that all of the transfers had been completed, and he needed to go. He asked if I still had a front door key, and would I lock up for him. I thought this was very odd, as if I had just bought a seven figure asset, the first thing I would do is change the bloody locks. However, the chap said goodbye and just disappeared leaving myself, a broker and Ron, the guy representing Greene King with whom all of my sale negotiations had been conducted.

As all transfers of monies were completed, I shook hands with Ron and the broker and they both departed. I was alone in The Compton. It was quite a surreal moment, knowing that this was actually the last point in time that I would ever spend in a pub as anything but a normal punter on the social side of the ramp. I spent a minute or two sat on a tall stool against the bar, just looking around at the chairs neatly stacked on the tables, the well trodden wooden floor with the small hole that Greene King still hadn't fixed, and the hundreds of old pump badges adorning the wooden beams on the ceiling. It was eerily quiet.

I recall my thoughts drifting back to The Clanger. It doesn't exist anymore. It got horribly hit by an IRA bomb that killed three people back in the early nineties. A shocking experience for everyone involved, but thankfully all of my friends and the team escaped physically unhurt. It eventually fell foul of "progress" in The City, and the building was knocked down for redevelopment. Upon rebuilding, it became a Drum and Monkey, then an All Bar One - although about fifty feet further down Houndsditch.

A couple more pubs that I did a relief in back in the day aren't around too. The Old Mill at Takeley, found in a small village near Stansted Airport closed down years ago, as did the Tiger Tavern, which used to be situated at the gates of the Tower of London. The Hayfield pub on the Mile End Road that I ran for a few weeks back in 1990 is now the Hayfield Masala. I heard the curries are better than mine were, but the beer is nothing to write home about.

To my knowledge, all of my other pubs are still standing. All have changed hands numerous times - different freeholders, different landlords or managers, new companies formed, companies going bust.... and one or two even have different names. It's a really fluid industry, pubs. I once worked for four different companies or parts of a company in two and a half years, without actually moving venues.

As my mind drifted, I began to compile a greatest ever Staff XI that I had employed throughout my time in the industry, but gave up after a couple of minutes. I figured that it would probably take some serious time and thought. I'd perhaps need a really long walk for that...

I gave the bar top a pat, let myself out of the front door, turned the chubb lock shut and slipped the key back through the letterbox, dropping down onto the mat inside. I got into my car and drove away, to begin my next chapter.

www.ingramcontent.com/pod-product-compliance
Lightning Source LLC
LaVergne TN
LVHW051922240325
806714LV00036BA/170